INTELLIGENT SYSTEM

Edited by **Chatchawal Wongchoosuk**

Intelligent System
http://dx.doi.org/10.5772/intechopen.70018
Edited by Chatchawal Wongchoosuk

Contributors

Alexey Germanovich Finogeev, Anton Finogeev, Ludmila Fionova, Mikhail Deev, Fateh Boutekkouk, Vladimir Robles-Bykbaev, Yaroslava Robles-Bykbaev, Salvador Naya, Silvia Díaz Prado, Daniel Calle-López, Luis Garzón-Muñoz, Clara Sanjurjo Rodríguez, Javier Tarrío-Saavedra, Washington Silva, Priscila Rocha, Allan Kardec Barros, Adang Suwandi Ahmad, Arwin Datumaya Wahyudi Sumari, Tatiana Kosovskaya, Oleh Berezsky, Aman Chandra Kaushik, Ajay Kumar, Avinash Dhar, Shiv Bharadwaj, Hadi Jahanshahi, Naeimeh Najafizadeh Sari

First published in London, United Kingdom, 2018 by IntechOpen
IntechOpen is the global imprint of INTECHOPEN LIMITED, registered in England and Wales, registration number: 11086078, The Shard, 25th floor, 32 London Bridge Street
London, SE19SG – United Kingdom
Printed in Croatia

British Library Cataloguing-in-Publication Data
A catalogue record for this book is available from the British Library

Additional hard copies can be obtained from orders@intechopen.com

Intelligent System, Edited by Chatchawal Wongchoosuk
p. cm.
Print ISBN 978-1-78923-606-4
Online ISBN 978-1-78923-607-1

For EU product safety concerns:
IN TECH d.o.o., Prolaz Marije Krucifikse Kozulić 3, 51000 Rijeka, Croatia,
info@intechopen.com or visit our website at intechopen.com.

Meet the editor

Chatchawal Wongchoosuk received his PhD and MSc degrees from the Mahidol University and his BSc degree with first-class honors in Physics from the Prince of Songkla University, Thailand, in 2011, 2007, and 2005, respectively. Currently, he is a faculty member of the Kasetsart University. He is a specialist in the development of smart sensors for food, agricultural, and environmental applications. He received over 18 research awards. He has published several dozens of articles in reputed journals and proceedings. He served as a reviewer of over 18 ISI journals. His research interests cover the topics of modern nanoscience and nanotechnology ranging from theoretical modeling to fabrication of intelligent nanodevices, such as hybrid gas sensors, printed electronics, and flexible electronics.

Contents

Preface

Intelligent system is an advanced machine that can perceive, learn, and solve the problems with a great accuracy. Technologies with intelligent system are currently available in the market and used in real-world applications, i.e., self-driving cars, Siri, Alexa, video games, Facebook, robot, and so on. To exceed human cognitive capabilities, the important keys rely on the developments of sensors and algorithms that allow to be a fundamental building block for design and construction of intelligent system with particular applications. Intelligent system including *artificial intelligence (AI)* is one of the *hottest* subjects in this era. The AI market is predicted to grow from USD 21.46 billion in 2018 to USD 190.61 billion by 2025. Big world change from these technologies results from the real-world problems and systems that are too complex with solving based on the static mathematical models. Intelligent system with machine learning has thus become the best solution, which can learn information through pattern recognition, classification, data mining, decision-making process, and adaptation to dynamic environments without requiring precise math equations.

This book aims to describe the artificial intelligent (AI) systems ranging from the basic knowledge, i.e., engineering design of intelligent systems, intelligent sensing technologies, fundamentals of machine learning, and computational artificial intelligent techniques, to the current state-of-the-art applications. The contributions of the book are presented in two parts as follows: (I) "Basic Concepts and Theoretical Backgrounds of Intelligent Systems (Chapters 1–4) and (II) Developments and Advances in Intelligent Systems and Applications (Chapters 5–9). The first chapter presents the basic concepts of intelligent embedded systems. Chapter 2 presents the basic knowledges of artificial intelligent (AI) and a new perspective in AI called as cognitive artificial intelligence (CAI). Chapter 3 describes the algorithm and mathematical models for AI problem solving. Chapter 4 focuses on the computational analysis of genetic algorithm and the concept of fuzzy logic for satellite attitude control. Chapter 5 discusses the intelligent system tools for data collection, data mining, and forecasting of transport incidents as well as models for sensor data processing in a smart road system. Chapter 6 proposes an expert system for collagen degradation analysis through computer vision methods and statistical modeling techniques. Chapter 7 demonstrates the development of a multilevel speech signal pattern recognition system based on neural networks. Chapter 8 reviews the modern automated microscopy systems and proposes the diagnosis of breast precancerous and cancerous states based on histological image analysis. Chapter 9 presents the particle swarm optimization (PSO) techniques and their applications in biomedical problems.

Finally, I would like to express my deep appreciation to all the contributors who are experts in their research fields. It should be emphasized that all chapters have been submitted for re-review and revision in order to improve their presentation with several interactions among editor, authors, and publisher. It is hoped that this book will be a useful tool of knowledge for a better understanding of basic concepts to state-of-the-art applications of intelligent system as well as inspiration and motivation to readerships for further developments in the field.

Asst. Prof. Dr. Chatchawal Wongchoosuk
Department of Physics, Faculty of Science
Kasetsart University, Thailand

Section 1

Basic Concepts and Theoretical Backgrounds of Intelligent Systems

Chapter 1

Intelligent Embedded Software: New Perspectives and Challenges

Fateh Boutekkouk, Ridha Mahalaine, Zina Mecibah, Saliha Lakhdari, Ramissa Djouani and Djalila Belkebir

Additional information is available at the end of the chapter

http://dx.doi.org/10.5772/intechopen.72417

Abstract

Intelligent embedded systems (IES) represent a novel and promising generation of embedded systems (ES). IES have the capacity of reasoning about their external environments and adapt their behavior accordingly. Such systems are situated in the intersection of two different branches that are the embedded computing and the intelligent computing. On the other hand, intelligent embedded software (IESo) is becoming a large part of the engineering cost of intelligent embedded systems. IESo can include some artificial intelligence (AI)-based systems such as expert systems, neural networks and other sophisticated artificial intelligence (AI) models to guarantee some important characteristics such as self-learning, self-optimizing and self-repairing. Despite the widespread of such systems, some design challenging issues are arising. Designing a resource-constrained software and at the same time intelligent is not a trivial task especially in a real-time context. To deal with this dilemma, embedded system researchers have profited from the progress in semiconductor technology to develop specific hardware to support well AI models and render the integration of AI with the embedded world a reality.

Keywords: embedded systems, embedded software, Codesign, intelligent embedded systems, intelligent embedded software, artificial intelligence

1. Introduction

Embedded systems (ES) [1] are changing our daily life. They are commonly found in consumer electronics, games, telecommunication, industrial, control, automotive, aeronautics and military applications.

ES development represents a hot topic in both academic research and industry. Contrary to conventional information systems, ES design needs software and hardware to be designed in a concurrently synergistic fashion, so the system functional/nonfunctional requirements are met. This new style of design is called Codesign [2]. Codesign is a collaborative and creative task requiring some specific skills in hardware, software and system engineering.

Semiconductor technology evolution (Moore law) pushes ES to be implemented as System On Chip (SOC) where all system functional elements or components are integrated in only one chip. Under time-to-market pressure, special customer requirements, rapid technologies changing, increasing applications complexity and diversity of design styles, methodologies and associated tools, ES designers must be assisted along the design process efficiently and interactively in order to minimize the cost of development and increase the productivity; many concepts have been borrowed from the software community, especially higher levels of abstraction, knowledge and experience reuse, project planning, cost/risk estimation and so on.

In contrast to traditional embedded systems which are central, simple, closed and reactive, nowadays embedded systems are becoming more complex, more autonomous, more open, more networked and more intelligent. For instance, they can execute very complex intelligent tasks to help invalid and aged persons in their daily activities with minor human intervention. These new features have pushed researchers and ES specialists to tune some well-known intelligence methods and paradigms. Consequently, a new class of ES called intelligent embedded systems (IES) has emerged. IES are discussed in some detail later in Section 6.

This book chapter puts the light on what we call intelligent embedded software.

First, we summarize all the specificities and the basic concepts which are related to traditional embedded system. Our focus is on embedded software models of computation and design methodologies. After that, we motivate the passage from embedded systems to intelligent embedded systems. Next, we define precisely what intelligent embedded software is and we discuss the possible models and approaches that can be used to model intelligent embedded software especially multiagent systems, expert systems, neural network, fuzzy logic, ontologies, bioinspired heuristics and hybrid models. We pass rapidly on organic computing. Finally, we present a possible intelligent embedded system design flow and present the main challenges and some future perspectives.

2. What are embedded systems?

An embedded system is a system that contains application-specific hardware and software suited to a particular task that is part of a larger system that is not necessarily computer (e.g., electronic, mechanical, electrical and so on). ES interact with the outside world via the sensors/actuators and are subjected to strict spatial, temporal and energy constraints. Indeed, ES are heterogeneous in nature. They typically combine software components (general-purpose processors, digital signal processors, etc.) and hardware components (ASIC, FPGA). Unlike a hardware implementation, a software implementation has the advantage of providing flexibility (i.e., the possibility of reprogramming), but at the price of satisfying performance constraints. ES are called real time if it is able to meet its timing constraints.

3. What is embedded software?

The principal role of embedded software (ESo) is not the transformation of data as in conventional software, but rather the interaction with the physical world. It executes on machines that are not, first and foremost, computers. They are cars, airplanes, telephones, audio equipment, robots, appliances, toys, security systems, pacemakers, heart monitors, weapons, television sets, printers, scanners, climate control systems, manufacturing systems and so on [3]. Traditionally, embedded software consisted of simple device drivers with or without an operating system support. ESo functions are activated by external controls, either external actions of the device itself or remote input. Embedded software varies in complexity as much the devices it is used to control. But with an increasing demand for wired and wireless communication, embedded software has started to use middleware to hide the implementation details of low-level communication.

Now, embedded software is becoming a large part of the engineering cost of embedded systems. That makes embedded software a likely place to look for engineering efficiencies and time-to-market improvements. Efficiency and time-to-market improvements come from good methodologies, good tools and talented programmers.

4. Embedded system architectures: state of the art and practice

The rapid evolution in the semiconductor technology led to the emerging of a new paradigm called System On Chip or SOC. The SOC can typically include a collection of heterogeneous processing elements such as embedded processors (RISC) for general purpose usage, microcontrollers for control-oriented processing, DSP for digital signal processing, ASIC to implement specific optimized processing, FPGA to implement reconfigurable computing, on-chip memories, analog part, RF part for wireless communication, an on-chip communication infrastructure such as buses, crossbars, buses hierarchies or a micronetwork, diagnostic elements, power management components, specific I/O interface modules and so on. The SOC can be seen as a compromise between hardware and software solutions. **Table 1** summarizes the main hardware components found in a typical SOC. **Table 2** recaptures our possible classification of SOC architectures. In traditional SOC (TSOC), the SOC architecture is centered on one master Instruction Set Architecture (ISA) processor and the other components are slaves playing the role of hardware accelerators. When SOC comprises many processors, we obtain multiprocessor SOC (MPSOC); this architecture is inspired from the multiprocessor architecture in general computers. When most application functionalities are implemented as software, the bulk of processors are ISA, and the architecture is called Software SOC (SSOC). In this case, real-time operating system (RTOS) is a first class. In the extreme case, when most of the application functionalities are implemented in hardware, the bulk of processors are ASICs and the result is what we call Hardware SOC (HSOC).

With the rapid advance in reconfigurable circuits, SOC tends to integrate more FPGA; this tendency helps to create what we call RSOC or reconfigurable SOC. This class of SOCs targets rapid prototyping.

Component	Main application	Main characteristics
Embedded RISC processor (ex. ARM)	General computing	Low performance, high flexibility, low cost
Microcontroller	Control-dominated computing	High performance, good flexibility, high cost
DSP: digital signal processor	Data-dominated computing	High performance, good flexibility, high cost
ASIC: application-specific integrated circuit	Specific computing	Very high performance, low flexibility, very high cost
ASIP: application-specific instruction set processor	Specific application domain	High performance, good flexibility, high cost
FPGA	Reconfigurable computing	Good performance, high flexibility, high cost

Table 1. Typical SOC components.

SOC class	Main characteristics
TSOC: traditional SOC	One central processor (master) with many hardware accelerators (slaves)
MPSOC: multiprocessor SOC	Multiprocessors architecture
SSOC: software-oriented SOC	SOC where software implementation is the prominent part; the architecture is mainly composed of ISA processors
HSOC: hardware-oriented SOC	SOC where hardware implementation is the prominent part; the architecture is mainly composed of ASICs
RSOC: reconfigurable SOC	FPGA-based
NOC: network on chip	A microcommunication network
PPSOC: plug and play SOC	SOC with IP reuse
PNOC: photonic NOC	Photonic technology
WNOC: wireless NOC	A combination between wired and wireless communications
QSOC: quantum SOC	SOC that contains all the components needed for a quantum information processor
CSOC: chaotic SOC	Chaotic computing-based

Table 2. SOC architectures.

The shared bus architecture represents a bottleneck in performance and scalability; for these reasons, researchers in the field had resorted to the Internet technology and tailor the ISO stack to create what we call Network On Chip (NOC) that integrates a micronetwork generally with three layers (physical, linking and network) to manage the big communication traffic between processors. With this network, scalability is also improved. One of the major problems in NOC is high power dissipation due to wired communication. The WNOC or wireless NOC presents a promised solution where some communication is done wirelessly by adding some antennas and RF modules. PNOC is a particular case of NOC where photonic technology is used [4]. QSOC [5] and CSOC [6] represent some new tendencies and refer to a SOC implementing quantum computing and chaotic computing, respectively.

5. Embedded system's Codesign methodologies: state of the art and practice

It has been emphasized that the best way to meet system-level objectives is exploiting the trade-offs between hardware and software in a system through their concurrent design. That is what we call Codesign. In the traditional ES design approach, the software/hardware teams work independently and generally the "hardware first" approach is adopted; when the hardware engineers synthesize their design, the software engineers begin to develop their software, implement and tune it to fit the hardware architecture. We can say that this style of design was imposed (the only solution) due to the lack of a unified modeling substrate supporting both hardware and software modeling at higher level of abstraction and co-simulation.

But with the advancement in system level languages, EDA and CAD tools, simulation and emulation, both hardware and software teams are able to work in a collaborative fashion and communicate from the early stages of design and consequently to reduce the cost and optimize the quality of the final product. **Table 3** summarizes our taxonomy of the most important ES Codesign approaches. CCodesign refers to the conventional (traditional) Codesign approach. **Figure 1** depicts the main activities in the CCodesign. Starting from a unified system functional specification, the flow then proceeds toward Hw/Sw partitioning where decisions on parts that should be implemented as hardware and parts that should be implemented as software are made. Many optimization algorithms and metrics can be applied at this stage. Three

Codesign methodology	Main characteristics
CCodesign: Conventional Codesign	Traditional codesign
IP-based Codesign	CCodesign + IP reuse
Platform-based Codesign	CCodesign + platform reuse
Design pattern-based Codesign	CCodesign + design pattern reuse
Codesign for reuse	Codesign to produce reusable components
MDCodesign: model-driven Codesign	Codesign + model transformation technology
AsCodesign: aspect-oriented Codesign	Codesign based on aspect engineering
Web-based Codesign	Codesign in the context of Internet
Cloud-based Codesign	Codesign in the context of cloud computing
IDE-based Codesign	Codesign using an integrated development environment
FCodesign: Formal Codesign	Codesign-based formal specifications and verifications (for critical systems)
PCodesign: Prototypic Codesign	Rapid Codesign-based emulation/simulation

Table 3. SOC main Codesign methodologies.

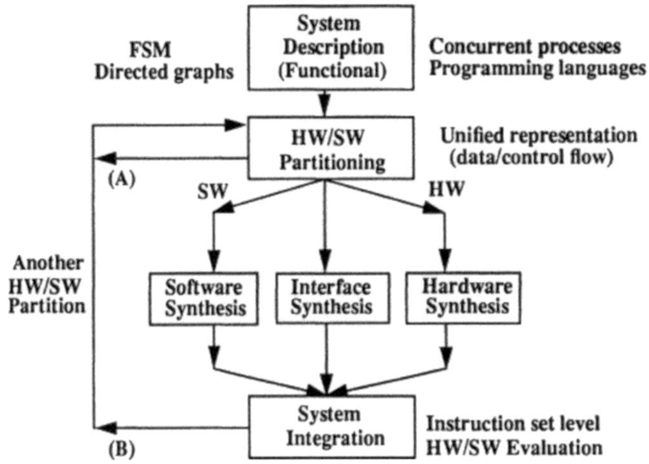

Figure 1. Conventional Codesign flow.

flows in parallel are outputted from Hw/Sw partitioning: the embedded software synthesis or compilation, the hardware synthesis, and the Hw/Sw interface synthesis. The outputs of these three flows will be then integrated for evaluation and co-simulation. As it is seen in the figure, the flow is iterative to seek for better partitions that satisfy the objectives of the design.

The system specification is the first key for the successfulness of the Codesign approach; the more the specification is expressive, complete and precise, the more the implementation will be efficient. Many requirements are identified for a good specification. Most authors prefer to use a unified unbiased model for both hardware and software. In the traditional method, such model did not exist. Embedded software is traditionally programmed in C or assembly language; such low-level languages are not portable and cannot anywhere meet system-level specification requirements. On the other hand, hardware parts were commonly specified using VHDL; but with the remarkable progress in modeling theory and programming language semantics, designers are now benefited from what we call model of computation or MOC. The latter defines formal syntax and semantic of computation and communication.

Table 4 summarizes a set of well-known untimed MOCs. Depending on the application domain, we find a collection of MOCs with different semantics. A multi-MOC denotes a MOC composing of multiple MOCs. The combination of heterogeneous MOCs is a hot research topic. Ptolemy is a good example of an environment allowing the combination of multiple MOCs hierarchically. We note the existence of a second class of MOCs called timed MOCs. The latter models and manipulates the time explicitly. As examples of timed MOCs, we find timed automata, timed Petri nets and so on.

Most existing specification/programming languages are based on one or more MOCs. We note that nowadays Codesign flows adopt SystemC [7] as the standard language for system-level specification. SystemC is an extension of the C++ language for both software and hardware programming. It supports many levels of abstraction such as transactional and RTL levels. In its earlier versions, SystemC used a discrete event simulator but with new versions it supports well other MOCs.

Model of computation	Application
DF: data flow	Data-oriented processing
SDF: synchronous DF	Data-oriented processing when the input/output size is known
KPN: Kahn process network	Deterministic data-oriented processing with infinite buffer
DE: discrete event	Discrete time processing
CT: continuous time	Continuous time processing (analog parts)
FSM: finite-state machine	Control-oriented sequential processing
DFSM: data path fsm	Control-/data-oriented processing
Statecharts	Control-oriented processing supporting concurrency and hierarchy
RS: reactive synchronous	Reactive systems with zero delay computing assumptions
Petri nets	Reactive systems (formal specification/verification)
Multi-MOC	Heterogeneous systems

Table 4. The most used models of computation.

EDA and CAD tools are also important in Codesign flow automation. Depending on the objective of the designer, we can find a plenty of tools for modeling, simulation, emulation, formal analysis, automatic code generation, optimization and verification, performances estimation, synthesis, and so on [8, 9]. The good choice of such tools may have a great impact on the quality of the final product.

The embedded software synthesis is part of the Codesign flow (**Figure 2**) [10].

Besides system-level description language (SLDL), which is able to capture both hard and software components, three major elements are needed in order to support the software aspect of the design flow:

1. Processor models that capture the processor at different levels of abstraction.
2. RTOS support for the processor.
3. A software generation tool that synthesizes user code targeted for the selected RTOS.

An RTOS provides at least the core real-time scheduling functionality, inter-task communication, timing and synchronization primitives. It is implemented and described as a real-time kernel or real-time executive. The scheduler in RTOS is designed to provide a predictable execution pattern. This is particularly of interest to embedded systems as embedded systems often have real-time requirements.

5.1. IP-based Codesign

Tends to shorten the time-to-market and minimize the cost of SOC design, the IP-based Codesign [11] emphasizes on reuse of predesigned and pre-verified components called

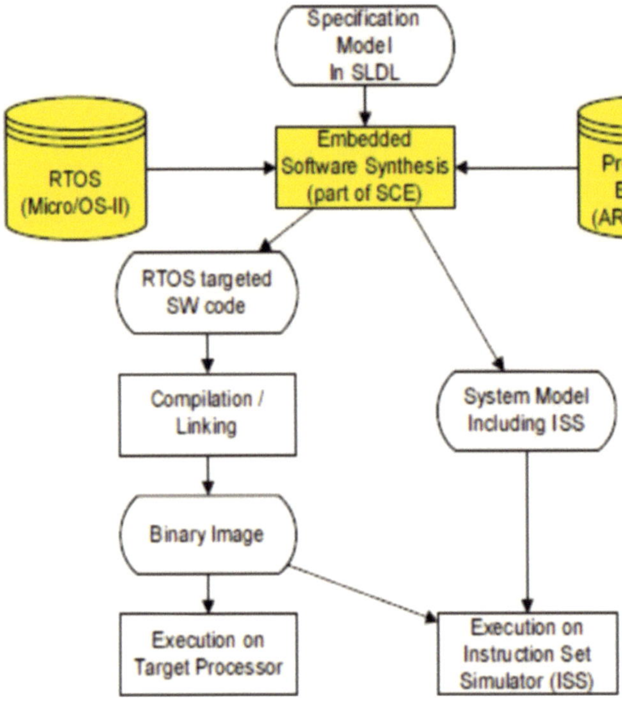

Figure 2. Embedded software synthesis flow.

intellectual properties (IPs). IPs may have many formats and specified at many levels of abstractions. In general, IPs are classified into three main classes called: soft IPs, firm IPs and hard IPs. IP reuse comes at the price of integration effort especially for incompatible IPs.

5.2. Platform-based Codesign

Instead of reusing individual IPs, this style of Codesign uses an entire platform specific for a certain application domain. The effort of design is limited to tuning the platform for the given application (bottom-up methodology) or to tuning the application for the given platform (top-down methodology). Certainly, this approach reduces considerably the effort of design, but at the price of nonoptimized designs furthermore, finding the existing platform that matches designer requirements is not trivial [12].

5.3. Design pattern-based Codesign

In software engineering, a pattern is a general repeatable solution to a commonly occurring problem. A pattern is an abstract template that needs to be refined and adapted before it can be integrated into the code. Patterns focus on descriptions that communicate the reasons for design decisions. In the field of SOC Codesign, the definition of generic patterns is more difficult. For instance, design patterns to generate wrappers for IPs integration have been already proposed and others to promote reuse beyond code reuse [13].

5.4. IDE-based Codesign

Putting a collection of tools that may be obtained from different providers and organizations in one environment to facilitate the SOC Codesign is the philosophy of the IDE-based Codesign. The main challenge in this style of Codesign is the interoperability between tools [14].

5.5. Codesign for reuse

Codesign for reuse tends to design reusable IPs. These reusable components can be soft, firm or hard, described in a standard format and well documented and catalogued for easy integration [15].

5.6. Aspect-oriented Codesign

The aspect-oriented engineering tends to increase reuse by separating in early stages between functional and nonfunctional aspects and to propose some mechanisms to integrate them lately to generate the full code. This new technology was rapidly borrowed by SOC designers [16]. This strategy will bring many advantages regarding the portability and reuse but at the price of time overhead.

5.7. Model-driven Codesign

This approach is relatively very recent and becomes very popular. It tends to apply the model-driven engineering technologies in SOC Codesign. The impetus behind this is to increase productivity by the use of a unified graphical notation (source models) to model different views of the system (functional, structural, behavioral, etc.) and the automatic transformation of such graphical notations to one or many other notations (target models). The source, the target meta-models and the transformation rules are expressed explicitly and can be used either to transform one model to another model or to refine the initial model. In this context, many UML profiles for SOC Codesign were proposed [17].

5.8. Web-based Codesign

By web-based Codesign, we refer to SOC Codesign in an Internet-based context. In this style of Codesign, designers develop their SOC online and, consequently, they can exploit available environments, tools and download what they need to accomplish their tasks. For instance, they can use sophisticated Internet research tools for IP selection, simulation and verification tools. They can also contact SOC experts and share the experience online [18].

5.9. Cloud Codesign

As a new form of Internet-based computing, cloud computing is an emerging computing style that tends to enable ubiquitous, on-demand access to a shared pool of configurable computing resources (e.g., computer networks, servers, storage, applications and services) which can be rapidly provisioned and released with minimal management effort. Cloud Codesign refers to CCodesign but in the context of cloud [19].

5.10. FCodesign: formal Codesign

Formal Codesign tends to develop SOCs implementing critical applications with hard constraints. This style of Codesign uses formal specification languages and formal verification techniques such as model checking and theorem proving to ensure the correctness of the system. The methodology itself starts from an initial formal specification and then proceeds by refinement till the code generation. Examples of such languages are B, Esterel, Lotos, Petri nets, abstract automata and so on. Generally, SOC designers are not very familiar with formal specifications requiring a deep mathematical background; for this reason, instead of dealing directly with such specifications, many tools have been developed to generate formal specification from graphical notations (UML) [20].

5.11. PCodesign: prototypic Codesign

The first objective of prototypic Codesign is to provide a rapid prototype of SOC to the customer. The prototype is generally implemented in FPGA. By exploiting existing tools of emulation/simulation, the customer requirements can be earlier validated without engaging into details. This style is very suitable when the customer requirements cannot be captured entirely in the requirements analysis phase or because the requirements change rapidly over time; in this case, SOC designers can incrementally validate the functionality using reconfigurable SOC.

6. What are intelligent embedded systems?

Intelligent embedded systems represent a novel and promising generation of embedded systems. The word "intelligent" or "smart" may imply many things: for instance, it can imply the ability to make decisions, the capability of learning from external stimuli, adapting to changes or the possibility of executing computationally intelligent algorithms.

In this context, we will define an IES as a conventional ES with the capacity of reasoning about their external environments and adapt their behavior accordingly. IES have some main characteristics such as self-learning, self-optimizing and self-repairing (**Figure 3**).

A good example where IES can be found is robotics. Robotics are basically intelligent machines whose functionality is controlled by embedded systems. Robotics contain embedded systems at their heart to perform the functions required for them, for example, pick and place systems in manufacturing industry, welding robots used in automobile assembly, and so on. Elmenreich [21] identified some potential reasons for employing an intelligent solution for embedded systems among them, such as dependability, efficiency, autonomy, easy modeling, maintenance costs and insufficient alternatives. Beyond these reasons, we can say that the first impetus behind IES is to render the human life easier, more comfortable and more secure. For instance, IES are now present in what we call smart homes, smart cities, Internet of things (IoT) and so on. IES can execute intelligent real-time tasks to manage power and water, help aged and invalid persons in their daily activities, and control smart cars and drones and many other smart devices. The presence of IES in our life becomes a necessity.

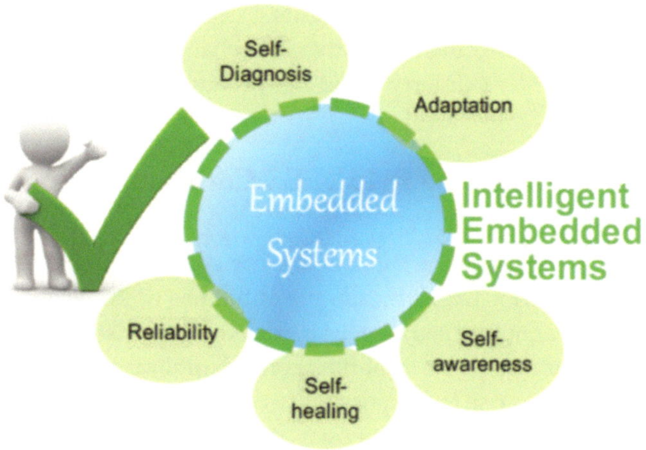

Figure 3. Intelligent embedded system features.

7. What is intelligent embedded software?

An IESo is first an ESo that has the capacity to gather and analyze data and communicate with other systems. Other criteria include the capacity to learn from experience, security, connectivity, the ability to adapt according to current data and the capacity for remote monitoring and management. As intelligent conventional software, IESo can also include sophisticated AI-based software systems, such as expert systems and other types of software. IESo exists all around us in terminals, digital televisions, traffic lights, automobiles, and airplane controls,

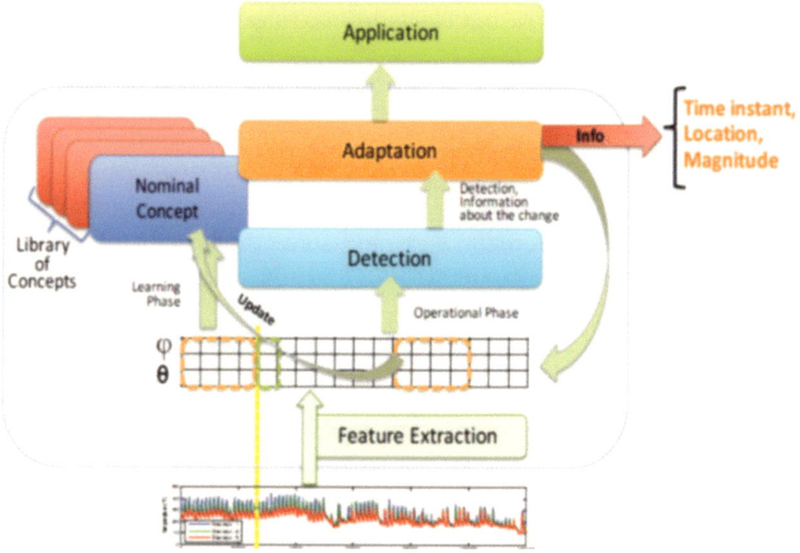

Figure 4. Adaptable embedded software flow.

among a great number of other possibilities. **Figure 4** depicts a possible flow for an adaptable IESo having the capability of learning from a dynamic changing environment. The IES have to resort to some concepts in order to interpret and comprehend the semantic of new features [22].

8. The application of AI in the field of ES Codesign

Artificial intelligence (AI) is becoming more and more attractive to model and simulate control intelligent system behavior [23]. An example is the use of knowledge-based technology for control systems that cannot be completely modeled mathematically. Recently, the use of artificial intelligence (AI) techniques in real-time control applications has emerged. In terms of embedded systems, this gives rise to the possibility of developing systems that can learn from their environment and that can change their own control programs to adapt to new situations, and these features are required to operate autonomous devices. In this section, we try to highlight some of AI methods that have been applied in the field of electronic and ES design at the same time and we will show the possibility of applying such methods in the context of IESo.

8.1. Expert systems, neural networks and fuzzy logic

The application of IA in the field of electronic design is not new. It returned to 1980s where EDA tools profited from expert system technology to assist electronic designers to make routing/placement and hardware synthesis [24].

With the ever-increasing in the semiconductor technology integration, using expert systems in IES design becomes questionable since they demand much time for reasoning, the knowledge base will be unmanaged, furthermore, rules of type if-else cannot model complex deduction process. Some works are proposed to implement expert systems in hardware, and other works are proposed to parallelize the inference process to gain time.

Expert systems have been maturated, and many environments and languages are now available to assist designers to develop their own domain-specific expert systems. Traditional expert systems are less interactive and have not the capabilities of learning; to overcome these drawbacks, researchers tend to integrate Neural Networks (NN) with expert systems, so they can learn and modify inference rules/knowledge base dynamically. Similarly, to deal with uncertain/incomplete information, fuzzy logic and some mathematical theories like rough sets have had been integrated with expert systems and NN.

In the context of IESo, fuzzy expert systems and neural networks can be applied especially in fault detection and diagnosis [25]. Cotton [26] proposed a solution for implementing neural networks on microcontrollers for many embedded applications. A new class of SOC called neural or nerve SOC implementing neural computing has been emerged [27].

8.2. Multiagent systems

Multiagent systems (MAS) have been successfully applied to model and manage complex distributed systems since they offer high capabilities for complex interactions, autonomy and reactive/cognitive behavior modeling. In the context of IES design, some authors proposed to model intelligent agents for IP research and web-based SOC design. An IP can be soft and consequently used to execute an IESo module. Other works have applied MAS to model complex IESo, and the result is what we call embedded agents. The latter can be later synthesized as software embedded agent or hardware embedded agent [28–30].

8.3. Ontologies

Recently, the use of ontologies in software engineering has gained popularity because they facilitate the semantic interoperability and machine reasoning. Ontology is a formal representation of domain-specific knowledge. In the context of ES Codesign, some researchers, used ontologies for IP research in web semantics, for instance authors in [31], defined a VHDL ontology. The work in [32] defined ontology for IP reuse-based SOC design. The IP can be of course soft. Other works have been tried to use ontologies in the context of the Internet of things (IoT) to guarantee interoperability [33]. For example, in **Figure 4**, we can use ontologies to model the set of concepts.

8.4. Nature/bioinspired approaches

Nature/bioinspired optimization meta-heuristics has gained more attention by ES designers especially in Hw/Sw partitioning and hardware synthesis. The latter is qualified as NP-hard problems. Among bioinspired meta-heuristics, we find genetic algorithms and their variants, simulated annealing, taboo search, ant colony, PSO and so on. In contrast to exact methods, meta-heuristics is more general and aims to compromise between solution quality and search time. In the context of IESo, optimization meta-heuristics can be applied to solve the RTOS energy aware scheduling problem or jointly with neural networks.

8.5. Constraint satisfaction

In AI, constraint satisfaction is the process of finding a solution to a set of constraints that impose conditions that the variables must satisfy. Many activities are considered as constraint satisfaction problems, especially the hardware/software partitioning including allocation, assignation and scheduling problems [34].

8.6. Logic programming

The effort of designing hardware capable of supporting the declarative programming model for logic derivations can now lead to intelligent embedded designs which are considerably more efficient compared to the traditional procedural ones. For instance, Panagopoulos et al. [35] proposed an extension of the RISC architecture microprocessor for knowledge representation, based on attribute grammar evaluation, in an effort of achieving design efficiency for intelligent embedded systems.

8.7. Hybrid models

Hybrid AI models refer to the combination of the above-mentioned models. For instance, we can combine between MAS and expert systems/NN/fuzzy logic and genetic algorithms to model the cognitive part of agents.

8.8. Organic computing

Organic computer (OC) is a new emerging computing paradigm inspired from the biological organic model. It is based on the insight that we will soon be surrounded by large collections of autonomous systems, which are equipped with sensors and actuators, aware of their environment, communicate freely, and organize themselves in order to perform the actions and services that seem to be required. An organic computing system is a technical system which adapts dynamically to exogenous and endogenous change. It is characterized by the properties of self-organization, self-configuration, self-optimization, self-healing, self-protection, self-explaining and context awareness. **Figure 5** depicts the IBM's MAPE cycle for autonomic computing which is the basis for OC. Here, M is for Monitor, A for Analyze, P for Plan, E for Execute, and K for Knowledge (the autonomic element). **Figure 6** shows the OC system generic architecture which is based on the observer/controller architecture. Here, SuOC designates system under observation and control. It is composed of a set of interacting elements/agents, and it does not depend on the existence of observer/controller [36, 37].

Recently, a new class of self-adaptive SOCs emerges as a new paradigm inspired from the organic computing and especially the self-x properties. This class of SOC is called organic

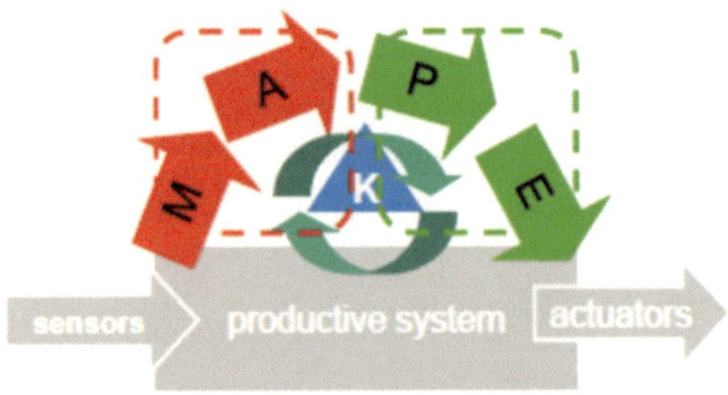

Figure 5. IBM's MAPE cycle for autonomic computing.

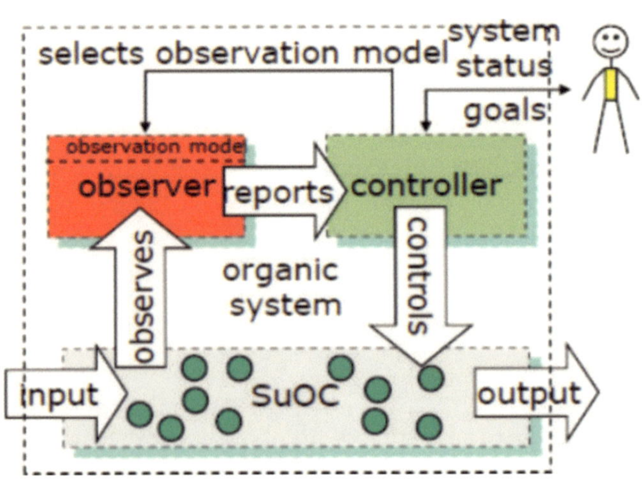

Figure 6. The generic OC system architecture.

SOC (OSOC), more suitable for smart applications having the capabilities of self-adaptation, self-control and evolvability. This new architecture is comprised of many layers and integrates more components to assure the self-x properties [38].

9. IA-based Codesign flow for intelligent embedded systems

As embedded systems become intelligent, the situation gets much more complicated regarding the application of traditional ES Codesign methodologies. In **Table 5**, we show some main differences between embedded computing and intelligent computing. The main challenge resides in how can we integrate these two styles or philosophies of computing?

In response to this aim, we propose what we call *AI-based Codesign flow for Intelligent Embedded Systems* (**Figure 7**). The idea is to enrich the conventional ES Codesign flow by another activity called *AI models partitioning* just before the HW/SW partitioning. During this activity, IES designer partitions his application functionalities or modules between a set of possible AI models such as neural network, expert system, genetic algorithm, fuzzy logic, intelligent agents, organic computing, etc., and other algorithmic modules. In other words, the objective of this step is to identify the system intelligent components and their associated AI models. At this stage, the designer can resort to some tools for modeling, simulation and formal verification. Combining AI heterogeneous models with different semantics in one framework is not an easy task and requires some validation to ensure the system correctness at higher level of abstraction. The Eclipse environment may offer an efficient solution for integration and interoperability between different AI tools and platforms. MATLAB, in turn, seems very appropriate to program and simulate some of the well-known AI paradigms such as NN, fuzzy logic and genetic algorithms. The objective of applying formal verification (i.e., model checking and/or theorem proving) at this stage is to ensure the correctness and termination properties especially in critical IES. But in order to be capable of doing formal verification, we have to define formal specification for AI models in specific formal specification languages. Depending on the used AI model, many formal languages can be employed. For example, Petri nets have been used

Embedded computing	Intelligent computing
Software and hardware are both first class	Software is first class
Resources constrained	Unlimited resources
Simple tasks	Very complex tasks
Small computing power	Significant computing power
Reactive	Cognitive
Low-level models and programming languages (Assembly, C)	High-level programming models beyond procedural paradigm
Static and completely specified environment	Dynamic and imprecise environments
Human intervention is weak	Human intervention is prominent

Table 5. Embedded computing vs. intelligent computing.

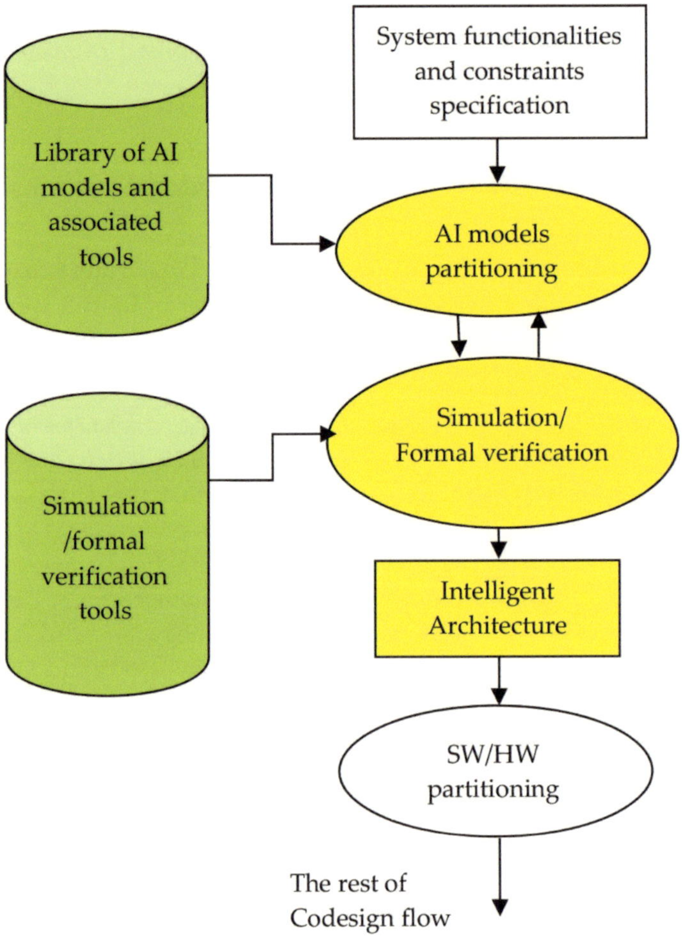

Figure 7. IA-based IES Codesign.

to formalize SMA [39]. Some authors have developed a new class of formal languages called Learning Regular Languages to formalize NN [40]. Some AI methods can be seen as formal models, especially the logic paradigm. A refinement step may also be needed to add the necessary details. The result of this step is what we call the *intelligent architecture*. After that comes the HW/SW partitioning to identify hardware/software components. For instance, we can implement a component modeled by a neural network as an ASIC, a FPGA or as a C code.

10. Challenges and perspectives

In the rapidly changing life requirements and technology, embedded software continues to dominate the values and costs of intelligent embedded systems industry. Despite the proliferation of IES over the last years, the industry of electronics and embedded systems has afraid from AI and the main question is: Can AI be a reality and apply it in IES industry efficiently without side effect?

If we know that when referring to AI, we automatically refer to human intellectual activities such as perception, learning, reasoning and memorization, self-optimization, self-adaptation and so on. The industry judgment is maybe due to the fact that the intellectual activities consume much time that can be a bottleneck for performance especially in a real-time context, where activities or tasks have deadlines or another form of timing constraints, or maybe due to the fact that AI does not reach a certain level of maturity especially at the pragmatic stage; so it can be applied efficiently in real physical systems.

For instance, multiagent systems and despite their solid theoretic basis and maturity, they are not well supported by industry. Experience from both academia and industry has proved that MAS have been used successfully to design complex, self-adaptable and even real-time systems. Currently, there are more than 80 MAS design methodologies. We think that most existing MAS methodologies in their current state are not able to deal with IES specificities; however, with some tuning and enhancement, MAS can be efficient to develop IES [41]. We note that the application of fuzzy expert systems and NN to model and simulate fault detection and diagnostics in IES is an attractive tendency. For instance, experience from both academy and industry has proved that NN have been used successfully to design self-adaptable IES.

Organic computing seems to be an attractive solution for IES but needs much effort to prove its efficiency in the industry.

In a real-time context, reasoning is known to be a bottleneck with regard to performances so in order to solve this dilemma, we can for instance parallelize reasoning or to implement it as hardware components. In all cases, we see that we must create a bridge between AI models and existing well-practiced ES Codesign methodologies and associated tools [42]. On the other hand, the progress in hardware technologies will certainly contribute in efficient implementations of IES, notably those targeting multicores and reconfigurable architectures like FPGA. Reconfigurable architectures match well dynamic and adaptable IES.

Author details

Fateh Boutekkouk[1]*, Ridha Mahalaine[2], Zina Mecibah[1], Saliha Lakhdari[1], Ramissa Djouani[1] and Djalila Belkebir[1]

*Address all correspondence to: fateh_boutekkouk@yahoo.fr

1 Research Laboratory on Computer Science's Complex Systems (ReLaCS²), University of Oum El Bouaghi, Algeria

2 École supérieure d'informatique (ESI), Algiers, Algeria

References

[1] Gajski DD, Vahid F, Narayan S, Gong J. Specification and Design of Embedded Systems. Englewood Cliffs, NJ: Prentice Hall; 1994

[2] Schaumont P. A Practical Introduction to Hardware/Software Codesign, 2nd ed. 2012. ISBN: 978-1-4614-3736-9

[3] Lee EA. Embedded Software. In: Zelkowitz M, editor. Advances in Computers. Vol. 56. London: Academic Press; 2002

[4] Bergman K, Carloni LP, Biberman A, Chan J, Hendry G. Photonic Network-on-Chip Design. 2014. Ebook. ISBN: 978-1-4419-9335-9

[5] Schuck C, Guo X, Fan L, Ma X, Poot M, Tang HX. Quantum Technology On A Chip. 2017. Available from: http://seas.yale.edu/news-events/news/quantum-technology-chip

[6] Ditto W, Murali K, Sinha S. Construction of a Chaotic Computer Chip. Applications of Nonlinear Dynamics; Part of the Understanding Complex Systems Book Series (UCS). 2009. pp. 3-13

[7] SystemC: www.systemc.org

[8] Mentor graphics: www.mentor.com

[9] Synopsis: www.synopsys.com/designware

[10] Schirner G, Sachdeva G, Gerstlauer A, Domer R. Modeling, Simulation and Synthesis in an Embedded Software Design Flow for an ARM Processor. Technical Report CECS-06-06 May 25. 2006

[11] Wagner F, Cesário W, Carro L. Jerraya A. Strategies for the integration of hardware and software IP components in embedded systems-on-chip. The VLSI Journal—Special Issue: IP and Design Reuse. 2004;**37**(4):223-252

[12] Sgroi M, Sangiovanni-Vincentelli A, Bernardinis F, Pinello C, Carloni L. Platform-Based Design for Embedded Systems. In: Zurawski R. editor. Embedded Systems Handbook. Print ISBN: 978-0-8493-2824-4, eBook ISBN: 978-1-4200-3816-3.2005. Chapter 22

[13] Manai Y, Haggège J, Benrejeb M. New approach for hardware/software embedded system conception based on the use of design patterns. Journal of Software Engineering and Applications. 2010;**3**(6)

[14] Carbone J. Doing embedded design with an Eclipse-based IDE. Express Logic. 2008. Available from: www.embedded.com/design/prototyping-and-development/

[15] Cavalloro P. System Level Design Model with Reuse of System IP. Kluwer Academic Publishers; 2016

[16] Deharbe D, Medeiro S. Aspect-oriented design in systemC: Implementation and applications. In Proceedings of the 19th annual symposium on Integrated circuits and systems design (SBCCI '06); 2006. p. 119-124

[17] Boutekkouk F, Benmohammed M, Bilavarn S, Auguin M. UML2.0 Profiles for embedded systems and systems on a chip (SOCs). Journal of Object Technology. 2009;**8**(1):135-157

[18] Witczyński M, Hrynkiewicz E, Pawlak A. A web services based approach for system on a chip design planning. In: Coordination of Collaborative Engineering—State of the Art and Future Challenges 5th International Workshop on Challenges in Collaborative Engineering (CCE'07). 2007

[19] Intel Labs. Single-chip Cloud Computer 2017. Available from: http://www.intel.com/go/terascale

[20] LIAMA. Formes: FORmal Methods for Embedded Systems.Visiting Committee Report. 2012

[21] Elmenreich W. Intelligent methods for embedded systems. In Proceedings of the First Workshop on Intelligent Solutions in Embedded Systems (WISES 2003); 2003

[22] Roveri M. Intelligence for embedded systems (introduction to the course) [Ph.D. and master course], Politecnico di Milano, DEIB, Italy, 2017. Available from: roveri.faculty.polimi.it/wp-content/uploads/Lecture_1.pdf

[23] Zilouchian A, Jamshidi M. Intelligent Control Systems Using Soft Computing Methodologies. CRC Press. 2001. ISBN 0-8493-1875-0

[24] Schwarz A.F. Handbook of VLSI Chip Design and Expert Systems. Academic Press Limited Harcourt Brace Jovanovich, Publishers ISBN: 0-12-632425-5. 1993

[25] Mostafa A, Elfattah M, Youssif A. An intelligent methodology for malware detection in android smartphones based static analysis. International Journal of Communications. 2016;**10**

[26] Cotton NJ. A neural network implementation on embedded systems [thesis]. Auburn, Alabama; 2010

[27] Johnson B, Lancaster K, Hogue I, Meng F, Kong Y, Enquist L, McAlpine M. 3D printed nervous system on a chip. Lab on a Chip—Miniaturisation for Chemistry and Biology. 2016;**16**(8):1393-1400

[28] Boutekkouk F, Benmohammed M. An agent-based framework for SOCs design. In Seminaire Nationale en Informatique, Biskra (SNIB'06). Algeria: Biskra; 2006

[29] Charles V. The design of a JADE-based autonomous workflow management system for collaborative SoC design. Journal of Expert Systems with Applications. 2009;**36**:2659-2669

[30] Jamont JP, Occello M. DIAMOND: Une approche pour la conception de systems multi-agents embarqués. France: Institut National Polytechnique de Grenoble-INPG; 2005

[31] Zdraveski V, Trajanov D. VHDL IP cores ontology. In: The 10th Conference for Informatics and Information Technology CIIT 2013. 2013

[32] Boutekkouk F. Towards an ontology-driven intellectual properties reuse for systems on chip design. In: Proceedings of the 2013 International Conference on Systems, Control, Signal Processing and Informatics; 2013; Greece

[33] Berrios V. Cross-Industry Semantic Interoperability, Part Three: The Role of a Top-level Ontology. 2017. Available from: http://embedded-computing.com/articles/

[34] Mitra R, Basu A. Hardware-software partitioning: A case for constraint satisfaction. IEEE Intelligent Systems. 2000;**5**(1):54-63

[35] Panagopoulos IP, Pavlatos CC, Papakonstantinou GK. An embedded system for artificial intelligence applications. International Journal of Computer, Electrical, Automation, Control and Information Engineering. 2007;**1**(4)

[36] Schmeck H. Organic computing—A new vision for distributed embedded systems. In Proceedings of the Eighth IEEE International Symposium on Object-Oriented Real-Time Distributed Computing (ISORC'05), 2005. p. 201-203

[37] Hartmut Schmeck Organic Computing—A Generic Approach to Controlled Self-organization in Adaptive Systems Institut AIFB, KIT Mars; 2009

[38] Herkersdorf A. Conquering MPSoC design and architecture complexity with bio-inspired self-organization. In: MPSoC Forum Margeaux, France, July 10. 2014

[39] Marzougui B, Hassine K, Barkaoui K. Formalism for modeling a multi agent systems: Agent petri nets. Journal of Software Engineering and Applications. 2010;**3**(12):1118-1124

[40] Madhusudan P. Learning Algorithms and Formal Verification. A Tutorial. University of Illinois at Urbana-Champaign VMCAI Nice; 2007

[41] Mecibah Z, Boutekkouk F. Comparative study between Multi Agents Systems methodologies according to intelligent embedded systems requirements. In: The 4th International Conference on Automation, Control Engineering and Computer Science (ACECS-2017); 28-30 March 2017; Tangier, Morocco

[42] Agarwal A, Shankar R, Pandya AS. Embedding intelligence into EDA tools. Series Frontiers in Artificial Intelligence and Application, Integrated Intelligent Systems for Engineering Design. 2006;**149**:389-408

Chapter 2

Cognitive Artificial Intelligence: Concept and Applications for Humankind

Arwin Datumaya Wahyudi Sumari and
Adang Suwandi Ahmad

Additional information is available at the end of the chapter

http://dx.doi.org/10.5772/intechopen.72764

Abstract

Computation within the human brain is not possible to be emulated 100% in artificial intelligence machines. Human brain has an awesome mechanism when performing computation with new knowledge as the end result. In this chapter, we will show a new approach for emulating the computation that occurs within the human brain to obtain new knowledge as the time passes and makes the knowledge to become newer. Based on this phenomenon, we have built an intelligent system called the Knowledge-Growing System (KGS). This approach is the basis for designing an agent that has ability to think and act rationally like a human, which is called the cognitive agent. Our cognitive modeling approach has resulted in a model of human information processing and a technique called Arwin-Adang-Aciek-Sembiring (A3S). This brain-inspired method opens a new perspective in AI known as cognitive artificial intelligence (CAI). CAI computation can be applied to various applications, namely: (1) knowledge extraction in an integrated information system, (2) probabilistic cognitive robot and coordination among autonomous agent systems, (3) human health detection, and (4) electrical instrument measurement. CAI provides a wide opportunity to yield various technologies and intelligent instrumentations as well as to encourage the development of cognitive science, which then encourages the intelligent systems approach to human intelligence.

Keywords: A3S, cognitive agent, cognitive artificial intelligence, knowledge extraction, Knowledge-Growing System, intelligent system

1. Introduction

The term artificial intelligence (AI) was coined over 20 years ago but the endeavor to emulate human intelligence, in this case is how humans think, has been around since the 19th century.

Why AI? Humans have intelligence that is not possessed by other living things. With this intelligence, humans can do almost everything, such as walking, talking, creating something worthy, doing business, leading an organization, inventing new technologies, and writing papers. How can humans do these things? There has to be something awesome inside that motivates humans to perform such actions. There will be no action if there is no knowledge, because it is something awesome that produces knowledge. It was then found that this something awesome is the brain with its complex structure as well as its mechanism. Without a brain, humans are just a pile of useless skin and bones. It is like a computer without a processor. So, the brain is the source of all human actions. The brain is the only "engine" that processes all information perceived by humans and the processed information becomes knowledge that creates human intelligence, namely, the ability to do almost everything.

Humans appear to do almost anything by orchestrating all of their apparatuses easily to perform the actions mentioned previously. What we can do is to emulate how the brain works by processing information to obtain knowledge. The brain works when humans think and this process is automatic when humans observe or see phenomena around them, meaning that there is a computation mechanism within the brain that will benefit humankind if it can be emulated in computer-based systems. There have been many approaches, techniques, and methods invented by many researchers all over the world. Some approaches are based on how the brain's neural networks work, use of stored knowledge or past learning, how humans think or act rationally, and the human infomation processing system. It is understood that computation within the human brain is very complex and cannot be emulated exactly 100%. Therefore, emulating some of its magnificence is something that can benefit humankind.

Based on the information in the previous paragraph, the first approach is called computational AI [1], the second is called knowledge-based AI or machine learning [2], the third according to [3] is called the agent approach, while the fourth according to [4] is called the Human Inference System (HIS) approach. Since the introduction of agent terminology as well as its definition by [3, 5], any kind of approach in AI is related to the agent because it is assumed to represent humans in real life. To become intelligent, an agent has to have knowledge and if we look at humans, an agent can obtain knowledge by any number of methods. With humans, knowledge does not come suddenly without process. Therefore, how can we get knowledge of something? First, we have to have information regarding that thing. This information is then sent to the brain to be processed to become knowledge of such thing. Based on this time knowledge, we can estimate the recognition of such thing. The knowledge of such thing can be added to or grown if we get more information from other sources. The more information we get, the more knowledge we have to more accurately estimate the recognition of a thing. **Estimating is making a decision about something that might happen in the future**. Estimation can only be done through thinking.

In this scheme of a real-life mechanism, we can see that the process of getting knowledge not only shows how neural networks work (as an example), namely, processing the information and how to store the knowledge in the brain's memory for later use, but also shows how the information, as the first source of knowledge, is gathered and processed within the brain with the ultimate aim of having comprehensive knowledge. This knowledge starts from nothing, grows with the increasing amount and kinds of information as well as the kinds of information source, and is stored and extracted when decisions need to be made. If other researchers focus their research on how the brain's cells work or how to create an intelligent agent with certain characteristics, we focus our research on how humans obtain their knowledge with a mechanism known as information extraction.

Our research was initiated from our curiosity that there has to be a unique mechanism within the brain that gives humans knowledge. It is an abstract thing but it is real. Therefore, we had a hypothesis that the brain does something that we call growing the knowledge. The knowledge will grow with the accretion of information as time passes. This is the essential matter of the system called the Knowledge-Growing System (KGS), a kind of cognitive agent. This system has been around since its first introduction in 2009 [6]. The aim of this chapter is as follows. Section 1 will give a brief introduction on what KGS is and a glance at AI. The approach perspectives to the development of KGS will be delivered in Section 2. In Section 3 we will show the steps needed to build a KGS. Examples of the utilization of KGS to real-world problems will be given in Section 4. Section 5 will provide some concluding remarks.

2. The idea and approach perspectives in building KGS

2.1. The idea

The idea was so simple. It emerged from a discussion in our laboratory in the mid-2000s. We had been observing the phenomenon of why humans are intelligent. Humans have a unique intelligence that differs one to another, and they are intelligent because they have knowledge. The question is how does the knowledge get there, where does it come from, when is it increased, and what mechanism processes it? We did not enquire why knowledge exists, because humans have a brain that differs from other living creatures. Our research is focused only on the above four mentioned questions, especially on the mechanism of the grown of the knowledge within human brain. This is a simple question but at that time we had not found any literature that had studied this matter. Therefore, we decided to conduct this research and have shared some of our research results in previous publications.

2.2. Psychological perspective

Why did we need to view our designed system from a psychological perspective? The primary consideration was that thinking is a cognitive process and it is easy to be viewed from the psychological side. We conducted a number of studies on some models that are considered as human thought models. There are so many models but we selected the ones that represented the mechanism that occurred when humans think and act rationally. Moreover, these models should be sufficiently representative. They are Galileo's four-step advancement of rational thinking, Piaget's schema, Feynman's model, which perfects Galileo's, Popper's three-world model, the cognitive psychology model, and Boyd's OODA model. The latest model can be used as part of our new human information processing model. A review of those selected

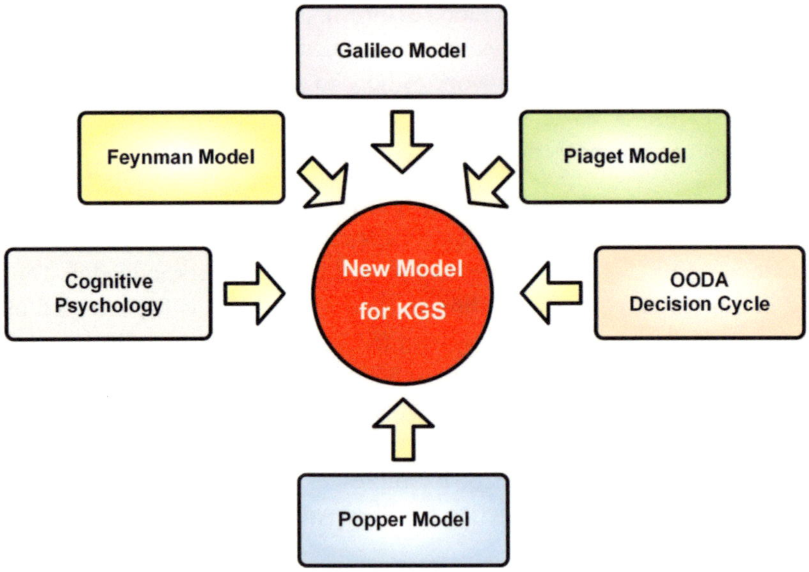

Figure 1. The psychological perspective of AI for building KGS.

models can be read in [4]. **Figure 1** summarizes all approaches from a psychological perspective to building new models of how humans think as the basis for KGS.

2.3. Mathematical perspective

In many cases, humans think probabilistically, especially when faced with situations that need a decision. In most situations, the decision to be made has to consider a plethora of data; on the other hand, there are also many decision alternatives or decision options that can be selected, e.g., plan A, plan B, etc. At the time we did the research, there was no method that was capable of coping with many data/indications, or many alternatives or hypotheses. We made three types of probabilistic thinking for mathematical verification as follows [7]:

2.3.1. Many-to-Estimated One (MEO) probability.

From processed data/indications, information will be obtained with a necessary certainty called degree of certainty (DoC), which leads to an inference regarding to the hypothesis being observed.

2.3.2. One-to-Many-to-Estimated-One (OMEO) probability.

Given processed single data/indication, information will be obtained regarding the DoCs of all available hypotheses, which in turn leads to a single hypothesis with the largest DoC.

2.3.3. Many-to-Many-to-Estimated-One (MMEO) probability.

Given processed multiple indications, information will be obtained regarding the DoCs of all available hypotheses, which in turn leads to a single hypothesis with the largest DoC. This is also called a multihypothesis multidata/indication problem, as illustrated in **Figure 1**. This is the case faced by most humans in real life.

The famous method that was designed to handle multiple data but with only one hypothesis is Bayes Inference Method (BIM). Later, we found that BIM is categorized as an MEO probability, as hypothesized above. **Figure 2** illustrates how MMEO probability works to obtain information with related DoCs.

2.4. Electrical engineering and informatics perspective

Even though AI is approached from various science and technology disciplines, it is mainly studied, researched, developed, applied, and implemented by researchers from the electrical engineering and informatics field. AI can be viewed from various angles. From this perspective, we had our own view, namely, the anatomy view. Based on our study, we found three theories that view AI from its anatomy. First, the theory of agent from Russel & Norvig [3], second, the theory of topology from Ahmad [1], and third, the types of processed data and the types of growing knowledge from Munakata [8] from which we can determine what type of data are grown by the system. **Figure 3** shows the three approaches that we use to develop our own KGS.

Another field that also attracts interest is information fusion, a method for integrating or combining information from diverse sources or mutliple sources into single comprehensive information to be used to estimate or predict an entity being observed. The information fusion

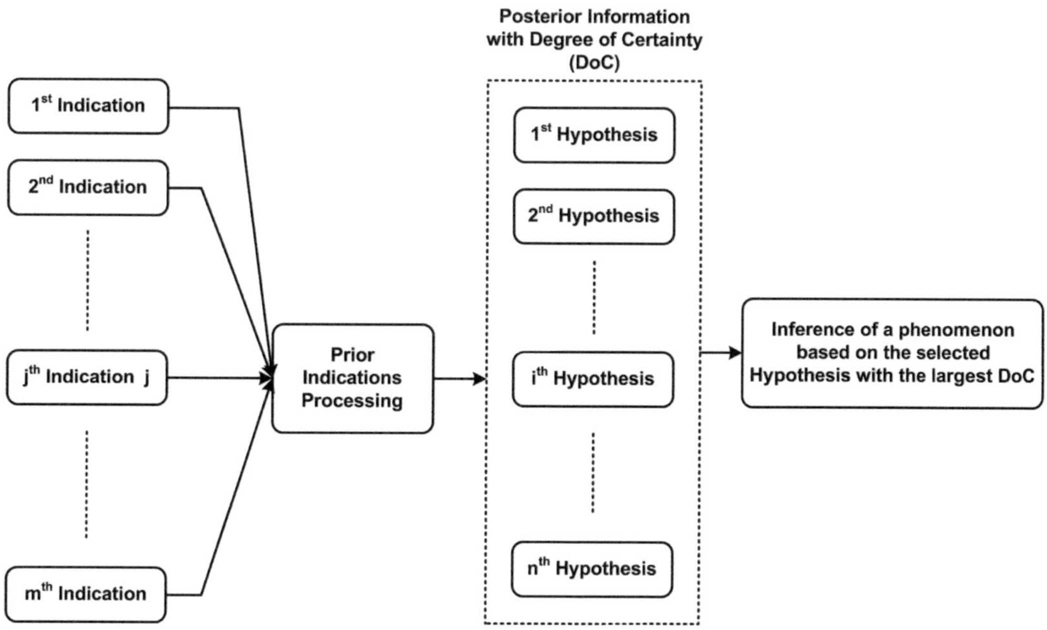

Figure 2. Illustration of the MMEO probability technique.

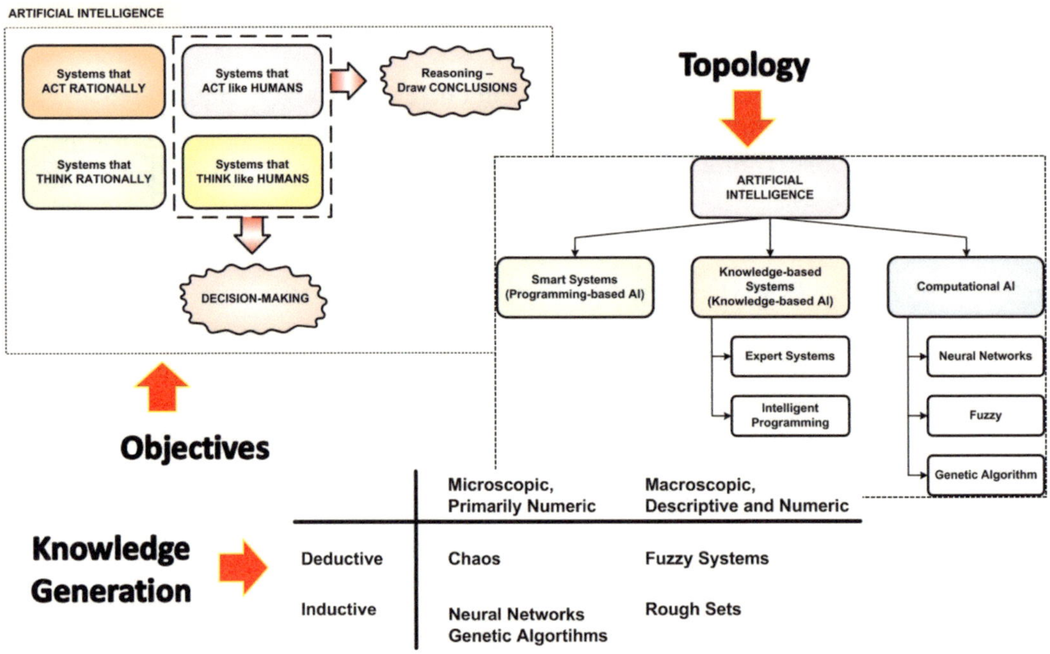

Figure 3. The engineering and informatics perspective of AI for building KGS.

field emerged from the desire to have better estimation of objects under observation from many sensors rather than just one.

Interestingly, humans already have multiple sensors to help them comprehend the environment. Normally, humans have five sensory organs, namely, eyes, ears, skin, tongue, and nose. Each sensor has its own kind of information. We believe that humans can acquire knowledge because of information delivered by the sensory organs and processed by the brain, which is then stored in a certain location in it. "Processed" in this case is the information from various sensory organs about something in the environment being observed, which is fused to become knowledge. **Fusing the information can be called knowledge extraction, meaning extracting knowledge from the fused information**.

2.5. Human information processing perspective

Essentially, the information processing model is a theory of human development that uses the computer as a metaphor for explaining thought processes. Similar to computers, humans transform information to solve cognitive problems. Development is viewed in terms of changes in memory-storage capacities and use of different types of cognitive strategies. On the other hand, information processing can be defined as the acquisition, recording, organization, retrieval, display, and dissemination of information.

We take a look at only three information processing models, namely, Wicken's model, Welford's model, and Whiting's model, the combination of which in our assessment can be adapted

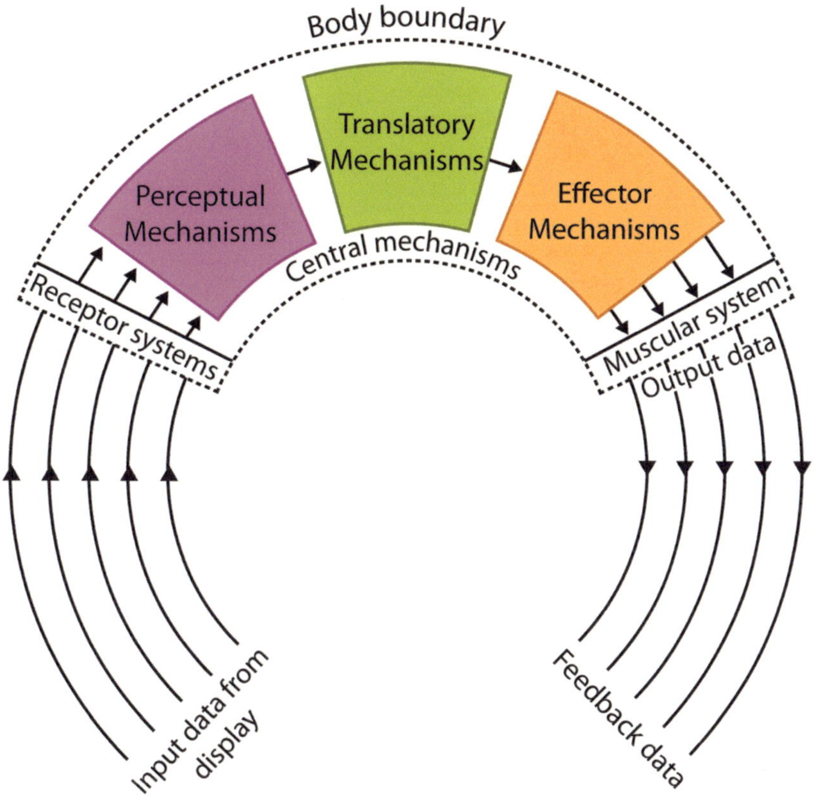

Figure 4. Whiting's model of information processing. Compare its similarity with Russel & Norvig's agent concept.

to our HIS design. Those three models are evaluated in [9]. **Figure 4** shows Whiting's model of information processing, which on thorough investigation is very close to Russel & Norvig's agent concept.

2.6. Social science perspective

In an endeavor to find a method that can complement BIM, from which two methods we can build our own method, we found a decision method taken from social science called Linear Opinion Pool (LOP) [10]. This method is designed to handle single data with multiple hypotheses. The method is important because agent is a social thing that cannot work alone in achieving its goal. In general, there are three types of social decision making as follows.

2.6.1. Linear Opinion Pool

LOP by [10], where ω_i is weighted between $0 \le \omega_i \le 1$ and $\sum_{i=1}^{n} \omega_i$:

$$P(B|A_1, A_2, \ldots, A_n) = \sum_{i=1}^{n} \omega_i P(B|A_i) \tag{1}$$

2.6.2. Independent Opinion Pool

Independent Opinion Pool (IOP) also known as Logarithmic Opinion Pool (LogOP) [11, 12]:

$$P(B|A_1, A_2, \ldots, A_n) \propto k \prod_{i=1}^{n} P(B|A_i) \tag{2}$$

2.6.3. Independent Likelihood Pool

Independent Likelihood Pool (ILP) by [13]:

$$P(B|A_1, A_2, \ldots, A_n) \propto P(B) \prod_{i=1}^{n} P(B|A_i) \tag{3}$$

The ILP method is the proper means for information combination in sensory cases because a priori information tends to come from the same source. However, the most used method in consensus theory is the LOP method, and in AI, LOP is the general method for combining probabilities from diverse agents to produce one social probability [14]. Later, we also found that LOP is categorized as OMEO probability, as hypothesized in Section 2.3.

3. Building the KGS

There is no exact definition of knowledge. For centuries there have been endeavors to understand what knowledge is. Essentially, knowledge is about knowing of something and knowing needs a means as well as a mechanism, such as thinking, perceiving, experience, learning, or interaction. An agent can do one of these means or more than one simultaneously, such as thinking while observing something. This is possible because humans have the ability to multitask. According to [15], there are four ways of knowing, namely:

- Some or all knowledge is innate.
- Some or all knowledge is observational.
- Some or all knowledge is nonobservational, attained by thought alone.
- Some or all knowledge is partly observational and partly not—attained at once by observing and thinking.

Back to our idea of building a KGS, that is, a cognitive agent that has the capability of growing knowledge as its intelligent primary characteristic. KGS is also a cognitive agent, which is designed to be able to think and act rationally like humans. Therefore, our design steps are as follows:

1. Determine the type of obtaining the knowledge.
2. Design the cycle for obtaining the knowledge and the model of information processing.
3. Design the cognitive agent.
4. Design the mechanism of obtaining the knowledge.

3.1. Determine the type of obtaining the knowledge

In the theory of knowledge generation, researchers in the field of psychology had different perspectives on knowledge generation in the human brain, but their idea is similar to what was later called constructivism. In its very simple definition, constructivism is a theory of learning or theory of knowledge (epistemology), which states that humans generate knowledge and meaning from experiences and interactions. Fundamentally, constructivists believe that humans "construct" their own knowledge and understanding through ideas, content, events, etc. that they come in contact with. This review can be read in [16].

From the perspective of agent, knowledge generation can be viewed from concept and method and terminology. From the first view, there are three types of methods, namely: (1) based on experience or past data [17], (2) based on interaction with the environment or cognitive computation [18], and (3) based on self-organizing [19]. From the latter view, at the time when we did the research, the only research that used this term was done for industrial application. It examined how knowledge grows old in the human brain and used the analogy to build a reconfiguration system for automobile application. It concentrated on the optimization of knowledge retrieval rather than emulating the way the human brain grows the knowledge over time [20].

There is an intersection of approach between past and current researchers that knowledge generation can be carried out by means of interaction with the environment. Therefore, we adopt the concept of constructivism in terms of interaction as the basis for growing knowledge in the human brain. This is the foundation of our new terminology, namely, knowledge growing, as a mechanism to grow knowledge in KGS.

3.2. Design the cycle for obtaining the knowledge and the model of information processing

Based on our study of various human information processing models, we conclude that the knowledge-growing cycle and human information processing models cannot be separated from each other. The cycle represents the mechanism of obtaining knowledge and uses it as the basis for making decisions or actions, while the human information processing models show how knowledge is grown within the brain.

From the models that have been studied, we have introduced a new human thought cycle called Sense-Inference and Decision Formulation-Decide and Act (SIDA) [3], which is part of the new human information processing model called HIS [20], as depicted in **Figure 5** and **Figure 6**, respectively. **Figure 6** became the basis for developing a mathematical model for knowledge growing.

3.3. Design the cognitive agent

In designing the agent, the essential points are that it has to have cognitive capability, namely, knowledge growing by means of information fusion. Our cognitive agent is depicted in **Figure 7**, an updated version from [22].

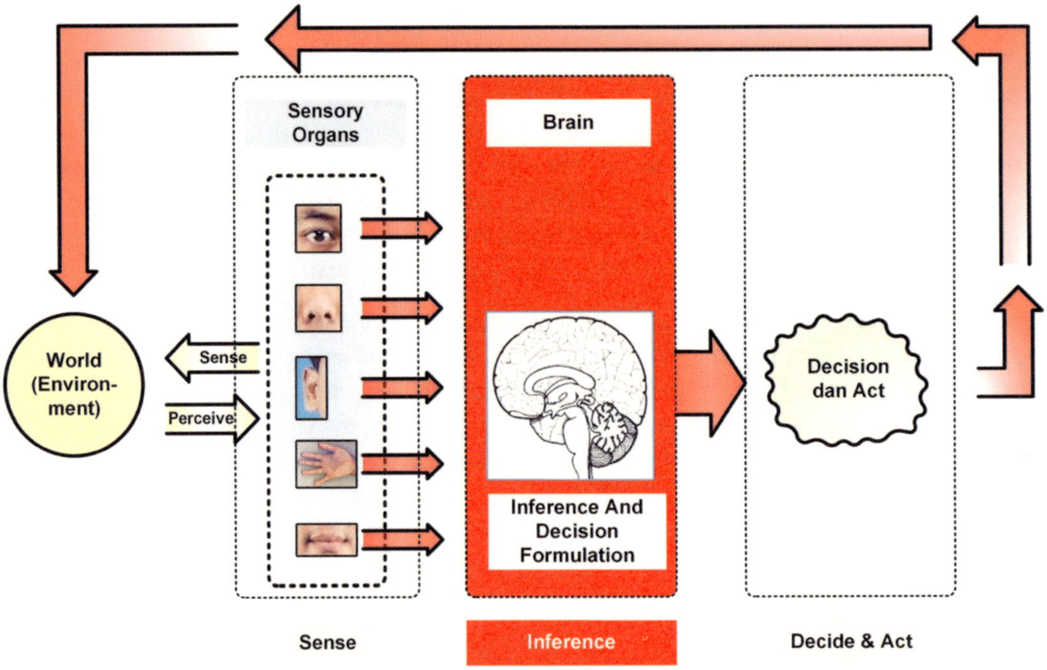

Figure 5. Sense-Inference and Decision Formulation-Decide and Act (SIDA) cycle.

3.4. Design the mechanism of obtaining the knowledge

This is the most important section of the chapter. The hardest way was to have the mathematical model of knowldege growing, because without it, it would not be possible to examine the mechanism depicted in **Figure 6**. However, first, we have to develop the formula for knowledge growing by taking advantage of the BIM and LOP methods, and obtain a mathematic formula that is designed to handle multiple data and multiple hypotheses called Maximum Score of the Total Sum of Joint Probabilities (MSJP) [22], as presented in Eq. (4). It is the representation of MMEO probability as hypothesized in Section 2.3. This method was then refined to become the A3S method [23] as the method for KGS knowledge growing as given in Eq. (5). To make it easy to remember, we replace the $\left(B_j|A_1\&\ldots\&A_i\&\ldots\&A_n\right)$ notation with $\left(B_j\boxplus A_i\right)$, where $\boxplus A_i$ is created to simplify $|A_1\&\ldots\&A_i\&\ldots\&A_n$ long notation:

$$P\left(B_j|A_1\&\ldots\&A_i\&\ldots\&A_n\right)=\frac{1}{n}\sum_{i=1}^{n}P\left(B_j|A_i\right)=\frac{\sum_{i=1}^{n}P\left(B_j|A_i\right)}{n} \tag{4}$$

$$P\left(B_j\boxplus A_i\right)=\frac{1}{n}\sum_{i=1}^{n}P\left(B_j|A_i\right) \tag{5}$$

where $P\left(B_j\boxplus A_i\right)$ is called New Knowledge Probability Distribution (NKPD).

Humans normally have five sensory organs that dynamically sense any kind of phenomenon that occurs in their environment. This phenomenon can be in physical or nonphysical form.

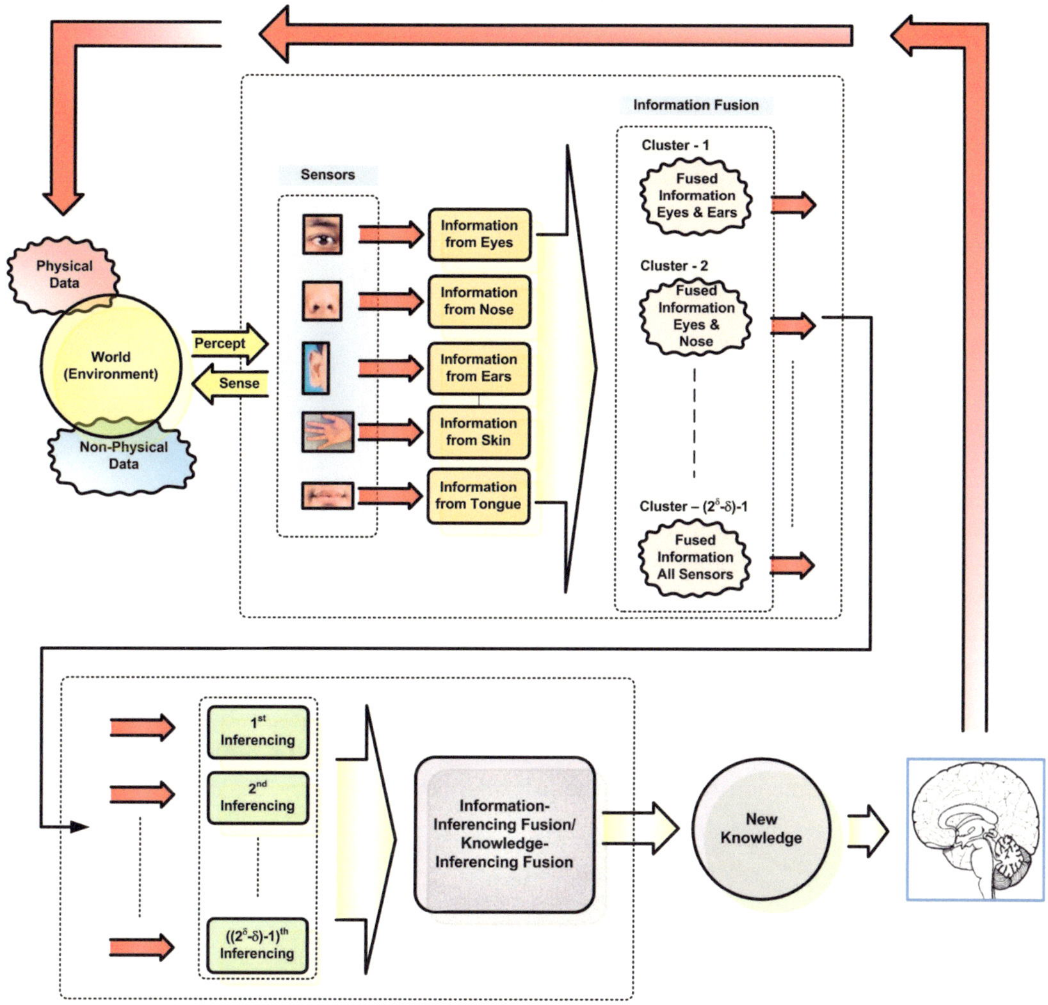

Figure 6. Human Inference System (HIS) model. The mechanism that occurred within SIDA is detailed in HIS.

The sensed phenomenon is then perceived by a sensory organ such as the ears for subsequent information processing. To gain comprehensive information, the information delivered by an individual sensory organ is then fused by the brain. In general, the amount of fused information can be obtained by using Eq. (6):

$$\lambda = \left(2^{\delta} - \delta\right) - 1 \tag{6}$$

where λ is the amount of fused information and δ is the number of sensors. In the case of humans with $\delta = 5$ there will be $\left(2^{5} - 5\right) - 1 = 26$ combinations of fused information or clusters (**Figure 6**).

The number of combinations is obtained under the assumption that there is no information fusion for information delivered from one-pair sensory organs such as eyes and ears. In

Information source	The possible combination of information from information sources					
	1	**2**	**...**	***i***	**...**	***λ***
1	X	X	...	X	...	X
2	X		...		...	X
...		X	...	X	...	X
j	...	...	...	X	...	X
...			...	X	...	X
δ			...		...	X
Fused information	1	2	...	*i*	...	*λ*

Table 1. Possible combinations of information from multisources (e.g. sensory organs).

general, the possible combination of information from a multisource that may be fused in KGS is shown in **Table 1**. Each combination will have its own information inferencing (**Figure 7**) and the fused information distribution is listed in the last row. **Table 2** presents the mathematical model of **Table 1**. As we can see in **Table 1**, the inputs to KGS are very simple and they have to be binary, after a certain conversion mechanism, of course, from their original inputs.

If we assume in general that $\delta = 1, \ldots, i, \ldots, n$ is the number of information multisources or multisensors, then $\lambda = 1, \ldots, j, \ldots m$ is a collection of hypotheses or multihypothesis of an environmental phenomenon regarding the information supplied by the multisensor. At the

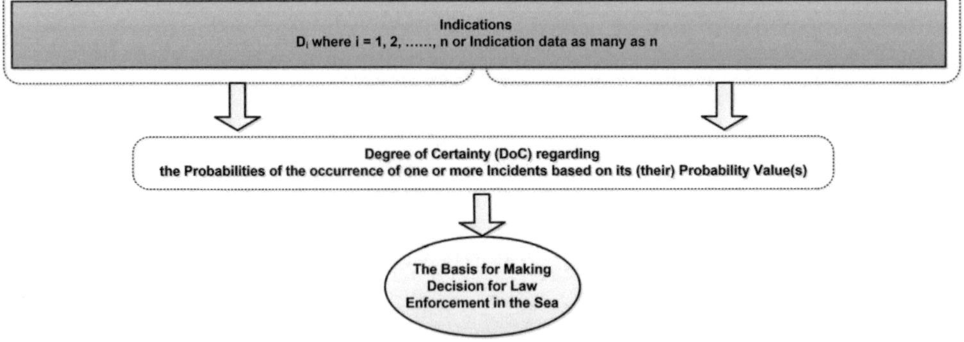

Figure 7. The cognitive agent for KGS.

Information source	The possible combination of information from information sources					
	1	**2**	**...**	***i***	**...**	**λ**
1	ϑ_1^1	ϑ_2^1	...	ϑ_i^1	...	ϑ_λ^1
2	ϑ_2^1	0	...	ϑ_i^2	...	ϑ_λ^2
...	...	...	...	...	...	...
j	0	0	...	ϑ_i^j	...	ϑ_λ^j
...	...	...	...	...	...	...
δ	0	0	...	0	...	ϑ_λ^δ
Ψ	ψ_1^1	ψ_2^1	...	ψ_i^1	...	ψ_λ^1

Table 2. The mathematical model of **Table 1**.

end of the computation, λ is also functioned as the number of fused information from a multisensor that explains a collection of individual phenomena based on the multihypothesis.

Notation $P\left(\vartheta_i^j\right)$ represents that the probability hypothesis j is true given information sensed and perceived by sensor i. The DoC represented by $P\left(\psi_1^j\right)$ defines that hypothesis j is selected based on the fusion of the information delivered from the multisensor, that is, from $P\left(\vartheta_i^j\right)$ to $P\left(\vartheta_\lambda^j\right)$, where $\lambda = 1, \dots, m$. The subscript "1" in the notation $P\left(\psi_1^j\right)$ means that the computation results are DoC at time 1 or the first observation time. This number is required if we want to have the next observation computed. Information fusion to obtain a collection of DoC is given in Eq. (7):

$$P\left(\psi_1^j\right) = \frac{\sum_{i=1}^{\delta} P\left(\vartheta_i^j\right)}{\delta} \tag{7}$$

where, for simplicty, $P\left(\psi_1^j\right)$ replaces $P(B_j \boxplus A_i)$, $P\left(\vartheta_i^j\right)$ replaces $P(B_j|A_i)$, and $P\left(\psi_1^j\right) \in \Psi$ and is NKPD. This is a collection of information that can be further extracted to obtain new knowledge. The new knowledge at this point can be obtained by applying Eq. (12):

$$P\left(\psi_1^j\right)_{\text{estimate}} = \odot\left[P\left(\psi_1^j\right)\right] \tag{8}$$

where $\odot[\dots] = \max[\dots]$. $P\left(\psi_1^j\right)_{\text{estimate}}$ is the inference of $P\left(\psi_1^j\right) \in \Psi$, which later becomes new knowledge of KGS. The growing of knowledge over time is obtained by replacing the first column of **Table 2** with a time parameter. The advancement of the A3S method that already involves the time parameter gives rise to a new method called Observation Multi-time A3S (OMA3S), and knowledge distribution resulting from the application of this method is called New Knowledge Probability Distribution over Time (NKPDT) [24]:

$$P(\theta_j) = \frac{\sum_{\gamma=1}^{\Gamma} P\left(\varphi_{\gamma}^{j}\right)}{\Gamma} \tag{9}$$

$$P(\theta)_{\text{estimate}} = \odot\left[P(\theta_j)\right] \tag{10}$$

where $j = 1, \ldots, \lambda$. The certainty of the phenomena that KGS observes in the environment is measured by using the DoC formula given in Eq. (11) for single observation time using A3S and Eq. (12) for multiple observation time using OMA3S (see the details in [25]).

$$\text{DoC} = |P(\psi)_{\text{estimate}} - \vartheta_1^j| \tag{11}$$

$$\text{DoC} = |P(\theta)_{\text{estimate}} - \varphi_1^j| \tag{12}$$

where $j = 1, \ldots, \lambda$, ϑ_1^j and φ_1^j is the knowledge in terms of probability value of the j best hypothesis at single observation time and multiple observation time γ_1, respectively.

3.5. Application examples

3.5.1. *CAI for intelligence decision making*

In this section we share our work on the application of CAI for intelligence decision making. "Intelligence" means "The product resulting from the collection, processing, integration, evaluation, analysis, and interpretation of available information concerning foreign nations, hostile or potentially hostile forces or elements, or areas of actual or potential operations" [25]. The process of obtaining this intelligence is carried out intelligently by KGS, a method of CAI.

Our work was supported by a national body that has responsibility for security at sea. It needs an automatic mechanism to extract knowledge from intelligence data delivered from direct observation by field personnel. By having such a mechanism, it is hoped that the abundance of data from the field can be processed quickly while maintaining their accuracy. The extracted knowledge obtained from the processed data will be used as the basis for making decisions and actions for law enforcement at sea. Based on the requirements, we customized our method so that it is suitable for the problems at hand. First, we have to build an intelligence tree based on an intelligence estimation table as well as indications of incidents related to the security and safety of certain aspects at sea. Second, the algorithm to represent the work of the required mechanism has also to be built. This algorithm becomes the basis for coding the mechanism, which is the core of the whole system. In general, the intelligence tree for security and safety at sea is depicted in **Figure 8**.

3.5.1.1. *Determining the hypotheses and indications*

The two important points that have to be determined are the number of hypotheses and indications. Determining the hypotheses is much easier because in general there are only eight possible incidents regarding security and safety at sea. For security at sea, there are seven hypotheses, namely, piracy, illegal mining, illegal fuel, illegal fishing, trafficking, drugs, and

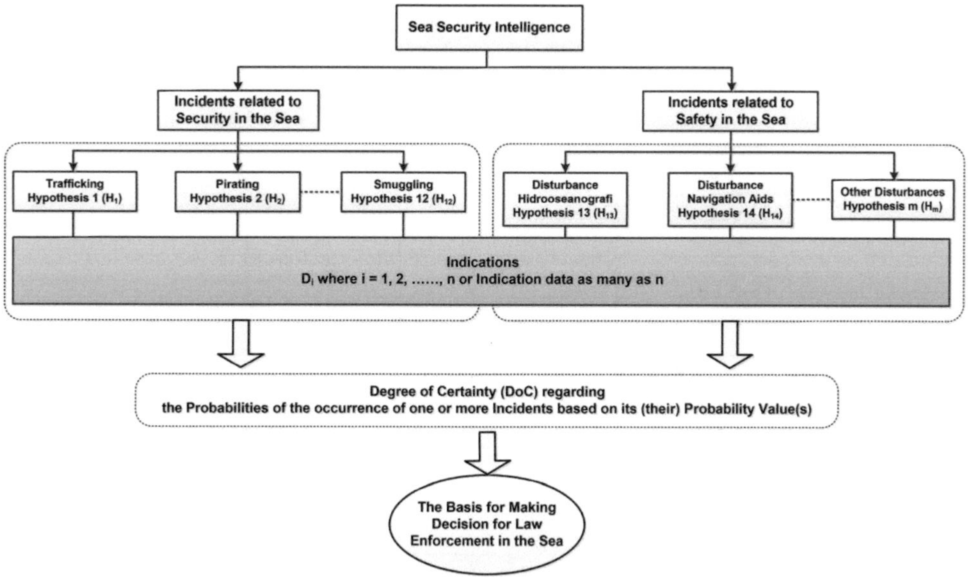

Figure 8. Intelligence tree for security and safety at sea.

smuggling. However, there is only one hypothesis for safety at sea, namely, safety from crime at sea. Each hypothesis has its own indications but some of them overlap one another. Therefore, we have to compare all indications. Initially, we have 54 indications altogether. After comparing and confirming them to the user, the number of indications narrows to 42. These indications are then placed in a table along with all hypotheses. One of the tables that contain the hypotheses and indications is shown in **Figure 9**. In this figure we show all hypotheses that are coded H[1] to H[8], while for indications we show only 12 of them, which are coded ID[1] to ID[12]. This table represents information within the intelligence tree for security and safety at sea as depicted in **Figure 8**.

3.5.1.2. Operating the intelligence decision-making system

In testing the system, we have created test inputs. The inputs to the system are in binary numbers. There are reasons why we select binary numbers (0 and 1, or "yes" and "no"). The first is that a decision cannot be blurred or cause ambiguity to the decision maker. The second is that the binary decision is a type of critical decision making [26]. This scheme is relevant to the situation faced by the user's field personnel because the information regarding the observed phenomenon has to be confirmed. If it is blurred or ambiguous, then the knowledge obtained by the system may not represent the real situation, meaning that the possibility of making an incorrect decision may be higher. In this test, we will use all hypotheses and only some indications. This is to observe that the system runs well and the knowledge obtained is relevant to human thought and decision when it is received.

For this test, we use 10 indications with eight hypotheses. To operate the system, we first run the application software with KGS already within it. The operation will be depicted

ID No.	Aspects of Sea Security and Safety Operation	Aspect of Security in the Sea							Aspect of Safety in the Sea
	Incident Alternatives (Hipothesis)	Piracy	Illegal Mining	Illegal Fuel	Illegal Fishing	Trafficking	Drugs	Smuggling	Safety from Sea Criminal
	H[j]	H[1]	H[2]	H[3]	H[4]	H[5]	H[6]	H[7]	H[8]
ID[i]	Indications								
ID[1]	There are two ships or more with different type and size are joining together in the sea								
ID[2]	The actor is using speedboat-type ship (traditional/modern)								
ID[3]	The gestures of the perpatrators are suspicious or there is unreasonable behavior of them								
ID[4]	The number of perpetrators are more than two persons								
ID[5]	The ship is using modified engine or the number of engine are more than two								
ID[6]	The perpetrators are indicated bringing firearms and sharp weapon								
ID[7]	The action is usually carried out at night (±22.00 PM) until approaching dawn (± 04.00 AM)								
ID[8]	If the ship is approached by the patrol ship, it will dodge (run away) or resist								
ID[9]	There are a group of people with suspicious behavior, especially at small port								
ID[10]	The ship used is small size but with big capacity engine								
ID[11]	The ship brings equipment which not accordance with sea activity function								
ID[12]	Ship which gets in or goes out from certain area by bringing illegal natural resources and no legal mark from the local Custom								

Figure 9. Intelligence table for security and safety at sea as the detailed representation of the intelligence tree.

chronologically in the following figures. **Figure 10** shows the empty field that is to be filled with inputs. **Figure 11** shows the field that is already filled with the combination of inputs. Field filling is based on the phenomenon observed by the personnel. Each observation will be compared with the available indications as well as the available hypotheses. A certain observation to the phenomenon may result an indication or indications which may be possessed by one or more incidents that are represented by hypotheses. The observed indications are then filled in the appropriated rows. This scheme that makes some rows are filled with "1." The next step is to execute the system by clicking the "Submit" button; the results of the computation are depicted in **Figure 12** and they can be saved as depicted in **Figure 13**.

The results of the computation can be easily extracted and then converted to a graphic to make them easy to understand, as depicted in **Figure 14**. From the results, we can extract the knowledge regarding the observed phenomenon. The computation results represent NKPD of the system and its DoC can be obtained by applying Eq. (12) as follows:

$$\begin{aligned}\text{DoC} &= |P(\theta)_{\text{estimate}} - \varphi_1^j| \\ &= |(0.12, 0.18, 0.08, 0.11, 0.20, 0.16, 0.10, 0.07) - 0| \\ &= |0.20 - 0| \\ &= 0.20\end{aligned}$$

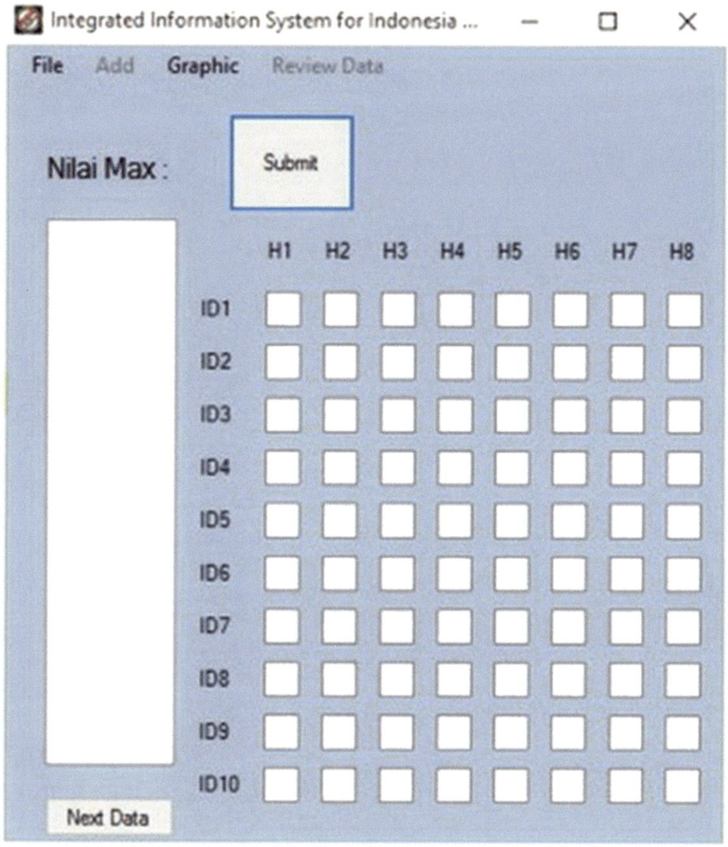

Figure 10. The empty field to accommodate the combination of inputs.

The value of $\vartheta_1^j = 0$ because at the beginning the system knows nothing about the phenomenon. After one observation, the system has knowledge regarding the phenomenon, with a DoC as much as 0.20 out of 1, where this value is in the H[5] column. This means that the system has only little certainty regarding the "Trafficking" situation. A single observation may be used as the basis for making a decision, but humans in general carry out more observations to ensure that the observed phenomenon is the same as the phenomenon observed in time 1 (the first observation). Based on that consideration, we put two more observation time inputs into the system and the results of computation are depicted graphically in **Figures 15** and **16**. After three observation times, we have a table with the computation results of each observation time (**Table 3**).

As we can see in **Table 3**, from three observation times the system has knowledge that the phenomenon it observes is H[5]. In each observation time, the system's DoC always goes to H [5]. To ensure that H[5] is the correct phenomenon, the system has to obtain the ultimate knowledge from all observation times. The resultant knowledge is represented with NKPDT where hypotheses with the highest DoC will become the ultimate knowledge of the system

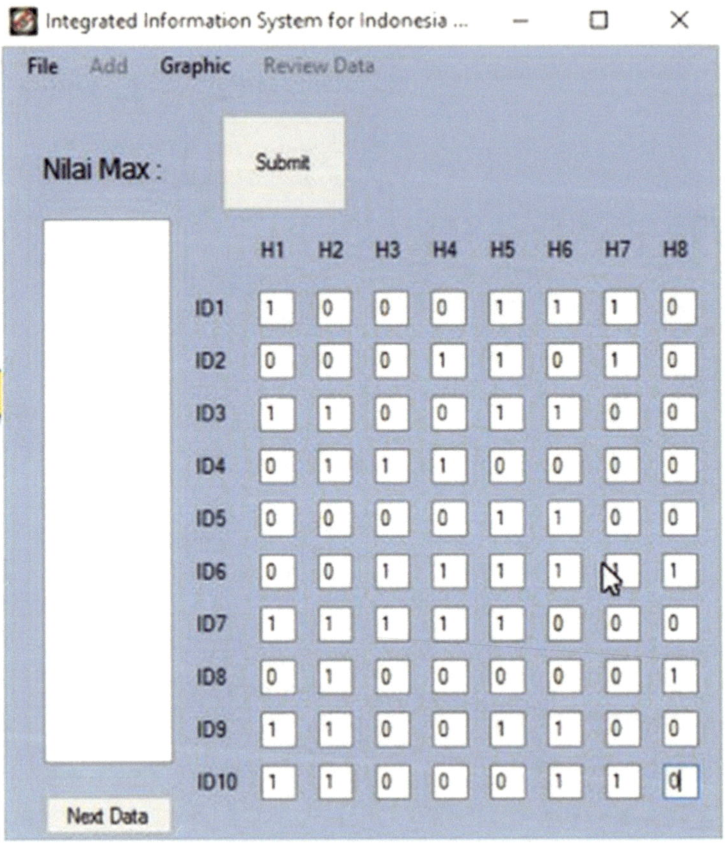

Figure 11. Inputs to the system that are being prepared for processing.

that determines the estimated phenomenon being observed. The application of Eqs. (9) and (10) will obtain NKPDT and DoC as follows. The DoC is depicted in **Figure 17**.

$$P(\theta_j) = (0, 0.11, 0, 0, 0.44, 0.44, 0, 0)$$

$$\begin{aligned} \text{DoC} &= |P(\psi)_{\text{estimate}} - \varphi_1^j| \\ &= |0, 0.11, 0, 0, 0.44, 0.44, 0, 0 - 0| \\ &= |0.44 - 0|, |0.44 - 0| \\ &= 0.44,\ 0.44 \end{aligned}$$

For this example, the system obtains knowledge that the phenomenon being observed is not just H[5] but it is also H[6]. In one view it is a good result because trafficking has a noticeable relation with drugs. According to research done by [27], there is a growing convergence of drug and human trade results from drug organizations entering into the businesses of smuggling and trafficking. Based on this knowledge, the decision maker can make a decision and action to cope with such a situation. The decision maker can set up a proper strategy, formulate the number of

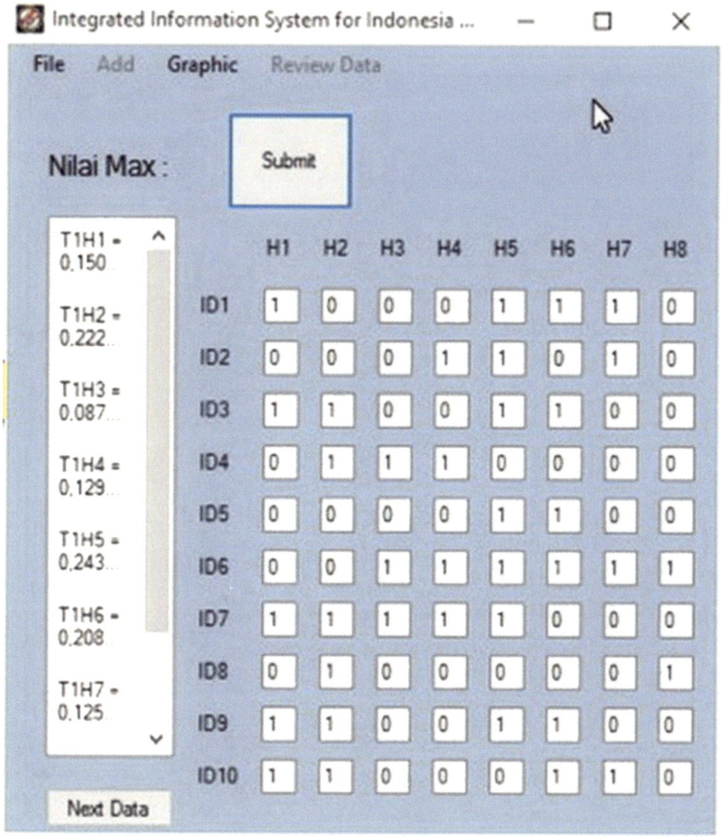

Figure 12. The results of the computation presented at the left-side field.

personnel who will carry out such a mission, and prepare a budget to support the mission. If the decision maker needs more detail of the situation, more observation time data can be added to the system. The more observation time, the more precise the knowledge obtained by the system.

3.5.2. *CAI for inferring the electrocardiography (ECG) data of heart block and arrhythmia*

This section is taken from the work of [28] where KGS is utilized to obtain knowledge regarding heart block and arrhythmia.

3.5.2.1. *Theory of ECG*

ECG is a medical instrument used to read the condition of the human heart. ECG works by receiving data from heart electrical signals and displaying them in graphical form known as a PQRST graph. Electrodes are placed at several points on the surface of the body to receive heart electrical signals. Usually, 12 leads of electrodes are used to receive heart electrical signals. The condition of the heart can be diagnosed by observing the shape, amplitudes, and wave periods of a PQRST wave. A normal ECG graph is shown in **Figure 18**. The vertical axis shows the

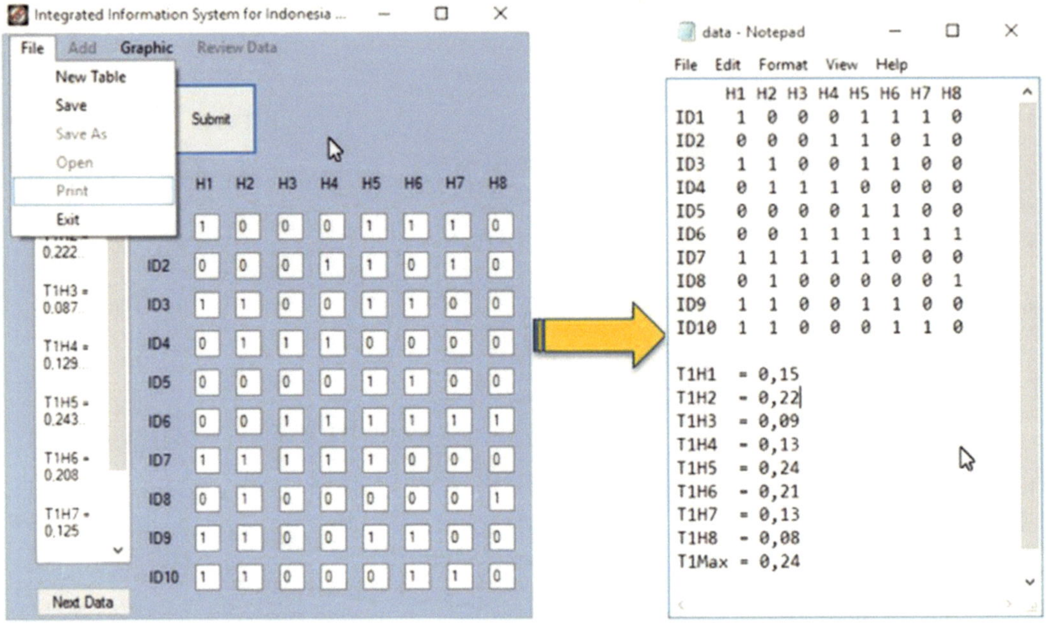

Figure 13. Saving the computation results.

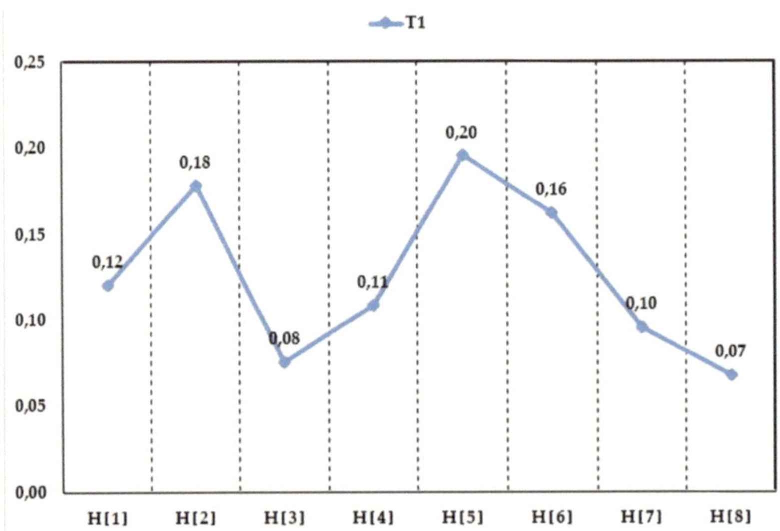

Figure 14. Graphical representation of the computation results.

amplitude of the PQRST (mV), and the horizontal axis defines the time parameter (s). The ECG graph is recorded on moving paper, which traces the heart activity, detected by the electrodes. **Figure 19** shows an example of normal ECG graph recording. A physician reads the graph result from the ECG machines by comparing the wave pattern from each of the 12 leads. Every

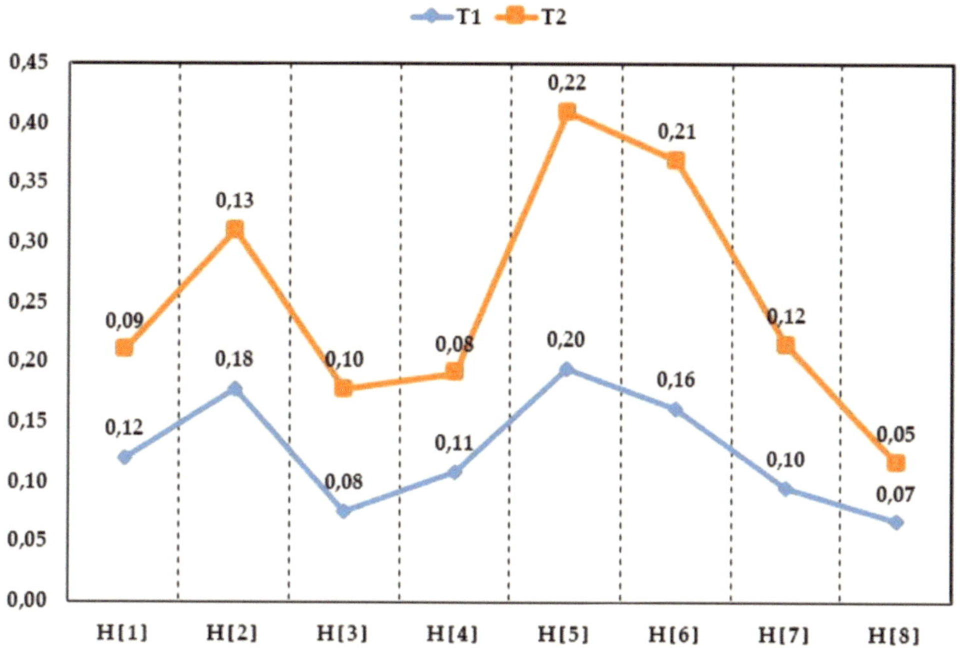

Figure 15. The computation results from two observation times.

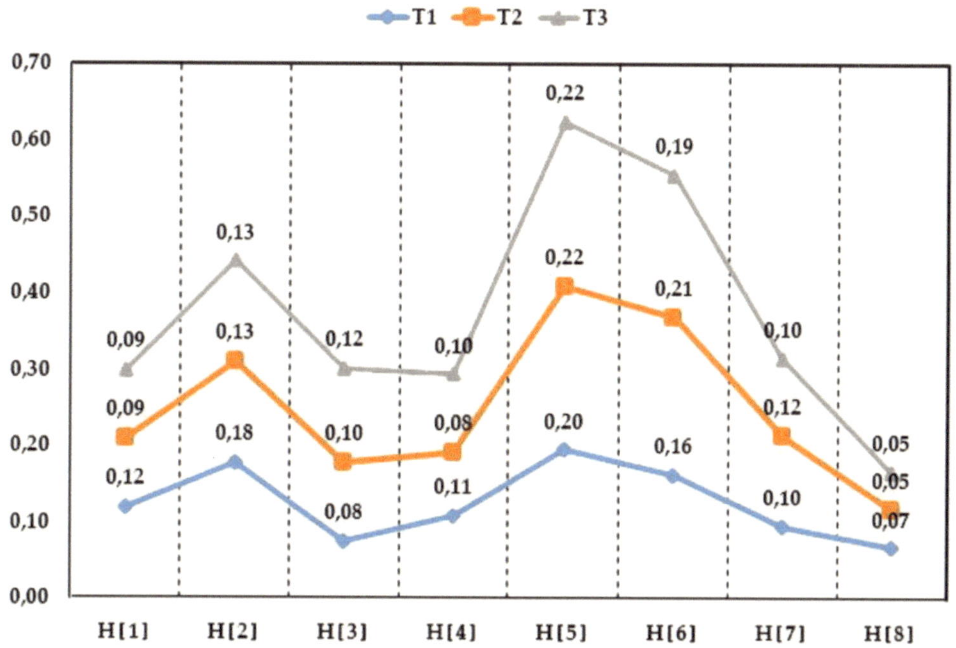

Figure 16. The computation results from three observation times.

Hypotheses	H[1]	H[2]	H[3]	H[4]	H[5]	H[6]	H[7]	H[8]
Category / -th time	Piracy	Illegal mining	Illegal fuel	Illegal fishing	Trafficking	Drugs	Smuggling	Safe from crime at sea
T-1	0.12	0.18	0.08	0.11	0.20	0.16	0.10	0.07
T-2	0.09	0.13	0.10	0.08	0.22	0.21	0.12	0.05
T-3	0.09	0.13	0.12	0.10	0.22	0.19	0.10	0.05

Table 3. The computation results from three observation times.

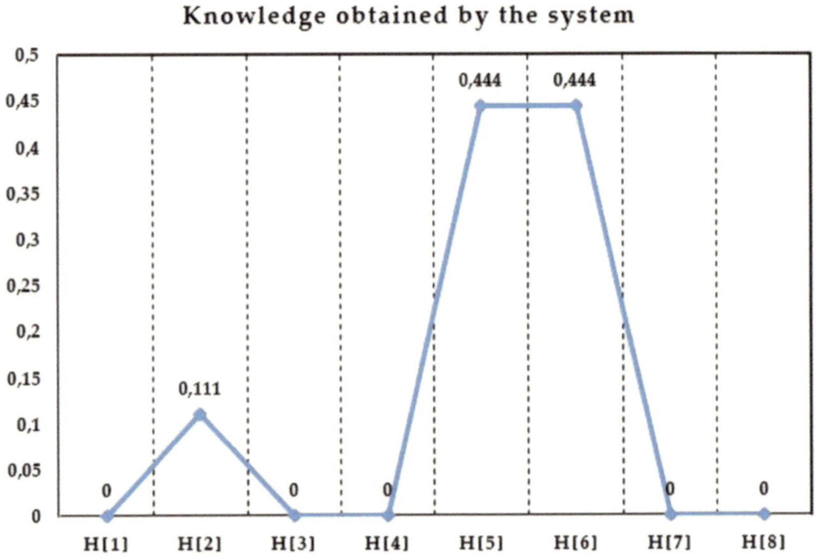

Figure 17. The DoCs resulting from the computation of the information from three observation times.

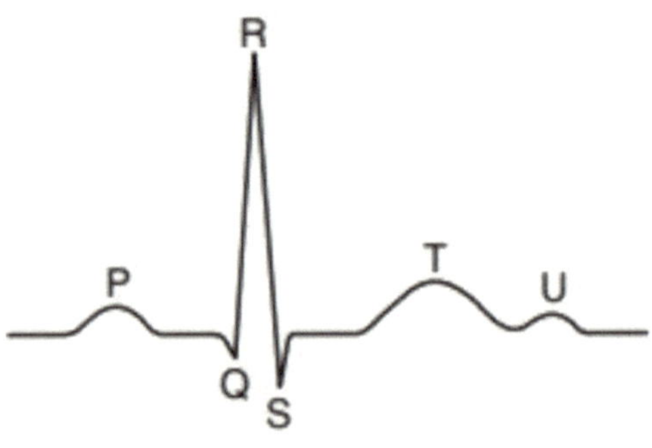

Figure 18. The normal ECG graph.

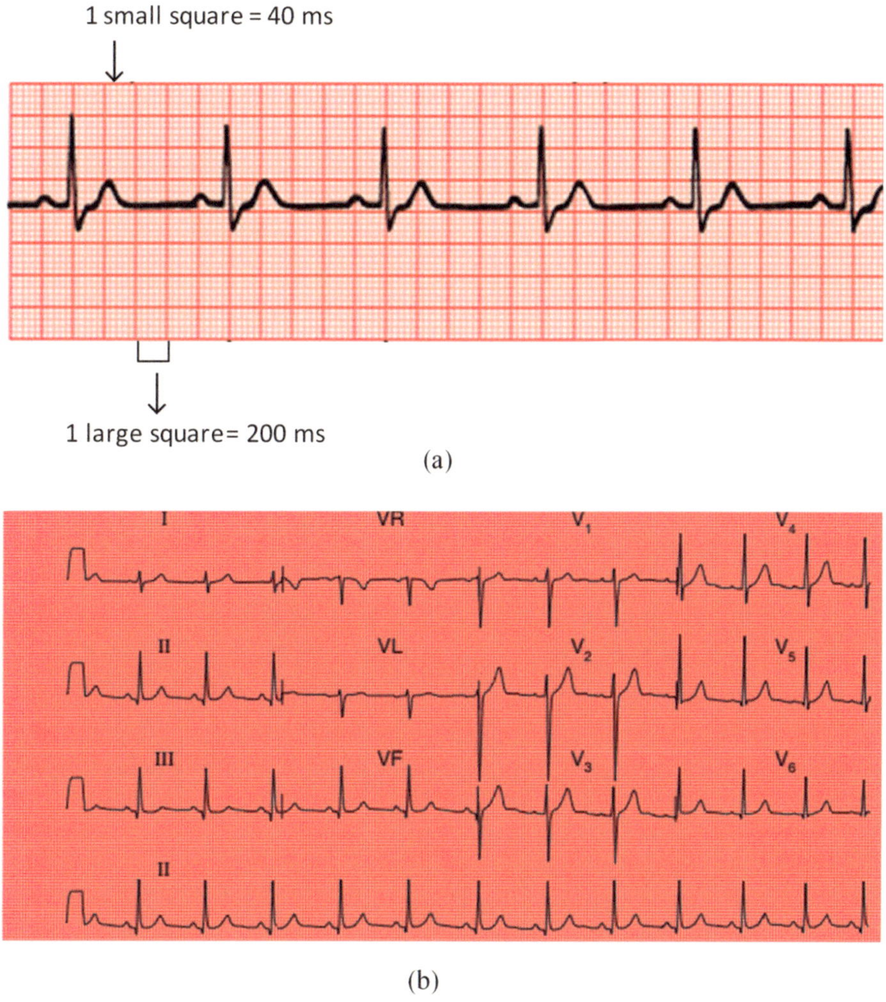

Figure 19. Example of the normal ECG graph recording. (a) Shown from one electrode, (b) the complete view of 12 lead electrodes [29].

abnormal pattern may signal one or more abnormalities or unhealthy conditions of the heart. Because in this section observation is limited to detecting heart block and arrythmia, information according to the hypotheses of heart conditions and the responses of the ECG graph when observing those conditions is gathered in **Table 4**.

3.5.2.2. Inferring the ECG data of heart block and arrhythmia

Calculation of the QRS angle can be used to detect a block in the bundle branch [30]. Otherwise, arrhythmia is an abnormal condition of heart beat rhythm. These two conditions can be used to analyze information regarding any possibility of heart disease. To implement the KGS computation for diagnosing heart conditions, first, information must be collected regarding all hypotheses and indications related to the observation of ECG resulting from heart block

No.	Hypothesis	ECG observation
1.	Normal	R wave in lead I + & R wave in lead avF +
2.	Normal	R: lead V6 +
3.	Normal	R: lead V1 –
4.	Normal	Normal heartbeat
5.	Left axis deviation (LAD)	R: lead I + & R: lead avF –
6.	Right axis deviation (RAD)	R: lead I – & R: lead avF +
7.	Left bundle branch block (LBBB) or right bundle branch block (RBBB)	Lead V1, interval QRS > 20 ms
8.	RBBB	Lead V6, S amplitude < 0.1 mV & S interval > 80 ms
…		…
14.	RBBB	In lead V3, merging together of the S wave and T wave
15.	LBBB	V5, Q amplitude < 0.1 mV
…	…	…
26.	LBBB	ST elevation in lead V4
27.	Arrhythmia	In one lead, varying interval of RR
…	…	…
31.	Arrhythmia	Slow heartbeat
32.	Atrial tachycardia	P wave morphology is abnormal
…	…	…
37.	Atrial tachycardia	Isoelectric baseline
38.	Ventricular tachycardia	P and QRS complexes at different rates
…	…	…
49.	Ventricular tachycardia	RSR complexes with taller R

Table 4. Correlation hypothesis and ECG observation [29, 30].

and arrhythmia. In this section, eight heart conditions are drawn to these two conditions as hypothesis information. All hypotheses and indications for inferring the ECG data can be seen in **Figures 20** and **21**.

The system will perform the computation by looking at the correlations between indications and appropriate hypotheses. Further details can be seen in **Figure 22**. Logic "1" denotes the correlation between a hypothesis and an indication. As shown in **Figure 22**, the relationship between H[1] and ID[1] is represented by logic 1. This means that at the time of examination the ECG results show the graph as described in ID1 (**Table 4**), number 1, which means this information relates to a normal heart condition. For a better understanding of the computation process in the system, an example using five indications as input is used. In this example the observation was done five times. The results of the computation can be seen in **Table 5**.

http://dx.doi.org/10.5772/intechopen.72764

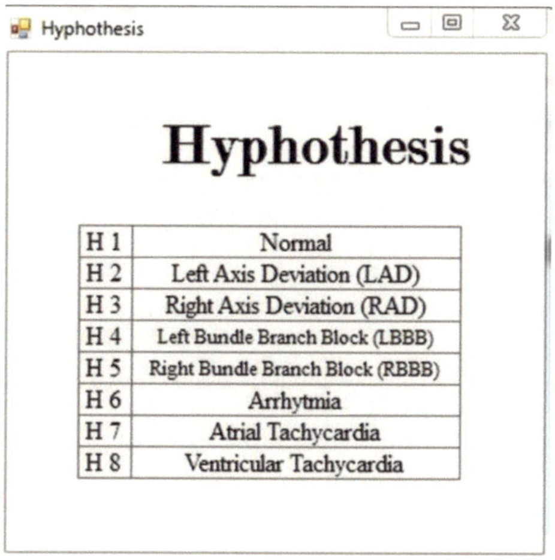

Hyphothesis

H 1	Normal
H 2	Left Axis Deviation (LAD)
H 3	Right Axis Deviation (RAD)
H 4	Left Bundle Branch Block (LBBB)
H 5	Right Bundle Branch Block (RBBB)
H 6	Arrhytmia
H 7	Atrial Tachycardia
H 8	Ventricular Tachycardia

Figure 20. The list of all hypotheses for inferring the ECG data according to **Table 4**.

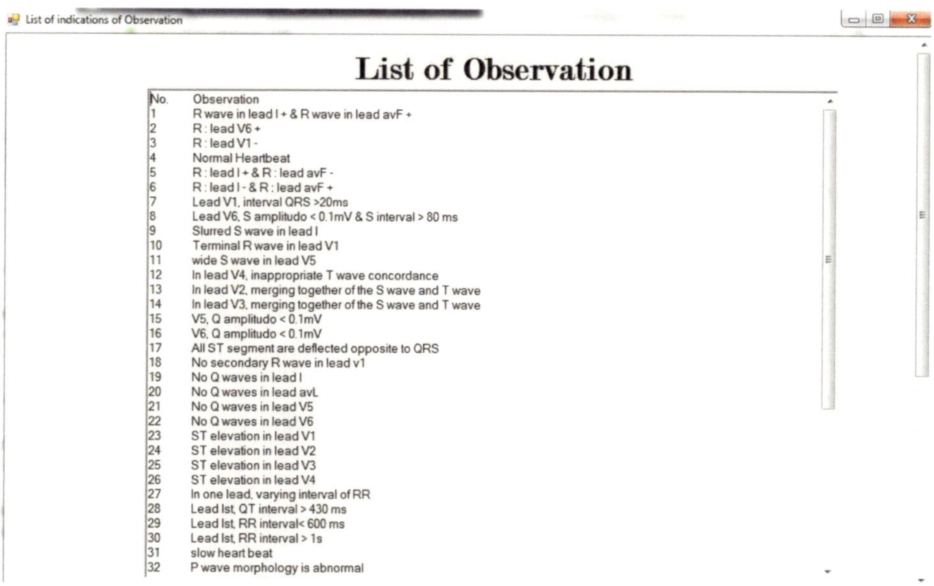

List of Observation

No.	Observation
1	R wave in lead I + & R wave in lead avF +
2	R : lead V6 +
3	R : lead V1 -
4	Normal Heartbeat
5	R : lead I + & R : lead avF -
6	R : lead I - & R : lead avF +
7	Lead V1, interval QRS >20ms
8	Lead V6, S amplitudo < 0.1mV & S interval > 80 ms
9	Slurred S wave in lead I
10	Terminal R wave in lead V1
11	wide S wave in lead V5
12	In lead V4, inappropriate T wave concordance
13	In lead V2, merging together of the S wave and T wave
14	In lead V3, merging together of the S wave and T wave
15	V5, Q amplitudo < 0.1mV
16	V6, Q amplitudo < 0.1mV
17	All ST segment are deflected opposite to QRS
18	No secondary R wave in lead v1
19	No Q waves in lead I
20	No Q waves in lead avL
21	No Q waves in lead V5
22	No Q waves in lead V6
23	ST elevation in lead V1
24	ST elevation in lead V2
25	ST elevation in lead V3
26	ST elevation in lead V4
27	In one lead, varying interval of RR
28	Lead Ist, QT interval > 430 ms
29	Lead Ist, RR interval< 600 ms
30	Lead Ist, RR interval > 1s
31	slow heart beat
32	P wave morphology is abnormal

Figure 21. The list of all indications for inferring the ECG data according to **Table 4**.

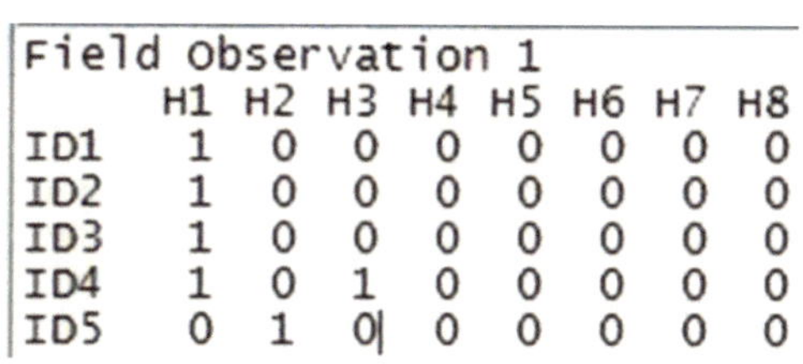

Field observation 1

	H1	H2	H3	H4	H5	H6	H7	H8
ID1	1	0	0	0	0	0	0	0
ID2	1	0	0	0	0	0	0	0
ID3	1	0	0	0	0	0	0	0
ID4	1	0	1	0	0	0	0	0
ID5	0	1	0	0	0	0	0	0

Figure 22. Example of inputs to the system.

Time (T)	Indica-tion (ID)	Hypotheses (H)							
		H1	H2	H3	H4	H5	H6	H7	H8
T1	ID1	1	0	0	0	0	0	0	0
	ID2	1	0	0	0	0	0	0	0
	ID3	1	0	0	0	0	0	0	0
	ID4	1	0	0	0	0	0	0	0
	ID5	0	1	0	0	0	0	0	0
P(ω)1		**0.8**	**0.2**	**0**	**0**	**0**	**0**	**0**	**0**
T2	ID1	1	0	0	0	0	0	0	0
	ID2	1	0	0	0	0	0	0	0
	ID3	1	0	0	0	0	0	0	0
	ID4	0	1	0	0	0	0	0	0
	ID5	0	1	0	0	0	0	0	0
P(ω)2		**0.6**	**0.4**	**0**	**0**	**0**	**0**	**0**	**0**
T3	ID1	1	0	0	0	0	0	0	0
	ID2	1	0	0	0	0	0	0	0
	ID3	1	0	0	0	0	0	0	0
	ID4	1	1	0	0	0	0	0	0
	ID5	0	1	0	0	0	0	0	0
P(ω)3		**0.7**	**0.3**	**0**	**0**	**0**	**0**	**0**	**0**
T4	ID1	1	0	0	0	0	0	0	0
	ID2	1	0	0	0	0	0	0	0
	ID3	1	0	0	0	0	0	0	0
	ID4	1	1	0	0	0	0	0	0
	ID5	1	1	0	0	0	0	0	0
P(ω)4		**0.8**	**0.2**	**0**	**0**	**0**	**0**	**0**	**0**
T5	ID1	1	0	0	0	0	0	0	0
	ID2	1	0	0	0	0	0	0	0
	ID3	1	0	0	0	0	0	0	0
	ID4	1	1	0	0	0	0	0	0
	ID5	1	1	0	0	0	0	0	0
P(ω)5		**0.8**	**0.2**	**0**	**0**	**0**	**0**	**0**	**0**
P(O)		**0.74**	**0.26**	**0**	**0**	**0**	**0**	**0**	**0**

Table 5. The results of system computation using five indications (ID1–ID5) for five observation times (T1–T5) for all hypotheses (H1–H8).

According to **Table 5**, computation of the system can be explained as follows. After collecting the information from the correlation among indications and hypotheses, the value of $P(\omega)$ is counted, creating a value of DoC for every hypothesis in one observation time. Then, after all DoCs for each hypothesis are collected, the system will compute the value of DoC for the whole observation time using the OMA3S equation. For this example, five observation times are applied. The system gives the results as shown in **Figure 23**. By looking at each correlation between the hypothesis and the indication of each observation time, using the OMA3S formula, the results of the observations can be summarized as depicted in **Figure 24**, which shows the results from all observation times, according to the data sample from **Table 4**. From the graphic, it can be seen from the observation results that the heart condition that has been observed has a 74% normal condition, which tends to have 26% of the left axis deviation (LAD) condition. Another example of observation results can be seen in **Figures 25** and **26** for different cases of heart condition. **Figure 25** shows the condition of left bundle branch block (LBBB), which tends to have an LAD condition, and **Figure 26** shows the condition for arrhythmia, which tends to have an atrial tachycardia condition.

3.5.3. Other CAI applications for humankind

KGS as the main engine of CAI has been applied to some real-life problems. Its applications range from decision making to biomedical engineering such as military decision making

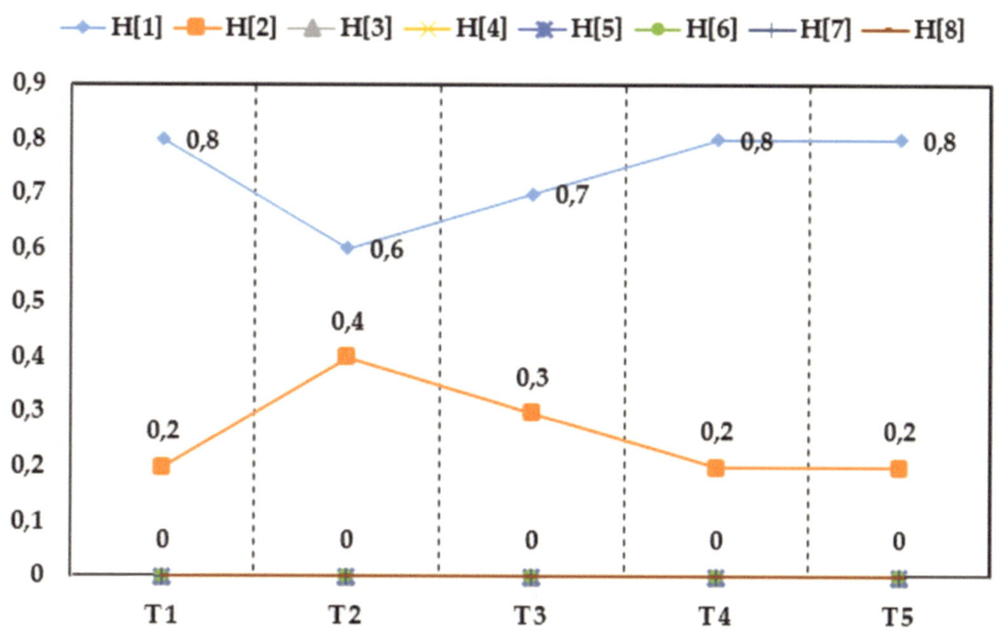

Figure 23. The results of system observation from time to time.

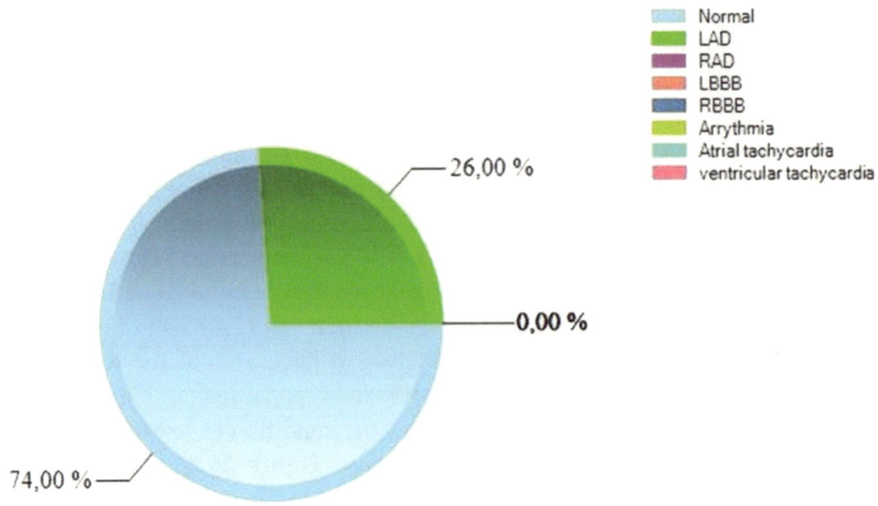

Figure 24. Knowledge obtained after applying OMA3S from the observation results given in **Table 4**, namely, a normal condition that tends to have LAD.

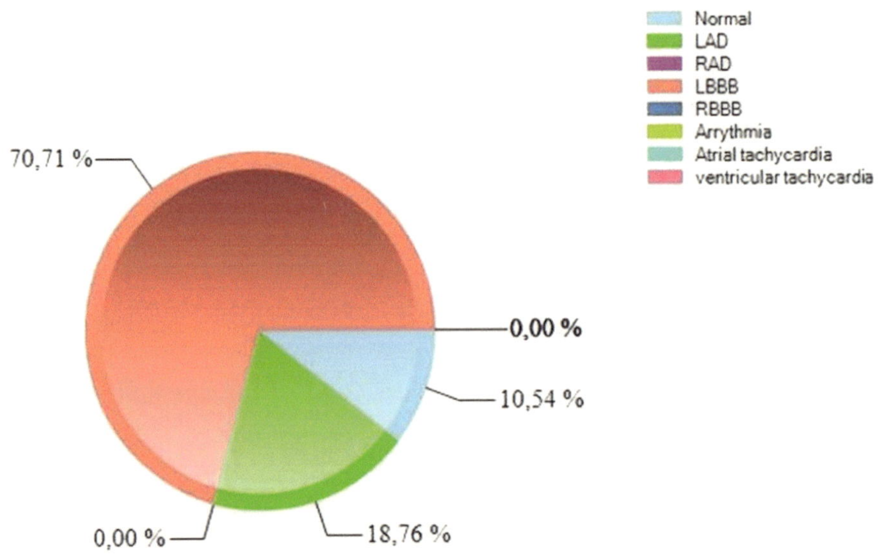

Figure 25. An example with different inputs, which results in LBBB that tends to have LAD.

in [21, 22] and [31], power plant energy management in [32], gene behavior estimation in [33], dissolved gas analysis for interpreting transformer condition in [34, 35], device encryption method in [36], and intelligence analysis and estimation in [37]. We have been making advances by transferring the KGS algorithm to hardware to develop a cognitive processor [38–40]. We have seen many opportunities that would suit this kind of processor for humankind such as for intelligent unmanned vehicles.

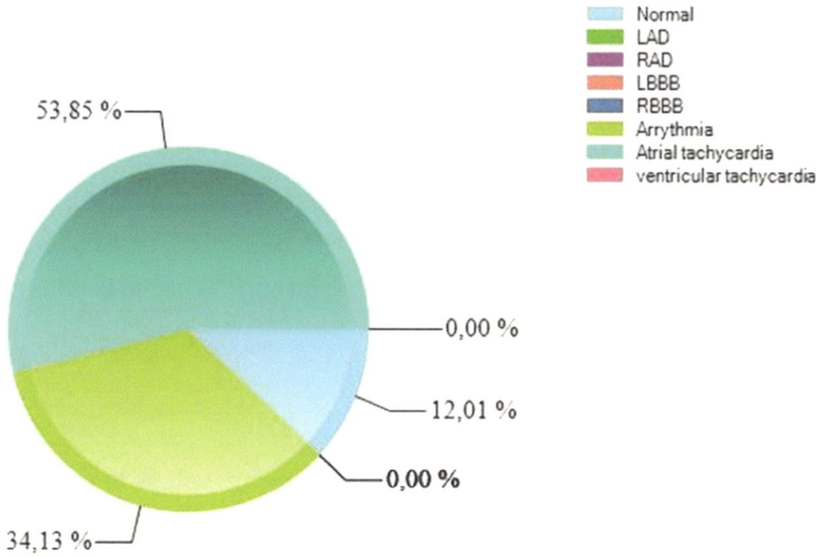

Figure 26. Another example with different inputs, which results in tachycardia that tends to have arrhythmia.

4. Concluding remarks

Applying AI to a simple idea was not an easy task until now. Our simple idea of emulating how the human brain grows knowledge or thinking over time, which makes humans intelligent, has been successfully achieved in the AI field. These novelties cover the cognitive agent KGS, which can think and act rationally like humans, the A3S and OMA3S formula for growing knowledge, and new HIS and SIDA cycles as part of HIS. KGS is one of the methods in CAI we have developed since 2006, and its computation method matures as time passes and as the number of fields where it is applied grows wider. Our research also proved that humans can become intelligent by interacting with the environment as stated in constructivism theory. Also important was that our research showed that to have a comprehensive model of human intelligence, it must be approached from diverse disciplines.

In this chapter we have also delivered two examples of CAI application for humankind. One example is related to obtaining knowledge for intelligence decision making, and the other is related to obtaining knowledge for e-health application. Our examples show that KGS is able to grow its knowledge from nothing to a certain extent depending on the number of observation times. The more information is processed, the more knowledge can be obtained, and the more intelligent it becomes. Equally important is that the outcome of this knowledge is more precise decisions and actions that can be taken by the decision maker. However, the most important is our research has opened a new perspective in AI. We are proud to call this new perspective as Cognitive Artificial Intelligence, abbreviated as CAI.

Author details

Arwin Datumaya Wahyudi Sumari[1,2] and Adang Suwandi Ahmad[1,2]*

*Address all correspondence to: adangsahmad@yahoo.com

1 Cognitive Artificial Intelligence Research Group (CAIRG), School of Electrical Engineering and Informatics, Institut Teknologi Bandung, Indonesia

2 University Center of Excellence on Microelectronics, Institut Teknologi Bandung, Indonesia

References

[1] Ahmad AS. Natural computation as future computation paradigm to support life quality enhancement. Scientific Oration on 47th ITB Anniversary, 2 March 2006

[2] Mitchell T. Machine Learning. New York: McGraw-Hill; 1997. 414 p

[3] Russell SJ, Norvig P. Artificial Intelligence: A Modern Approach. 2nd ed. New Jersey: Prentice-Hall; 2003. 960 p

[4] Sumari ADW, Ahmad, AS, Wuryandari, AI, Sembiring J. Constructing brain-inspired Knowledge-Growing System: a review and a design concept. In: Proceedings of the Second International Conference on Distributed Framework and Applications 2010 (DFMA '10); 2–3 August 2010; Yogyakarta: IEEE; 2010. p. 95-102

[5] Wooldridge M. An Introduction to Multiagent Systems. Chichester: John Wiley & Sons; 2002. 484 p

[6] Sumari ADW, Ahmad AS. The development of Knowledge Growing System as a new perspective in Artificial Intelligence. In: Proceedings of the Conference on Information Technology and Electrical Engineering 2009 (CITEE '09); 4 August 2009; Yogyakarta. p. 46-51

[7] Sumari ADW, Ahmad AS, Wuryandari AI, Sembiring J. A mathematical model of Knowledge-Growing System: a novel perspective in Artificial Intelligence. In: Proceedings of IndoMS International Conference on Mathematics and Its Applications 2009 (IICMA '09); 13 October 2009; Yogyakarta. p. 229-240

[8] Munakata T. Fundamentals of the New Artifical Intelligence. 2nd ed. London: Springer-Verlag; 2008. 256 p

[9] Sumari ADW. A new model of information processing based on human brain mechanism: toward a cognitive intelligent system. In: Proceedings of the 1st Conference on Information Technology, Computer, and Electrical Engineering (CITACEE '13); 16 November 2013; Yogyakarta. p. 56-61

[10] Stone M. The opinion pool. Annals of Mathematical Statistics. 1961;**32**(4):1339-1342

[11] Benediktsson JA, Sveinsson JR, Ersoy K, Swain PH. Parallel consensual neural networks. IEEE Transactions on Neural Networks, 1997;**8**(1):54-64

[12] Chen Y, Chu CH, Mullen T, Pennock DM. Information markets vs. opinion pools: an empirical comparison. In: Proceedings of ACM Conference in Electronic Commerce; 5–8 June 2005; Vancouver. p. 58-67

[13] Punska O. Bayesian approaches to multi-sensor data fusion [Internet]. 31 August 1999. Available from: http://www-sigproc.eng.cam.ac.uk/~op205/mphil.pdf. [Accessed: 25-05-2010]

[14] Chambers CP. An ordinal characterization of the linear opinion pool. Economic Theory, 2007;**3**(3):457-474

[15] Hetherington S. Knowledge [Internet]. Available from: http://www.iep.utm.edu/knowledg/ [Accessed: 20-06-2017]

[16] Ahmad AS, Sumari ADW. Cognitive Artificial Intelligence: brain-inspired intelligent computation in Artificial Intelligence. In: Proceedings of SAI Computing Conference 2017 (SAI '17); London: IEEE, 18–20 July 2017. p. 135-141

[17] Dodig-Crnkovic G. Knowledge generation as natural computation. Systemics, Cybernetics and Informatics, 2008;**6**(2):12-16

[18] Castelli G, Menezes R, Zambonelli F. **S**elf-organized control of knowledge generation in pervasive computing systems. In: Proceedings of the 2009 ACM Symposium on Applied Computing; 8–12 March 2009. p. 1202-1208

[19] Sumari ADW, Ahmad AS, Wuryandari AI, Sembiring J. Knowledge sharing in knowledge-growing-based systems. In: Proceedings of the First International Conference on Green Computing 2010 and the Second AUN/SEED-Net Regional Conference on ICT (ICGC-RCT '10); Yogyakarta; 2–3 March 2010. p. 329-333

[20] Sumari ADW, Ahmad AS, Wuryandari AI, Sembiring J. Brain-inspired Knowledge Growing-System: towards a true cognitive agent. International Journal of Computer Science & Artificial Intelligence (IJCSAI), 2012;**2**(1):26-36

[21] Sumari ADW, Ahmad AS. Multiagent collaborative computation paradigm for decision-making support system. In: Proceedings of International Industrial Informatics Seminar 2009 (IIIS '09); Yogyakarta; 15 August 2009. p. 17-22

[22] Sumari ADW, Ahmad AS. Design and implementation of multi agent-based information fusion system for supporting decision making (a case study on military operation). ITB Journal of Information and Communication Technology (JICT), 2008;**2**(1):42-63

[23] Ahmad AS, Sumari ADW. Multi-agent information inferencing fusion in integrated information system. Bandung: ITB Publisher; 2008. 144 p

[24] Sumari ADW, Ahmad AS, Wuryandari AI, Sembiring J. The application of knowledge-growing system to multiagent collaborative computation for inferring the behavior of

genes interaction. International Journal of Computer Science & Network Security (IJCSNS). 2009;**9**(11):82-92

[25] Joint Chiefs of Staff. Publication 1-02: Department of Defense Dictionary of Military and Associated Terms. Washington DC: US Department of Defense; 2008. 780 p

[26] Snow RM, Phillips PH. Making Critical Decision: A Practical Guide for Nonprofit Organizations. San Francisco: John Wiley & Sons; 2008. 256 p

[27] Shelley L. The relationship of drug and human trafficking: a global perspective. European Journal on Criminal Policy and Research. 2012;**18**:241-253. DOI 10.1007/s10610-012-9175-1

[28] Sereati CO, Sumari ADW, Adiono T, Ahmad AS. Cognitive Artificial Intelligence (CAI) software based on Knowledge Growing System (KGS) for detecting heart block and arrhythmia. In: Proceedings of the International Conference on Electrical Engineering and Informatics 2017 (ICEEI '17); Langkawi: IEEE, 25–27 November 2017

[29] Hampton JR. The ECG Made Easy. New York: Churchill Livingstone; 2003

[30] Goeirmanto L, Mengko R, Rajab TL. Comparison of the calculation QRS angle for bundle branch block detection. IOP Conference Series: Materials Science and Engineering 128, 012037. 2016: 1-3

[31] Sumari ADW, Ahmad AS, Wuryandari AI, Sembiring J. Strategic decision making based on A3S information-interferencing fusion method. In: Proceedings of the 3rd International Conference on Electrical Engineering and Informatics 2011 (ICEEI '11); Bandung: IEEE; 17–19 July 2011. p. 430-435

[32] Mitayani A, Priandana ER, Mareta R. Knowledge Growing System application in hybrid power plant energy management in Nemberala village Rote Island. Procedia Technology, 2013;**11**:641-649

[33] Sumari ADW, Ahmad AS, Wuryandari AI, Sembiring J. Brain-Inspired Knowledge-Growing System and its application in biomedical engineering: inferring genes behavior in Genetic Regulatory System. Journal of eHealth Technology and Application (JETA), 2011;**8** (2):141-151

[34] Bachri KO, Anggoro B, Ahmad AS. Dissolved gas analysis interpretation using OMA3S information fusion algorithm. In: Proceedings of the 2nd International Conference on Electrical Engineering and Computer Science (ICEECS '16); Taipei; 28–29 October 2016. p. EE1

[35] Bachri KO, Anggoro B, Sumari ADW, Ahmad AS. Cognitive Artificial Intelligence method for interpreting transformer condition based on maintenance data. Advances in Science, Technology and Engineering Systems Journal (ASTESJ) 2017;**2**(1):1137-1146

[36] Putra SD, Ahmad AS, Sutikno S. Securing encryption device with Knowledge Growing System. In: Proceedings of the 2nd International Conference on Electrical Engineering and Computer Science (ICEECS '16); Taipei; 28–29 October 2016. p. EE4

[37] Sumari ADW, Ahmad AS. Information fusion as knowledge extraction in an information processing system. In: Proceedings of the Fourth International Conference on Advances in Computing, Electronics and Communication (ACEC '16); Roma; 15–16 December 2016. p. 22-27

[38] Sumari ADW, Sereati CO, Ahmad AS, Adiono T. Constructing an architecture for cognitive processor based on Knowledge-Growing System algorithm. In: Proceedings of 2015 International Symposium on Nano Science and Technology (ISNST '15); Tainan City; 30–31 October 2015. p. O-04

[39] Sereati CO, Sumari ADW, Adiono T, Ahmad AS. VHDL design for KGS's information fusion algorithm. In: Proceedings of the 2nd International Conference on Electrical Engineering and Computer Science (ICEECS2016); Taipei; 28–29 October 2016. p. EE3

[40] Sereati CO, Sumari ADW, Adiono T, Ahmad AS. Implementation Knowledge Growing System algorithm using VHDL. In: Proceedings of International Symposium on Electronics and Smart Devices 2016 (ISESD2016); Special Session on Cognitive Artificial Intelligence Research (CAIR); 29–30 November 2016; Bandung: IEEE, Indonesia: IEEE p. 12-16

Chapter 3

Predicate Calculus as a Tool for AI Problems Solution: Algorithms and Their Complexity

Tatiana Kosovskaya

Additional information is available at the end of the chapter

http://dx.doi.org/10.5772/intechopen.72765

Abstract

The chapter is devoted to the use of predicate calculus for artificial intelligence (AI) problem solving. Here, an investigated object is represented as a set of its elements and is characterized by a fixed number of predicates. Its description is a set of all constant literals (with the chosen predicates), which are valid on the object. The NP-complete problem, "whether an object satisfies a goal formula," is under consideration. The upper bound of number of its solution steps is exponential. The notion of common up to the names of arguments subformula of two predicate formulas and one of their isomorphisms allows to construct a level description of the set of goal formulas and essentially to decrease the upper bounds of the problem solving. The level description permits to define a self-training predicate network, which may change its configuration during the process of training. The extraction of common up to the names of arguments subformulas permits to construct a multiagent description of an object when every agent does not know the true number of the object elements and uses her own notifications for the names of elements. A model example illustrating all algorithms is presented.

Keywords: predicate calculus, NP-completeness, level description, predicate network, multi-agent description

1. Introduction

The choice of initial attributes for description of an object in an artificial intelligence (AI) problem is the first stage of any simulation of an informational process (representation of information for its further use).

At the 60–70th of the twentieth century, many authors (see, for example, [1]) offered to use predicate calculus for AI problem solving. The resolution method seemed to be a very easy and clear tool to solve problems dealing with compound objects, which can be described by properties of its elements and relations between these elements.

Until the notion of NP-complete problem (in particular, described in [2, 3]) was not widely adopted, such an approach seemed to be very convenient, but many such-a-way formalized problems occurred to be NP-complete or even algorithmic unsolvable.

While developing the effective algorithms deciding discrete problems, determination of estimations for number of steps of their run becomes one of the important problems. The absence of the proved estimations for number of an algorithm run steps is considered as an insufficient research of this algorithm. It is especially relevant for problems with big input. It concerns, in particular, to the algorithms deciding various AI problems. At practical use of an algorithm, it is important that it has polynomial upper bound of number of its run steps. The NP-completeness or NP-hardness of a problem means now that the polynomial algorithm of its decision is not known.

In 2007, the author proved NP-completeness of a series of AI problems formalized with the help of predicate calculus formulas [4], proved upper bounds for number of steps of algorithms solving these problems [5], and offered a level description of goal formulas for decreasing the number of proof steps [6]. Such a level description is based on the extraction of a common up to the names of its arguments sub-formula of the set of elementary conjunctions of atomic predicate formulas. These sub-formulas define generalized characteristics of an object.

Extraction of such sub-formulas allows to construct logic-predicate networks [7], which may change its configuration (the number of layers and the number of cells in the layer) during the process of training.

Extraction of these sub-formulas may serve as an instrument for constructing a multi-agent description of an object, when every agent can describe only a part of the object (these parts are intersected), but every agent gives its own names to the elements of the whole object [8].

Here, some AI problems formalized in such a way are under consideration. For these problems, the solving algorithms and upper bounds of their run are obtained. These upper bounds permit to point out the parameters of the problem, which mostly influence on the complexity of the algorithm, and to offer approaches permitting to decrease the complexity.

A model example illustrating the described approach and algorithms is given.

2. Logic-predicate approach to some AI problems and number of steps of these problems solution

Let an investigated object be presented as a set of its elements $\omega = \{\omega_1,\dots, \omega_t\}$. The set of predicates $p_1,\dots, p_n$ (every of which is defined on the elements of ω) characterizes properties of these elements or relations between them. Logical description $S(\omega)$ of an object ω is a collection of all true formulas in the form $p_i(\overline{\tau})$ or $\neg p_i(\overline{\tau})$ (where $\overline{\tau}$ is an ordered subset of ω) describing the properties of ω elements or relations between them.

Let the set Ω of all investigated objects be a union of classes Ω_k, ($k = 1,\ldots, K$), i.e., $\Omega = \bigcup_{k=1}^{K}\Omega_k$. Logical description of the class Ω_k is such a formula $A_k(\overline{x})$ that if the formula $A_k(\overline{\omega})$ is true then $\omega \in \Omega_k$. The class description may be represented as a disjunction of elementary conjunctions of atomic formulas.

Here and below, the notation $\overline{x}$ is used for an ordered list of the set x. To denote that there exists such a list $\overline{x}$ that all values for variables from the list $\overline{x}$ are distinct the notation $\exists\overline{x}_{\neq}A_k(\overline{x})$ is used.

The introduced descriptions allow to solve many artificial intelligence problems [9]. Main of these problems may be formulated as follows.

Identification problem: to pick out all parts of the object ω that belongs to the class Ω_k.

Classification problem: to find all such class numbers k that $\omega \in \Omega_k$.

Analysis problem: to find and classify all parts τ of the object ω.

The solution of these problems may be reduced to the proof of logic sequents

$$S(\omega) \Rightarrow \exists\overline{x}_{\neq}A_k(\overline{x}), \tag{1}$$

$$S(\omega) \Rightarrow \bigvee_{k=1}^{K}A_k(\overline{x}), \tag{2}$$

$$S(\omega) \Rightarrow \bigvee_{k=1}^{K}\exists\overline{x}_{\neq}A_k(\overline{x}), \tag{3}$$

respectively, and determination of the values for $\overline{x}$ and k. The number of $A_k(\overline{x})$ variables in the sequent (2) must be equal to the number of constants in ω.

Note that the proof of any of the sequent (1), (2), or (3) answers only the question "whether it is true?" Strictly speaking, in the sequents (1)–(3), instead of the symbols $\exists\overline{x}$ and $\bigvee_{k=1}^{K}$ there must be words "what are the distinct values of $\overline{x}$" denoted as $(?\overline{x})$ and "what are the values of k?" denoted as $?_{k=1}^{K}$, respectively. In such a case, the sequents (1)–(3) would take the form

$$S(\omega) \Rightarrow (?\overline{x}) \neq A_k(\overline{x}), \tag{4}$$

$$S(\omega) \Rightarrow ?_{k=1}^{K}A_k(\overline{x}), \tag{5}$$

$$S(\omega) \Rightarrow ?_{k=1}^{K}(?\overline{x}) \neq A_k(\overline{x}). \tag{6}$$

If one uses an exhaustive or a logical algorithm (derivation in a sequent calculus or proof by resolution method), the algorithm gives the values for $\overline{x}$ and k.

The proof of sequents (1) and (3) is based on the proof of the sequent

$$S(\omega) \Rightarrow \exists\overline{x}_{\neq}\ A(\overline{x}), \tag{7}$$

where $A(\overline{x})$ is an elementary conjunction. It follows from the fact that $A_k(\overline{x})$ is a disjunction of the form $C_1\vee\ldots\vee C_r$ of elementary conjunctions of atomic formulas $C_1,\ldots,C_r$, and $\exists\overline{x}_{\neq}\ (C_1\vee\ldots\vee C_r)$ $\Leftrightarrow$ $(\exists\overline{x}_{\neq}\ C_1\vee\ldots\vee\ \exists\overline{x}_{\neq}\ C_r)$. That is why we can consecutively check the sequents of the form

$S(\omega) \Rightarrow \exists \overline{x}_{\neq}\ C_j$. Here, the maximal value for j is r for the sequent (1), and the sum of the number of elementary conjunctions in all class descriptions for the sequent (3).

An **exhaustive algorithm** is widespread to prove (4). The total estimate for the number of steps (i.e., the number of comparisons) for the exhaustive algorithm solving (4) is

$$t(t\text{–}1)\ldots(t\text{–}m+1)\sum_{i=1}^{n} a_i s_i \tag{8}$$

or, more roughly,

$$O(t^m as). \tag{9}$$

While using a **logical algorithm** (derivation in a predicate sequent calculus or proof by resolution method for predicate calculus), one must find unifier of the formula $A(\overline{x})$ and some subset of $S(\omega)$.

The number of steps (i.e., the number of comparisons) required for the solution of the system and, hence, for the logical algorithm solving (4) is

$$O\left(s_1^{a_1}\ldots s_n^{a_n}\right), \tag{10}$$

a_i and s_i be the numbers of literals with the predicate p_i in $A(\overline{x})$ and in $S(\omega)$, respectively. More roughly

$$O\left(s'^{a}\right), \tag{11}$$

where $s' = \max\{s_1,\ldots, s_n\}$.

The above-received estimations are exponential over the length of $A(\overline{x})$. The ones for an exhaustive algorithm are exponential over the number of variables, and for a logical algorithm they are exponential over the maximal number of literals with the same predicate. It allows to choose the algorithm depending on characteristics of the concrete problem under consideration. Note that the reverse Maslov's method [10, 11] has the same estimations for the solution of the sequent (4), but makes essentially smaller number of steps on the average.

The received estimations cannot be essentially decreased up to polynomial ones if **P** $\neq$ **NP** (classes **P** and **NP** are the classes of predicates checked in polynomial time by a deterministic or nondeterministic Turing machine respectively). More precisely, the problem (4) is NP-complete and, hence, the problems (1) and (3) are NP-complete, and the problems (4) and (5) are NP-hard [4, 5].

Problem (2) is strictly connected with the so-called "open" problem ISOMORPHISM OF GRAPHS [3], for which it is not proved neither its polynomiality nor its NP-completeness.

http://dx.doi.org/10.5772/intechopen.72765

2.1. Model example of description and the estimations for the number of an algorithm steps

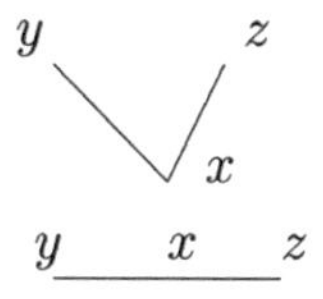

Given two predicates $V(x, y, z) \Longleftrightarrow$ "$\angle yxz < \pi$" and and $L(x, y, z,) \Longleftrightarrow$ "*x belongs to the segment* (y, z)" describe (in the perms of these predicates) the class of "boxes"according to the training set represented in the **Figure 1**.

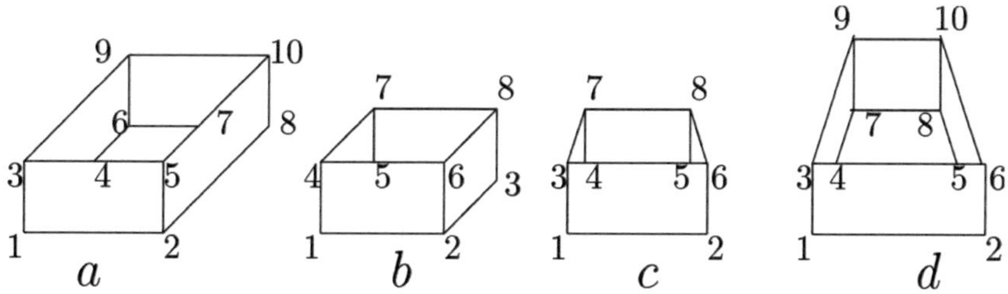

Figure 1. Standard different contour images of a "box".

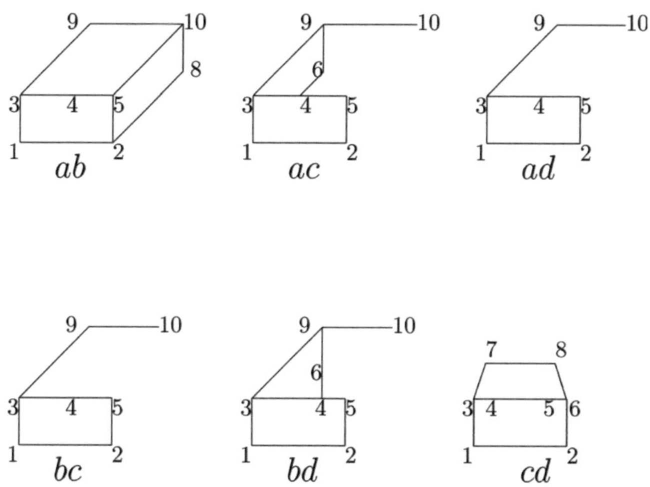

Figure 2. Images corresponding to extraction of common sub-formulas.

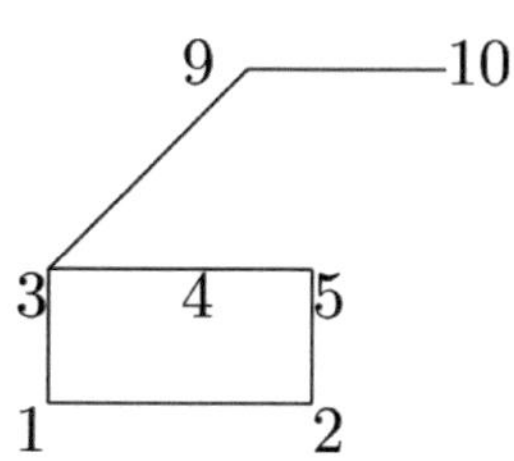

Figure 3. Image corresponding to the second extraction of common sub-formulas.

These standard images allow to form a description (up to mirror image) of almost all boxes. Such a description is a disjunction of four elementary conjunctions containing, respectively, 10, 8, 10, 8 variables and 30 + 2, 23 + 1, 28 + 4, 33 + 4 atomic formulas with predicates V and L, respectively. The elementary conjunctions corresponding to the images are

$$\begin{aligned}A_a(x_1,x_2,x_3,x_4,x_5,x_6,x_7,x_8,x_9,x_{10}) = {} & V(x_1,x_3,x_2)\&V(x_2,x_1,x_5)\&V(x_2,x_5,x_8)\&V(x_3,x_4,x_1)\& \\ & V(x_3,x_5,x_1)\&V(x_3,x_9,x_4)\&V(x_3,x_9,x_5)\&V(x_3,x_9,x_1)\&V(x_4,x_3,x_6)\&V(x_4,x_6,x_5)\& \\ & V(x_5,x_2,x_3)\&V(x_5,x_2,x_4)\&V(x_5,x_3,x_7)\&V(x_5,x_3,x_{10})\&V(x_5,x_4,x_7)\&V(x_5,x_4,x_{10})\& \\ & V(x_5,x_7,x_2)\&V(x_5,x_{10},x_2)\&V(x_6,x_4,x_9)\&V(x_6,x_7,x_4)\&V(x_6,x_9,x_7)\&V(x_7,x_5,x_6)\& \\ & V(x_7,x_6,x_{10})\&V(x_8,x_2,x_{10})\&V(x_9,x_6,x_3)\&V(x_9,x_{10},x_6)\&V(x_9,x_{10},x_3)\&V(x_{10},x_7,x_9)\& \\ & V(x_{10},x_8,x_7)\&V(x_{10},x_8,x_9)\&L(x_4,x_3,x_5)\&L(x_7,x_5,x_{10}),\end{aligned}$$

$$\begin{aligned}A_b(x_1,x_2,x_3,x_4,x_5,x_6,x_7,x_8) = {} & V(x_1,x_4,x_2)\&V(x_2,x_1,x_6)\&V(x_2,x_6,x_3)\&V(x_2,x_1,x_3)\& \\ & V(x_3,x_2,x_8)\&V(x_4,x_5,x_1)\&V(x_4,x_6,x_1)\&V(x_4,x_7,x_5)\&V(x_4,x_7,x_6)\&V(x_4,x_7,x_1)\& \\ & V(x_5,x_4,x_7)\&V(x_5,x_7,x_6)\&V(x_6,x_2,x_5)\&V(x_6,x_2,x_4)\&V(x_6,x_5,x_8)\&V(x_6,x_4,x_8)\& \\ & V(x_6,x_8,x_2)\&V(x_7,x_5,x_4)\&V(x_7,x_8,x_5)\&V(x_7,x_8,x_4\&V(x_8,x_3,x_6)\&V(x_8,x_6,x_7)\& \\ & V(x_8,x_3,x_7)\&L(x_5,x_4,x_6),\end{aligned}$$

$$\begin{aligned}A_c(x_1,x_2,x_3,x_4,x_5,x_6,x_7,x_8) = {} & V(x_1,x_3,x_2)\&V(x_2,x_1,x_6)\&V(x_3,x_4,x_1)\&V(x_3,x_5,x_1)\& \\ & V(x_3,x_6,x_1)\&V(x_3,x_7,x_4)\&V(x_3,x_7,x_5)\&V(x_3,x_7,x_6)\&V(x_3,x_7,x_1)\&V(x_4,x_3,x_7)\& \\ & V(x_4,x_7,x_5)\&V(x_4,x_7,x_6)\&V(x_5,x_3,x_8)\&V(x_5,x_4,x_8)\&V(x_5,x_8,x_6)\&V(x_6,x_2,x_5)\& \\ & V(x_6,x_2,x_4)\&V(x_6,x_2,x_3)\&V(x_6,x_5,x_8)\&V(x_6,x_4,x_8)\&V(x_6,x_3,x_8)\&V(x_6,x_2,x_8)\& \\ & V(x_7,x_8,x_4)\&V(x_7,x_8,x_3)\&V(x_7,x_4,x_3)\&V(x_8,x_6,x_5)\&V(x_8,x_5,x_7)\&V(x_8,x_6,x_7)\& \\ & L(x_4,x_3,x_5)\&L(x_4,x_3,x_6)\&L(x_5,x_4,x_6)\&L(x_5,x_3,x_6),\end{aligned}$$

$$\begin{aligned}A_d(x_1,x_2,x_3,x_4,x_5,x_6,x_7,x_8,x_9,x_{10}) = {} & V(x_1,x_3,x_2)\&V(x_2,x_1,x_6)\&V(x_3,x_4,x_1)\& \\ & V(x_3,x_5,x_1)\&V(x_3,x_6,x_1)\&V(x_3,x_9,x_4)\&V(x_3,x_9,x_5)\&V(x_3,x_9,x_6)\&V(x_3,x_9,x_1)\& \\ & V(x_4,x_3,x_7)\&V(x_4,x_7,x_5)\&\&V(x_4,x_7,x_6)\&V(x_5,x_4,x_8)\&V(x_5,x_3,x_8)\&V(x_5,x_8,x_6)\& \\ & V(x_6,x_2,x_5)\&V(x_6,x_2,x_4)\&V(x_6,x_2,x_3)\&V(x_6,x_5,x_{10})\&V(x_6,x_4,x_{10})\&V(x_6,x_3,x_{10})\& \\ & V(x_7,x_4,x_9)\&V(x_7,x_8,x_4)\&V(x_7,x_9,x_8)\&V(x_8,x_5,x_7)\&V(x_8,x_7,x_{10})\&V(x_8,x_{10},x_5)\&\& \\ & V(x_9,x_7,x_3)\&V(x_9,x_{10},x_3)\&V(x_9,x_{10},x_7)\&V(x_{10},x_6,x_8)\&V(x_{10},x_8,x_9)\&V(x_{10},x_6,x_9)\& \\ & L(x_4,x_3,x_5)\&L(x_4,x_3,x_6)\&L(x_5,x_4,x_6)\&L(x_5,x_3,x_6).\end{aligned}$$

Given a "box" inside a complex contour image containing t nodes and s be the maximal number of occurrences of the predicate V in the description $S(\omega)$, it would be recognized (according to the estimations (5′) and (6′)) in $O(t^{10})$ steps by an exhaustive algorithm and in $O(s^{37})$ steps by a logical algorithm.

Can seem that many atomic formulas such as $V(x_5,x_2,x_4)$, $V(x_5,x_3,x_7)$, $V(x_5,x_4,x_7)$, and $V(x_5,x_7,x_2)$ in $V(x_5,x_2,x_3)$ & $V(x_5,x_2,x_4)$ & $V(x_5,x_3,x_7)$ & $V(x_5,x_3,x_{10})$ & $V(x_5,x_4,x_7)$ & $V(x_5,x_4,x_{10})$ & $V(x_5,x_7,x_2)$ & $V(x_5,x_{10},x_2)$ are unnecessary. But if we delete such "unnecessary" formulas, it would be needed to add to a premise of a sequent, a condition that every point that belongs to a segment (y,z) may be substituted instead of y or z (be the second or the third argument) in every atomic formula with the predicate V. It would be another setting of a problem. Moreover, such "unnecessary" formulas can help to decrease the number of algorithm run steps if we use branch and bound algorithm inside the exhaustive algorithm or the reverse Maslov's method for a logical one [11].

3. Level description of classes

Below, the designation $A_k(\overline{x}_k)$ will be used for elementary conjunctions, which are disjunctive terms of a class description.

The notion of level description of classes was introduced in [6]. Such a description essentially allows to decrease the number of steps for an algorithm solving every of the above-formulated problems. This notion is based on the extraction of "frequently" appeared "sub-formulas" $P_i^1(\overline{y}_i^1)$ $(i = 1,\ldots, n_1)$ of $A_1(\overline{x}_1),\ldots, A_K(\overline{x}_K)$ with "small complexity" and changing them in these formulas by atomic formulas $p_i^1(y_i^1)$ defined by an equivalence of the form $p_i^1(y_i^1) \Leftrightarrow P_i^1(\overline{y}_i^1)$. New predicates p_i^1 having new first-level arguments y_i^1 for lists $\overline{y}_i^1$ of initial variables are called first-level predicates. The formula $A_k^1(\overline{x}_k^1)$ is received from $A_k(\overline{x}_k)$ by means of a substitution of $p_i^1(y_i^1)$ instead of $P_i^1(\overline{y}_i^1)$

Repeat the above-described procedure with all formulas $A_k^1(\overline{x}_k^1)$. After L repetitions, an L-level description in the following form is received:

$$\begin{cases} A_k^L(\overline{x}^L) \\ p_1^1(y_1^1) \Leftrightarrow P_1^1(\overline{y}_1^1) \\ \vdots \\ p_{n_1}^1\left(y_{n_1}^1\right) \Leftrightarrow P_{n_1}^1\left(\overline{y}_{n_1}^1\right) \\ \vdots \\ p_i^l(y_i^l) \Leftrightarrow P_i^l(\overline{y}_i^l) \\ \vdots \\ p_{n_L}^L\left(y_{n_L}^L\right) \Leftrightarrow P_{n_L}^L\left(\overline{y}_{n_L}^L\right) \end{cases} \qquad (12)$$

The solution of the problem of the form (4) with the use of the level description of classes is decomposed on the sequential ($l = 1, \ldots, L$) implementation of the actions 1–4:

1. For every i $(i = 1,\ldots, n_l)$ check $S^{l-1}(\omega) \Rightarrow \exists\overline{y}_i^1 \neq P_i^1(\overline{y}_i^1)$ and find all lists $\overline{\tau}_i^1$ of previous levels constants for the values of the variable list y_i^1 such that $S^{l-1}(\omega) \Rightarrow P_i^1(\overline{\tau}_i^1)$.
2. Introduce new l-level atomic formulas $p_i^1(y_i^1)$ defined by the equalities $p_i^1(y_i^1) \Leftrightarrow P_i^1(\overline{y}_i^1)$ with new l-level variables.
3. Substitute $p_i^1(y_i^1)$ instead of $P_i^1(\overline{y}_i^1)$ into $A_k^{l-1}(\overline{y}_k^{l-1})$ and obtain $A_k^l(\overline{y}_k^l)$.

4. Add all constant atomic l-level formulas in the form $p_i^1(\tau_i^1)$ (τ_i^1 were received at the first step) to $S^{l-1}(\omega)$ and obtain $S^l(\omega)$. Here τ_i^1 τ_i^l are new l-level constants for the lists of $(l-1)$-level constants

5. At last check $S^L(\omega) \Rightarrow \exists \overline{y}_k^L \neq A_k^L(\overline{y}_k^L)$.

The decreasing of the number of steps for an algorithm solving every of the above formulated problems (1)–(3) with the use of a level description follows from the fact that in items 1, 2, and 5, we solve the same problem as it was formulated in Section 1 and has the number (4). The estimations of number of steps exponentially depend on the parameters of the formula, i.e., on the right part of implication. That is why the term "small complexity" for $P_i^l(\overline{y}_i^l)$ must be interpreted as "small number of variables in $P_i^l(\overline{y}_i^l)$" for an exhaustive algorithm, and "small number of literals in $P_i^l(\overline{y}_i^l)$" for a logical algorithm

Why did we use quotation marks for the term "sub-formulas?" Such formulas (elementary conjunctions) $P_j^l(\overline{y}_j^l)$ are not obliged to be precisely sub-formulas of $A_1(\overline{x}_1), \ldots, A_K(\overline{x}_K)$ but may differ from these sub-formulas in names of variables and order of conjunctive terms

Definition 1. *Elementary conjunctions P and Q are called isomorphic if there is an elementary conjunction R and substitutions $\lambda_{R,P}$ and $\lambda_{R,Q}$ of the arguments of P and Q, respectively, instead of the variables in R such that the results of these substitutions coincide up to the order of literals*

The substitutions $\lambda_{R,P}$ and $\lambda_{R,Q}$ are called unifiers of R with P and Q, respectively.

Definition 2. *Elementary conjunction C is called a common up to the names of arguments sub-formula of two elementary conjunctions A and B if it is isomorphic to some sub-formulas A′ and B′ of A and B, respectively*

For example, let $A(x,y,z) = p_1(x) \,\&\, p_1(y) \,\&\, p_1(z) \,\&\, p_2(x, y) \,\&\, p_3(x, z)$, $B(x,y,z) = p_1(x) \,\&\, p_1(y) \,\&\, p_1(z) \,\&\, p_2(x, z) \,\&\, p_3(x, z)$

Is the formula $P(u,v) = p_1(u) \,\&\, p_1(v) \,\&\, p_2(u, v)$ their common sub-formula?

The formula $P(u,v)$ is their common up to the names of variables sub-formula with the unifiers $\lambda_{P,A}$—substitution of x and y instead of u and v, respectively, and $\lambda_{P,B}$—substitution of x and z instead of u and v, respectively. It is so because $P(x,y) = p_1(x) \,\&\, p_1(y) \,\&\, p_2(x,y)$ is a sub-formula of A(x,y,z) and $P(x,z) = p_1(x) \,\&\, p_1(z) \,\&\, p_2(x,z)$ is a sub-formula of $B(x,y,z)$.

An algorithm of extraction of a maximal (having a maximal number of literals) common up to the names of arguments sub-formula C of two elementary conjunctions A and B and determining the unifiers $\lambda_{c,A'}$ and $\lambda_{c,B'}$ is described in [12]. The number of steps of this algorithm is $O(a^a b^b)$, where a and b are the numbers of literals in A and B, respectively. The minimal number of steps of this algorithm is $O((ab)^2)$, the middle estimate is $O((ab)^{1/2 \log(ab)})$.

This algorithm allows to construct a level description for a set of goal elementary conjunctions. Essential difference between maximal common up to the names of arguments sub-formulas and sub-formulas in the level description consists in the fact that in the level description it is needed to extract sub-formulas with "small complexity" but not a maximal one. An algorithm of level description construction is in [6]. It consists in sequential pairwise extraction of common up to the names of variables sub-formulas of $A_i(\overline{x}_i)$ and $A_j(\overline{x}_j)$ with finding their unifiers and then the analogous procedure with the obtained sub-formulas.

Let N be the maximal number of literals $A_k(\overline{x}_k)$ in $(k = 1,\dots, K)$. The upper bound of this algorithm number of steps is $O(K^2N^{2N})$.

3.1. Example of sub-formula extraction and a level description construction

Return to the example in the previous section. There, we have seen a description of a class of "boxes" represented in **Figure 1**. According to these descriptions, we have received that given a "box" inside a complex contour image containing t nodes it would be recognized in $O(t^{10})$ steps by an exhaustive algorithm and in $O(s^{37})$ steps by a logical algorithm (here, s is the maximal number of occurrences of the same predicate in the object description $S(\omega)$).

Pairwise extraction of common up to the names of variables of elementary conjunctions, corresponding to these images, allows to extract common up to the names of variables sub-formulas corresponding to the images represented in **Figure 2**

These sub-formulas contain, respectively, 8, 8, 7, 7, 7, 8 variables and 18, 15, 11, 11, 15, 16 atomic formulas.

The following extraction by means of pairwise partial deduction between common sub-formulas corresponding to images *ab, ac, ad, bc, bd, cd* gives a sub-formula corresponding to the image represented in **Figure 3**.

Elementary conjunction $P^1(x_1,x_2,x_3,x_4,x_5,x_9,x_{10}) = V(x_1,x_3,x_2)$ & $V(x_2,x_1,x_5)$ & $V(x_3,x_4,x_1)$ & $V(x_3,x_5,x_1)$ & $V(x_3,x_9,x_4)$ & $V(x_3,x_9,x_5)$ & $V(x_3,x_9,x_1)$ & $V(x_5,x_2,x_4)$ & $V(x_5,x_2,x_3)$ & $V(x_9,x_{10},x_3)$ & $T(x_4,x_3,x_5)$, corresponding to this image, defines a first-level predicate $p^1(x^1)$. The first-level variable x^1 is a variable for a list of seven initial variables $x^1 = (x_1,x_2,x_3,x_4,x_5,x_9,x_{10})$. The unifier of $P^1(x_1,x_2,x_3,x_4,x_5,x_9,x_{10})$ with the description of ab, ac, ad, ac, and bd is an identical substitution, but its unifier with the description of cd is a substitution of x_6 instead of x_5.

Elementary conjunctions $P_1^2(x^1,x_1,x_2,x_3,x_4,x_5,x_8,x_9,x_{10})$, $P_2^2(x^1,x_4,x_5,x_6,x_9,x_{10})$, $P_3^2(x^1,x_3,x_4,x_5,x_{10})$, $P_4^2(x^1,x_2,x_5,x_6,x_{10})$, corresponding to the images *ab, ac, bd, cd* and written with the use of the predicate $p^1(x^1)$, define second-level predicates $p_1^2(x_1^2)$, $p_2^2(x_2^2)$, $p_3^2(x_3^2)$, $p_4^2(x_4^2)$ with the second-level variables $x_1^2 = (x^1,x_1,x_2,x_3,x_4,x_5,x_8,x_9,x_{10})$, $x_2^2 = (x^1,x_4,x_5,x_6,x_9,x_{10})$, $x_3^2 = (x^1,x_3,x_4,x_5,x_{10})$, $x_4^2 = (x^1,x_2,x_5,x_6,x_{10})$.

For example, a sub-formula corresponding to the image ab is $P_1^2(x^1,x_1,x_2,x_3,x_4,x_5,x_8,x_9,x_{10}) = p^1(x^1)$ & $V(x_2,x_5,x_8)$ & $V(x_2,x_1,x_8)$ & $V(x_5,x_4,x_{10})$ & $V(x_5,x_3,x_{10})$ & $V(x_8,x_2,x_{10})$ & $V(x_{10},x_8,x_5)$ & $V(x_{10},x_5,x_9)$ & $V(x_{10},x_8,x_9)$. The unifier of $P_1^2(x^1,x_1,x_2,x_3,x_4,x_5,x_8,x_9,x_{10})$ with the description of a is an identical substitution, and with the description of b, it is a substitution of x_4,x_5,x_6,x_7,x_8 instead of x_2,x_4,x_5,x_9,x_{10}. Descriptions of images c and d are not unified with it.

The three-level description of the image b takes the form $A_b^2(x_1^2,x_4,x_5,x_6,x_7) = p_1^2(x_1^2)$ & $V(x_5,x_4,x_7)$ & $V(x_5,x_7,x_6)$ or $A_b^2(x_3^2,x_4,x_5,x_6,x_7) = p_3^2(x_3^2)$ & $V(x_3,x_2,x_8)$ & $V(x_5,x_4,x_7)$ & $V(x_5,x_7,x_6)$.

Given a "box" inside a complex contour image containing t nodes, the proof the sequence from S(ω) of elementary conjunction $P^1(x_1,x_2,x_3,x_4,x_5,x_9,x_{10})$ defining the first-level predicate $p^1(x^1)$ and the denotation of variables $x_1,x_2,x_3,x_4,x_5,x_9,x_{10}$ would be done in O(t^7) steps by an exhaustive algorithm and in O(s^{11}) steps by a logical algorithm.

Elementary conjunctions $P_1{}^2(x_1{}^1)$, $P_2{}^2(x_1{}^1)$, $P_3{}^2(x_1{}^1)$, $P_4{}^2(x_1{}^1)$ contain respectively only 1, 1, 0, 1 "new" variables (not containing in the first-level variables) and 7, 4, 4, 5 "new" atomic formulas. The proof of the sequence from $S^1(\omega\ )$ of these elementary conjunctions defining the second-level predicates $p_1{}^2(x_1{}^2)$, $p_2{}^2(x_2{}^2)$, $p_3{}^2(x_3{}^2)$, $p_4{}^2(x_4{}^2)$, and the denotation of the "new" variables would be done in O(t) steps by an exhaustive algorithm and in O(s^7) steps by a logical algorithm.

Elementary conjunctions obtained from the class description by means of second-level predicates instead of the corresponding sub-formulas contain respectively 2, 0, 2, 2 "new" variables and 7, 4, 11, 16 "new" atomic formulas. The proof of the sequence from S^2(ω) of these elementary conjunctions and the denotation of the "new" variables would be done in O(t^2) steps by an exhaustive algorithm and in O(s^{16}) steps by a logical algorithm.

As O(t^7) + O(t) + O(t^2) = O(t^7) < O(t^{10}) and O(s^{11}) + O(s^7) + O(s^{16}) = O(s^{16}) < O(s^{37}) then both an exhaustive algorithm and a logical algorithm using the built level description of the class of "boxes" make the less number of steps then the same ones using the initial description. At the same time, the decreasing of number of steps of a logical algorithm is more noticeably.

4. Logic-predicate network

Traditional neuron network deals with binary or many-valued characteristics of an object and is an adder of weighted inputs followed by a function mapping the result into the segment [0, 1]. The neuron network configuration is fixed and only the weights may be changed.

A logic-predicate network is described later. The inputs for this network are atomic formulas setting properties of the elements composing an investigated object and relations between them [7]. The proposed model of logic-predicate network has two blocks: a training block and a recognition block. The input of every block is an elementary conjunction of atomic predicate formulas or their negations. Configuration of the recognition block is formed after an implementation of the training block and may be changed with its help.

The training block is a "slowly running" block. At the same time, the recognition block is a "quickly running" one. The base of the proposed predicate network is a logic-objective approach to AI problems and level description of classes.

The scheme of the logic-predicate network is presented in **Figure 4**

At a training stage of logic-predicate network construction, we have a training set of objects. Let a training set of objects $\omega_1,\ldots,\omega_K$ be given to form an initial variant of the network training block. Replace every constant ω_k^j in S(ω_k) by a variable x_k^j ($k = 1,\ldots, K$, $j = 1,\ldots, t_k$) and substitute the sign & between the atomic formulas. Initial goal formulas $A_1(\overline{x}_1), \ldots, A_K(\overline{x}_K)$ are obtained.

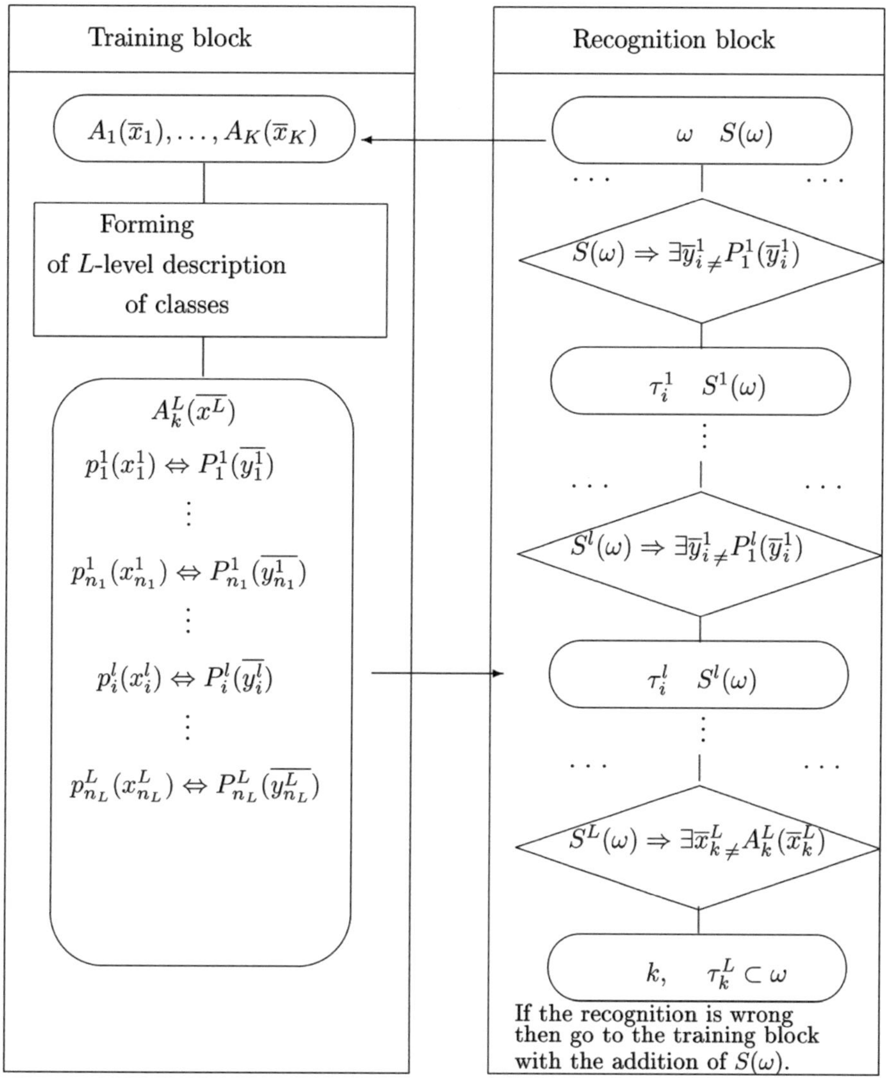

Figure 4. Scheme of the logic-predicate network.

Construct a level description for these goal formulas with the use of algorithm of level description. The first approximation to the recognition block is formed. Formulas $P_i^l(\overline{y}_i^l)$ ($i = 1,\ldots, n_l$, $l = 1,\ldots, L$) obtained in the training block (together with the unifiers) are the contents of the cells forming the recognition block. This block runs as it was described in the section level description of classes.

The recognition block tries to identify a new object according to the level description of classes, obtained in the training block.

If after the "recognition block" run an object is not recognized or has wrong classification, then it is possible to train anew the network. The description of the "wrong" object must be added to the input set of the training block. The training block extracts common sub-formulas of this description and previously received formulas forming the recognition block. Some sub-formulas in the level description would be changed. Then, the recognition block is reconstructed.

4.1. Model example of a logic-predicate network construction

Given a training set for the class of contour images of "boxes" presented in **Figure 1** (Section 2). Pairwise extraction of common up to the names of variables of elementary conjunctions, corresponding to these images, allows to extract common sub-formulas corresponding to the images presented in **Figures 2** and **3** (Section 3). Fragments of the images corresponding to a three-level network are presented in **Figure 5**.

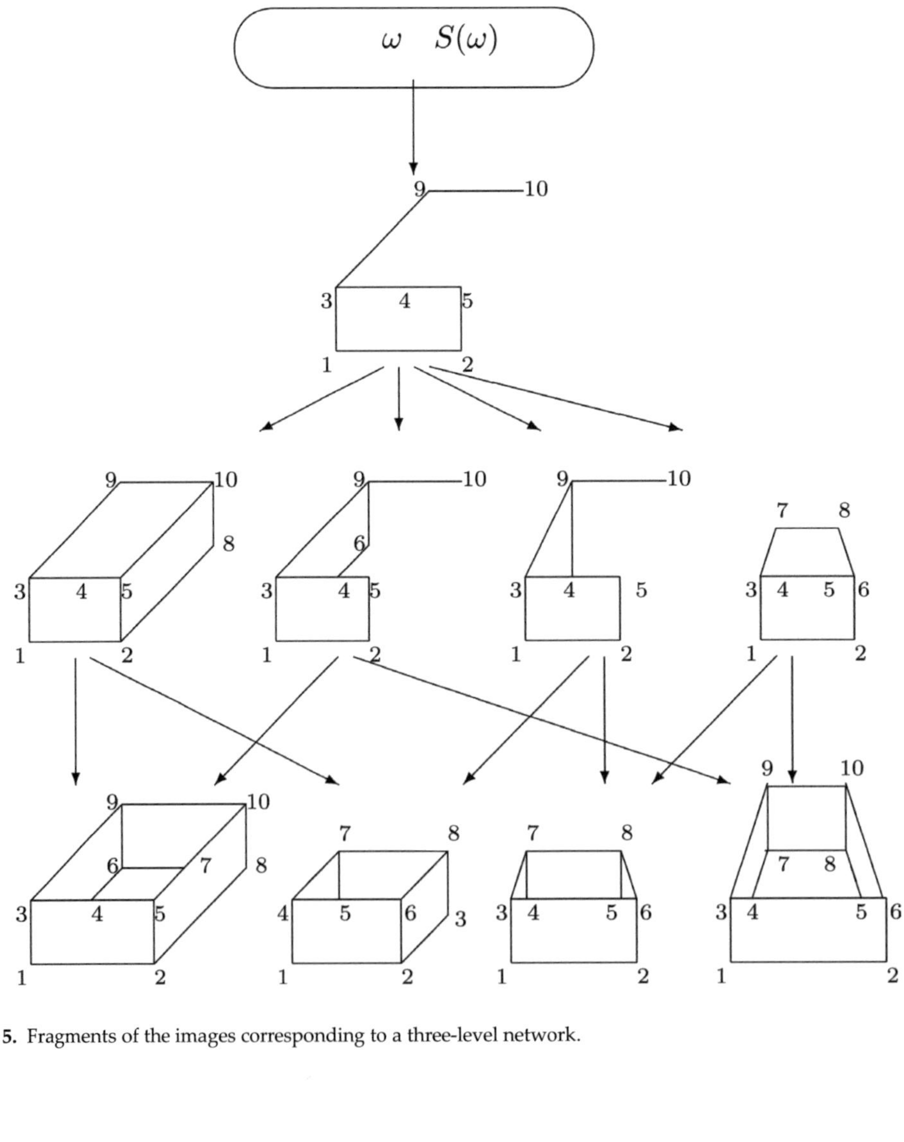

Figure 5. Fragments of the images corresponding to a three-level network.

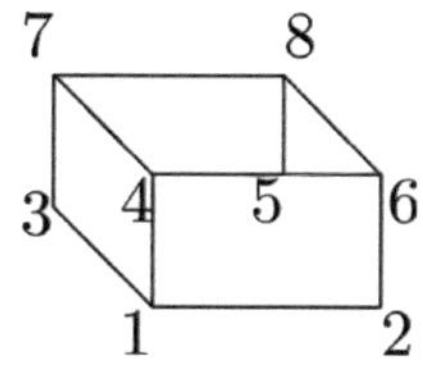

Figure 6. Control image.

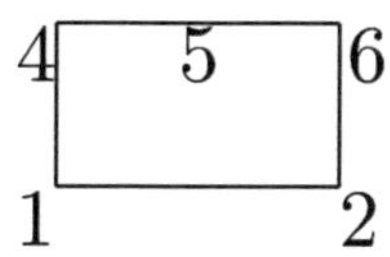

Figure 7. Image corresponding to the new first-level predicate.

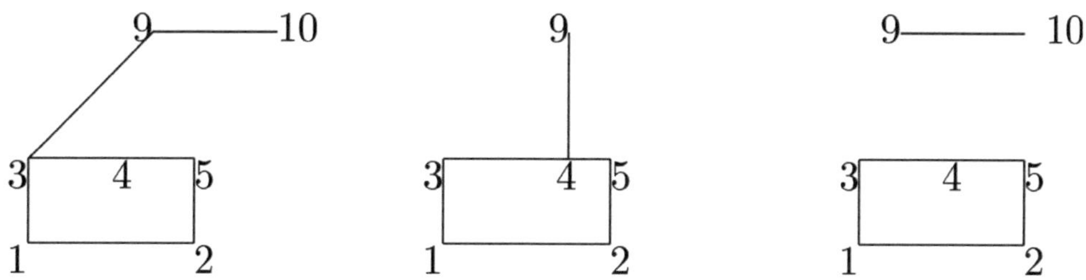

Figure 8. Images corresponding to three new second-level predicates.

Given, a new image represented in **Figure 6** for recognition, the network would not recognize it because the first-level predicate is not valid.

Add the description of this control image to the input data of the training block. The extraction of common sub-formulas for this description and the formula defining the first-level predicate gives a formula corresponding to the image represented in **Figure 7**.

New second-level predicates correspond to three images represented in **Figure 8**.

The set of the third-level predicates coincides with the set of previous second-level predicates. So, the recognition block is constructed anew and represents four-level description of the class. Fragments of the images corresponding to a four-level network are presented in **Figure 9**.

5. Multi-agent description of an object

A problem of multi-agent description of a complex object is under consideration in this section. It is supposed that every agent knows only a part of an investigated object description. Moreover, she does not know the true names of elements and gives them names arbitrary. It is similar to the parable about tree blind men who feel an elephant. To overcome such a

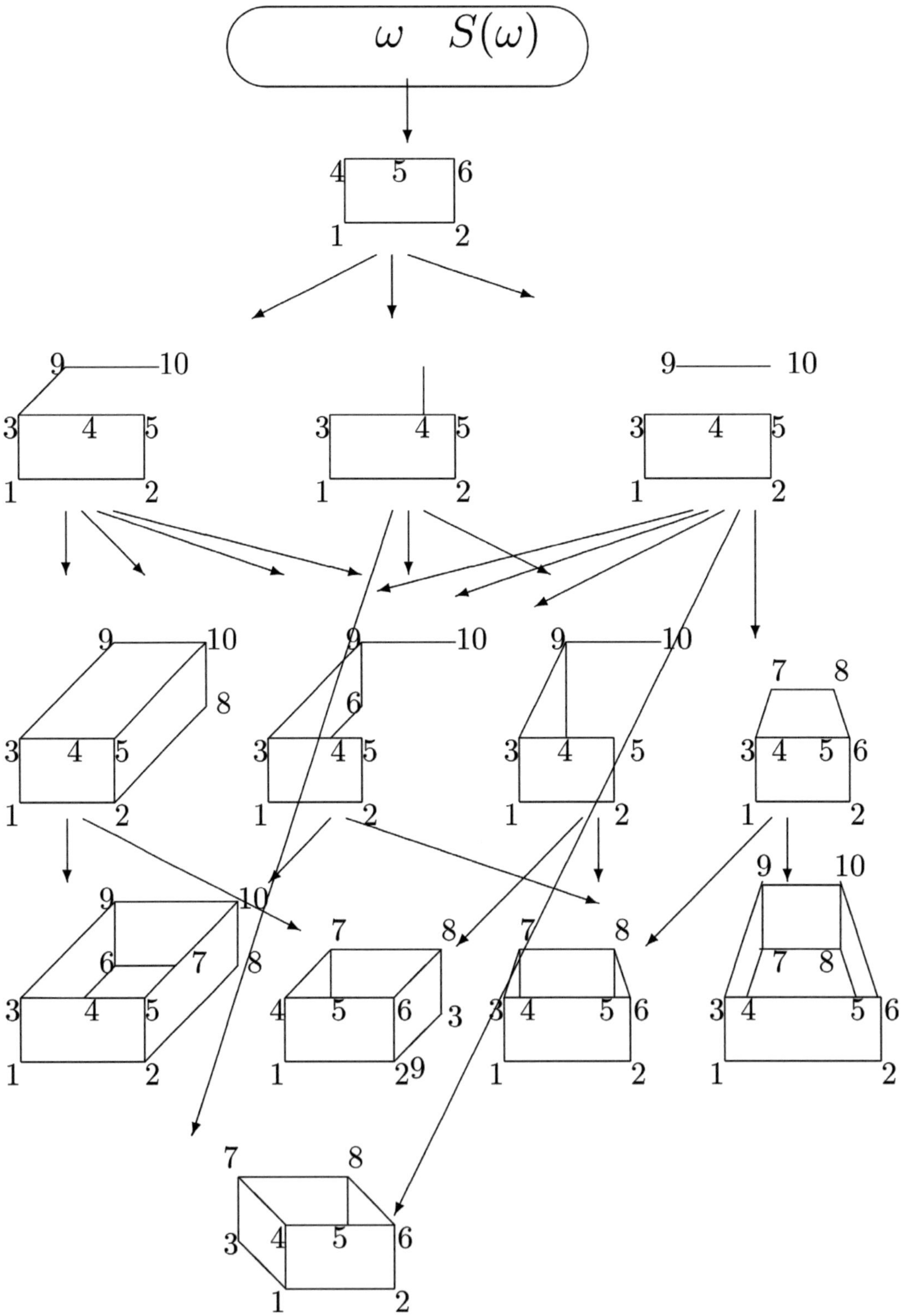

Figure 9. Fragments of the images corresponding to a four-level network.

paradox, it is supposed that every two agents have information concerning some common part of an object. The main difficulty in this problem is to find and identify these parts [8].

5.1. Setting of the problem

Let an investigated object is represented as a set of its elements $\omega = \{\omega_1, \ldots, \omega_t\}$ and is characterized by the set of predicates $p_1, \ldots, p_n$, every of which is defined on the elements of ω and gives properties of these elements or relations between them.

Information (description) of an object is an elementary conjunction of atomic formulas with predicates $p_1, \ldots, p_n$ and some constants as arguments.

There are m agents $a_1, \ldots, a_m$ which can measure some values for some predicates of some elements of ω. The agent a_j does not know the true number of the ω elements and suppose that she deals with the object $\omega_j = \left\{\omega_1^j, \ldots, \omega_{t_j}^j\right\}$. That is, the agent a_j has the information $I_j\left(\omega_1^j, \ldots, \omega_{t_j}^j\right)$ in the form of elementary conjunction of atomic formulas. It is required to reconstruct the full description $I(\omega_1, \ldots, \omega_t)$ of ω (if it is possible).

As every agent uses her own notifications for the names of the object elements, it is needed to find all common up to the names of arguments sub-formulas C_{ij} of the information $I_i\left(\omega_1^i, \ldots, \omega_{t_i}^i\right)$ and $I_j\left(\omega_1^j, \ldots, \omega_{t_j}^j\right)$ $(i \neq j)$ and their unifiers, i.e., such substitutions for the argument names that the extracted pairs of sub-formulas are identical.

5.2. Algorithm of multi-agent description

Below, the arguments of information will be omitted. Let every agent a_j has information I_j about the described object ω $(j = 1, \ldots, m)$. To construct a description of ω the following algorithm is offered.

1. Change all constants in $I_1, \ldots, I_m$ by variables in such a way that different constants are changed by different variables and the names of variables in Ii and Ij $(i \neq j)$ does not coincide. Obtain $I'_1, \ldots, I'_m$.

2. For every pair of elementary conjunctions I'_i and I'_j $(i = 1, \ldots, m-1, j = i+1, \ldots, m)$ find their maximal common up to the names of arguments sub-formula C_{ij} and unifiers $\lambda_{i,ij}$ and $\lambda_{j,ij}$. Every argument of C_{ij} has a unique name.

3. For every pair i and j $(i > j)$ check if I'_i and I'_j contain a contradictory pair of atomic formulas or two sub-formulas which cannot be satisfied simultaneously (for example, "x is green" and "x is red"). If such a contradiction is established, then delete from C_{ij} atomic formulas containing the variables, which are in the contradictory sub-formulas. Change the unifiers by means of elimination of these variables.

4. For every i, identify the variables in C_{ij} $(i \neq j)$ which are substituted in I'_i and I'_j instead of the same variable. The names of the identified variables are changed in unifiers by the same name.

5. With the use of the unifiers obtained in items 2–4 change the names of variables in $I'_1, \ldots, I'_m$. Obtain $I''_1, \ldots, I''_m$.

6. Write down the conjunction $I''_1 \& \ldots \& I''_m$ and delete the repeated atomic formulas.

5.3. Upper bound of the number of steps

To estimate the number of the algorithm run steps, we estimate every item of the algorithm.

1. Item 1 requires not more than $\sum_{j=l^m} \|I_j\|$ "steps."

2. Item 2 requires $O\left(t_i^{t_j} \cdot 2^{\|I_j\|}\right)$ "steps" for an exhaustive algorithm and $O\left(s_i^{\|I_j\|} \cdot \|I_i\|^3\right)$ "steps" for an algorithm based on the derivation in the predicate calculus.

   It is needed to summarize the above estimates for $i = 1, \ldots, m - 1$, $j = i, \ldots, m$. So, we have $O\left(t^t \cdot 2^s m^2\right)$ "steps" for an exhaustive algorithm and $O\left(s^{s+3} \cdot m^2\right)$ "steps" for an algorithm based on the derivation in the predicate calculus. Here, t and $\|I\|$ are the maximal numbers of variables and atomic formulas in I_j ($j = 1, \ldots, m$), respectively.

3. Consistency checking of the formulas I_i and I_j requires $\|I_i\|\|I_j\|$ "steps." This item of the algorithm requires not more than $\sum_{i=1}^{m} (m - i)\|I_i\|$ "steps" that is $O(m^2 s)$ "steps."

4. For every i, identification of the variables in C_{ij} ($i > j$) consists in the comparison of the replaced part of the unifiers $\lambda_{i,ij}$ and $\lambda_{j,ij}$. It requires not more than $(m - i)t_i^2$ "steps." Summarizing it for $i = 1, \ldots, m$ we have not more than $\sum_{i=1}^{m} (m - i)t_i^2 = O\left(m^2 t^2\right)$ "steps".

5. The number of "steps" required for the changing of the names of variables in $I1, \ldots, Im$ is linear under $\sum_{i=1}^{m} \|I_i\| = O(m\|I\|)$ "steps."

6. The number of "steps" required for the deleting of the repeated conjunctive terms is not more than $\sum_{i=1}^{m-1} \sum_{j=i+1}^{m} \|I_i\|\|I_j\|$ "steps."

The whole number of the algorithm run steps is $O(t^t\, 2^s\, m^2)$ for an exhaustive algorithm and $O(s^{s+3}\, m^2)$ for an algorithm based on the derivation in the predicate calculus.

The analysis of the received estimation shows that the main contribution is made by the summarized number of partial deduction checking (item 2).

5.4. Example of a multi-agent description

Let the initial predicates be V and L described in Section 2. Each of the three agents has a description of one of the fragment presented in **Figure 10**.

According to the item 1 of the algorithm, all constants in the fragment descriptions are replaced by variables in such a way that different constants are changed by different variables and the names of variables in I_i and I_j ($i \neq j$) does not coincide. The fragment descriptions take the form:

I′1(x1,…,x6) = V(x1,x2,x4) & V(x1,x5,x4) & V(x1,x3,x2) & V(x1,x3,x5) & V(x1,x3,x4) & V(x2,x1, x3) & V(x2,x3,x5) & V(x3,x2,x1) &V(x3,x6,x2) & V(x3,x6,x1) & L(x2,x1,x5),

I′2(y1,…,y6) = V(y3,y1,y4) & V(y1,y2,y3) & V(y1,y5,y3) & V(y1,y6,y2) & V(y1,y6,y5) & V(y1,y6, y3) & L(y2,y1,y5),

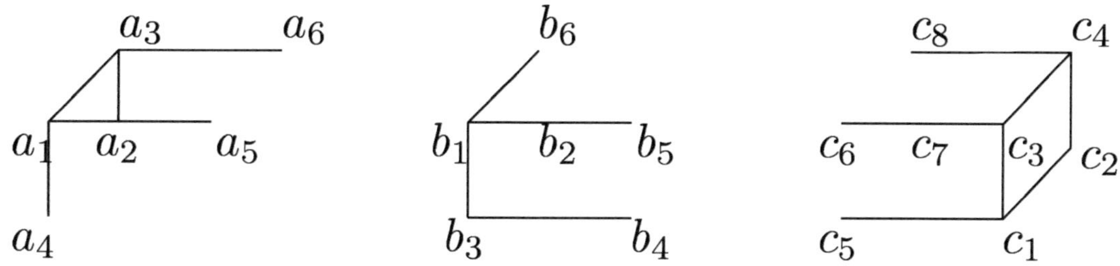

Figure 10. Fragments of the image received by three agents.

I′3(z1,…,z8) = V(z1,z5,z3) & V(z1,z3,z2) & V(z1,z5,z2) & V(z3,z1,z7) & V(z3,z1,z6) & V(z3,z7, z4) & V(z3,z6,z4) & V(z3,z4,z1) & V(z4,z2,z3) & V(z4,z3,z8) & V(z4,z2,z8) & L(z7,z6,z3).

According to the item 2 of the algorithm, find maximal common up to the names of arguments sub-formula of formulas I′1(x1,…,x6) and I′2(y1,…,y6). It is C12(u0,…,u4) of the form C12(u0, …,u4) = V(u0,u1,u2) & V(u0,u3,u2) & V(u0,u4,u1) & V(u0,u4,u3) & V(u0,u4,u2) & L(u1,u0,u3).

It has unifiers $\lambda_{I1,C12}$—substitution of u0, u1, u4, u2, u3 instead of x1, x2, x3, x4, x5, respectively, and $\lambda_{I2,C12}$—substitution of u0, u1, u2, u3, u4 instead of y1, y2, y3, y5, y6, respectively. Besides,

I′1(u0,u1,u2,u3,u4,x6) = V(u1,u0,u4) & V(u1,u4,u3) & V(u4,u1,u0) & V(u4,x6,u1) & V(u4,x6,u0) & C12(u0, …, u4),

I′2(u0,u1,u2,y4,u3,u4) = V(u2,u0,y4) & C12(u0,…,u4).

Maximal common up to the names of arguments sub-formula of I′2(y1,…,y6) and I′3(z1,…,z8) is C23(v0,v2,v4,v5,v6,v7) of the form

C23(v0,v2,v4,v5,v6,v7) = V(v6,v2,v7) & V(v2,v4,v6) & V(v2,v5,v6) &V(v2,v0,v4) & V(v2,v0,v5).

It has unifiers $\lambda_{I2,C23}$—substitution of v2, v4, v6, v7, v5, v0 instead of y1, y2, y3, y4, y5, y6, respectively, and $\lambda_{I3,C23}$—substitution of v0, v2, v6, v5, v4, v7 instead of z1, z3, z5, z6, z7, z8, respectively. Besides,

I′2(v2,v4,v6,v7,v5,v0) = V(v2,v0,v6) & L(v4,v2,v5) & C23(v0,v2,v4,v5,v6,v7),

I′3(v0,z2,v2,v6,z5,v5,v4,v7) = V(v2,v6,v0) & V(v0,z5,v2) & V(v0,v2,z2) & V(v0,v5,z2) & V(v6, z2,v2) & V(v6,v2,v7) & L(v4,v5,v2) & C23(v0,v2,v4,v5,v6,v7).

As I′2(v2,v4,v6,v7,v5,v0) contains V(v2,v0,v6) and I′3(v0,z2,v2,v6,z5,v5,v4,v7) contains V(v2, v6,v0) and according to the definition of the predicate V, the formula V(x,y,z) & V(x,z,y) is a contradiction, so substitutions with this unifiers cannot give a consistent description of the object. After deleting from I′2(y1,…,y6) and I′3(z1,…,z8), the variables y1 and z3, respectively, a new maximal common up to the names of arguments their sub-formula C′23(v0,v2,v4,v5,v6, v7) of the form C′23(v0,v1,v2) = L(v1,v0,v2) will be received with the unifiers $\lambda_{I2,C'23}$— substitution of v0, v1, v2 instead of y1, y2, y3, respectively, and $\lambda_{I3,C'23}$—substitution of v2, v0, v1 instead of z3, z6, z7, respectively. Besides,

I′2(v0,v1,v2,y4,y5,y6) = V(v2,v0,y4) & V(v0,v1,v2) & V(v0,y5,v2) & V(v0,y6,v1) &V(v0,y6,y5) & V(v0,y6,v2) & C′23(v0,v1,v2),

I′3(z1,z2,v2,z4,z5,v0,v1,z8) = V(z1,z5,v2) & V(z1,v2,z2) & V(z1,z5,z2) & V(v2,z1,v1) & V (v2,z1, v0) & V(v2,v1,z4) & V(v2,v0,z4) & V(v2,z4,z1) & V(z4,z2,v2) & V(z4,v2,z8) & V(z4,z2,z8) & C′23(v0,v1,v2).

Maximal common up to the names of arguments sub-formula of I1(x1,…,x6) and I3(z1,…,z8) is C13(w0, …,w6) in the form

C13(w0, …,w6) = V(w2,w4,w6) & V(w2,w5,w6) & V(w2,w0,w4) & V(w2,w0,w5) & V(w0,w1,w2).

It has unifiers $\lambda_{I1,C13}$— substitution of w2, w4, w0, w6, w5, w6 instead of x1, x2, x3, x4, x5, x6, respectively, and $\lambda_{I3,C13}$—substitution of w0, w2, w6, w1, w5, w2 instead of z1, z3, z4, z5, z6, z7, respectively. Besides,

I′1(w2,w4,w0,w6,w5,w1) = V(w2,w0,w6) & V(w0,w1,w4) & V(w0,w4,w2) & L(w2,w4,w5) & C13(w0,…,w6),

I′3(w0,z2,w2,w6,w1,w5,w4,z8) = V(w0,w2,w3) & V(w0,w1,w3) & V(w2,w6,w0) & V(w6,w3, w2) & V(w6,w2,w7) & V(w6,w3,w7) & C13(w0,…,w6).

As I′1(w2,w4,w0,w6,w5,w1) contains V(w2,w0,w6), I3(w0,z2,w2,w6,w1,w5,w4,z8) contains V (w2,w6,w0) and according to the definition of the predicate V, the formula V(x,y,z) & V(x,z,y) is a contradiction, so substitutions with this unifiers cannot give a consistent description of the object.

After deleting from I′1(x1,…,x6) and I′3(z1,…,z8) literals with the variables x1 and z3, respectively, a new maximal common up to the names of arguments their sub-formula

C′13(w0,w1,w2) of the form C′13(w0,w1,w2) = L(w1,w0,w2)

will be received with the unifiers $\lambda_{I1,C'13}$—substitution of w0, w1, w2 instead of x1, x2, x5, respectively, and $\lambda_{I3,C'13}$—substitution of w2, w1, w0 instead of z3, z4, z5 respectively. Besides,

I′1(w0,w1,x3,x4,w2,x6) = V(w0,w1,x4) & V(w0,w2,x4) & V(w0,x3,w1) & V(w0,x3,w2) & V(w0,x3,x4) & V(w1,w0,x3) & V(w1,x3,w2) & V(x3,w1,w0) & V(x3,x6,w1) & V(x3,x6,w0) & C′13(w0,w1,w2),

I′3(z1,z1,w2,w1,w0,z6,z7,z8) = V(z1,w0,w2) & V(z1,w2,z2) & V(z1,w0,z2) & V(w2,z1,z7) & V (w2,z1,z6) & V(w2,z7,w1) & V(w2,z6,w1) & V(w2,w1,z1) & V(w1,z2,w2) & V(w1,w2,z8) & V (w1,z2,z8) & C′13(w0,w1,w2).

According to the item 4 of the algorithm, we identify new variables substituted instead of the same initial variable. That is we identify the following variables:
u0 and w0 (are substituted instead of the variable x1),

u1 and w1 (are substituted instead of the variable x2),

u2 and w2 (are substituted instead of the variable x4),

u0 and v0 (are substituted instead of the variable y1),

u1 and v1 (are substituted instead of the variable y2),

u2 and v2 (are substituted instead of the variable y3),

v0 and w0 (are substituted instead of the variable z6),

v1 and w1 (are substituted instead of the variable z3),

v2 and w2 (are substituted instead of the variable z7).

The identified variables denote as α 0, α 1, and α 2. So, we have the equalities u0 = v0 = w0 = α 0, u1 = v1 = w1 = α 1, u2 = v2 = w2 = α 2.

As a result, we have the following descriptions of the fragments:

I″1(α 0, α 1,u4,u2, α 2,x6) = V(α 0, α 1,u2) & V(α 0, α 2,u2) & V(α 0,u4, α 1) & V(α 0,u4, α 2) & V (α 0,u4,u2) & V(α 1, α 0,u4) & V(α 1,u4, α 2) & V(x3, α 1, α 0) & V(u4,x6, α 1) & V(u4,x6, α 0) & L(α 1, α 0, α 2),

I″2(α0, α 1,u2,y4, α 2,u4) = V(u2, α 0,y4) & V(α 0, α 1,u2) & V(α 0, α 2,u2) & V(α 0,u4, α 1) & V (α 0,u4, α 2) & V(α 0,u4,u2) & L(α 1, α 0, α 2),

I″3(z1,z2, α 2,z4,z5, α 0, α 1,z8) = V(z1,z5, α 2) & V(z1, α 2,z2) & V(z1,z5,z2) & V(α 2,z1, α 1) & V(α 2,z1, α 0) & V(α 2, α 1,z4) & V(α 2, α 0,z4) & V(α 2,z4,z1) & V(z4,z2, α 2) & V(z4, α 2,z8) & V(z4,z2,z8) & L(α 1, α 0, α 2).

Their conjunction

V(α0, α 1,u2) & V(α 0, α 2,u2) & V(α 0,u4, α 1) & V(α 0,u4, α 2) & V(α 0,u4,u2) &

V(α 1, α 0,u4) & V(α 1,u4, α 2) & V(x3, α 1, α 0) & V(u4,x6, α 1) & V(u4,x6, α 0) &

V(u2, α 0,y4) & V(z1,z5, α 2) & V(z1, α 2,z2) & V(z1,z5,z2) & V(α 2,z1, α 1) &

V(α 2,z1, α 0) & V(α 2, α 1,z4) & V(α 2, α 0,z4) &V(α 2,z4,z1) & V(z4,z2, α 2) &

V(z4, α 2,z8) & V(z4,z2,z8) & L(α 1, α 0, α 2)

allows to "stick together" the images of fragments according to the same variable. The image corresponding to the result of "sticking" is presented in **Figure 11**.

If a description of the investigated object is presented in the database, it may be found according the principle "the nearest neighbor" with the use of metric for predicate formulas presented in [13].

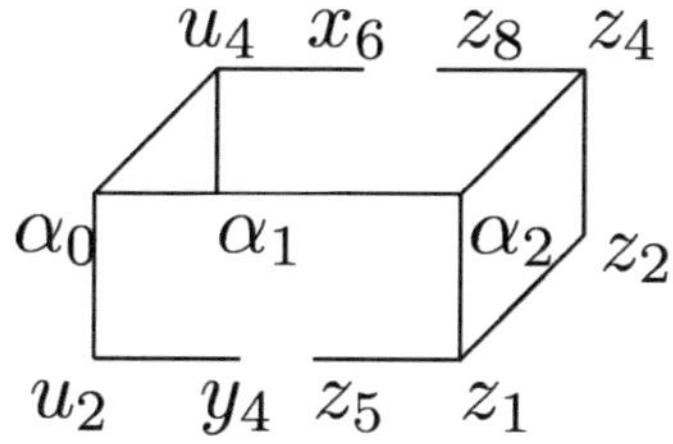

Figure 11. Image corresponding to the result of "sticking".

6. Conclusion

Logic-predicate approach to an AI problem has a rather powerful capability, essentially when an investigated object is a compound one and is characterized by properties of its elements and relations between them.

Setting of pattern recognition problems considered in Section 2 (except the problem (2)) differs from the classical one. The setting of the problems (1) and (3), in which it is needed to find parts of an investigated object, turns out to be a rather difficult one in the frameworks of a standard approach in the frameworks of which an object is regarded as a whole indivisible one.

In particular, an exponential estimation for number of propositional variables in a formula simulating a predicate formula in a finite domain for planning problems $T \cdot |Act| \cdot O^P$ is mentioned in [14]. Here, T is the number of time stages, $|Act|$ is the number of schemes of actions, O is the number of objects in the domain, P is the maximal number of parameters in schemes of actions. In Section 2, the analogous estimate (5′) was received for an exhaustive algorithm solving the problem (4).

The problem (2) is polynomial equivalent to an "open" problem ISOMORPHISM OF GRAPHS [3] and the problems (1) and (3) are NP-complete.

A notion of level description of classes has been introduced in Section 3 in order to decrease the number of steps of algorithms solving these problems. Such a description reduces the solution of the main problem to a series of solutions of the same form problems with the inputs with the essentially less notation lengths. At the same time, the constructing of a level description still deals with big input data. So, a problem with big input data is solving only once, and then the problem with the essentially less input data is solving repeatedly.

The idea of decomposition of a problem to a series of the "less dimension" problems is not a new one and is frequently used. The difficulty consists in a precise definition of the term "common sub-formula of small complexity."

The development of a precise definition and of an algorithm for the extraction of a common up to the names of arguments sub-formula of two elementary conjunctions (and their unifiers) allows not only to work out an algorithm of level description construction but also to find an approach to the solution of some else AI problems.

Note that the extracted sub-formulas define generalized characteristics of an object. This has an analogy in medical diagnostics: initial characteristics are symptoms and the generalized ones are syndromes.

Level description of classes allowed to introduce the notion of logic-predicate network described in Section 4. Such a network may be regarded as a self-training network which changes its configuration after an additional training. It corresponds to the fact that in the process of a man training, new notions and relations between them are formed in a human brain.

The presence of an algorithm for the extraction of a common up to the names of arguments sub-formula of two elementary conjunctions (and their unifiers) allows to find an approach to a problem of multi-agent description of an object described in Section 5. Just an extraction of such sub-formulas and determining of their unifiers with the input formulas makes possible to "stick together" such parts of descriptions in which different agents gives different names to one element of the whole object.

Note that the formulation of the problem (1) from Section 2 coincides with the one for a well-known problem CONJUNCTIVE BOOLEAN QUERY from [3]. The difference is in the implementation of these problems. While repeated implementation of the problem (1) the premise S(ω) of the sequent $S(\omega) \Rightarrow \exists \overline{x}_{\neq} A_k(\overline{x})$ is different, while every implementation and the conclusion $A_k(\overline{x})$ is a constant part. That is why just a collection of class descriptions $A_1(\overline{x}_1)$, …, $A_K(\overline{x}_K)$ permits to construct a level description.

While repeated implementation of the problem CONJUNCTIVE BOOLEAN QUERY, the premise S(ω) of the sequent $S(\omega) \Rightarrow \exists \overline{x}_{\neq} A_k(\overline{x})$ is constant while every implementation and queries $A_k(\overline{x})$ are different while every implementation. An approach to the construction of a level data base is presented in [15].

The possibility of reduction of an object description length by means of adding a formula setting some properties of initial predicates to the premise of a sequent was mentioned in the model example in Section 2. Properties of initial predicates also were used in the item 3 of the algorithm of multi-agent description. In fact, in the both cases instead the sequent of the form (4) $S(\omega) \Rightarrow \exists \overline{x}_{\neq} A(\overline{x})$ it is needed to check another sequent of the form $C(\overline{y})\ S(\omega) \Rightarrow \exists \overline{x}_{\neq} A(\overline{x})$, where $C(\overline{y})$ is a set of formulas setting properties of initial predicates. Investigation of computational complexity of such a form sequent may be an interesting problem in the further research.

To solve the problem (2) and to extract a maximal common up to the names of arguments sub-formula of two elementary conjunctions it is needed to check whether two elementary conjunctions are isomorphic. A polynomial in time rough algorithm for such a checking was offered in [12] by Petrov. Numerical experiments with this algorithm give over 99.95% of valid results.

Author details

Tatiana Kosovskaya

Address all correspondence to: kosovtm@gmail.com

St. Petersburg State University, St. Petersburg, Russia

References

[1] Nilson N. Problem-Solving Methods in Artificial Intelligence. New York: McGraw-Hill Book Company Press. Publ; 1971. 280p

[2] Du DZ, Ko KI. Theory of Computational Complexity. New York: John Wiley & Sons, Inc.; 2000:512 p. A Wiley-Interscience Publication

[3] Garey M, Johnson D. Computers and Intractability: A Guide to the Theory of NP-Completeness. San Francisco: Freeman Press; 1979. 340p

[4] Kossovskaya T. Proofs of the number of steps bounds for solving of some pattern recognition problems with logical description. Series 1. Mathematics, Mechanics, Astronomy. St. Petersburg: Vestnik of St. Petersburg State University; 2007. issue 4. pp. 82-90 (in Russian)

[5] Kosovskaya T. Some artificial intelligence problems permitting formalization by means of predicate calculus language and upper bounds of their solution steps. In: SPIIRAS Proceedings; No. 14; 2010. pp. 58-75 (in Russian)

[6] Kosovskaya T. Construction of class level description for efficient recognition of a complex object. International Journal Information Content and Processing. 2014;**1**(1):92-99

[7] Kosovskaya T. Self-modificated predicate networks. International Journal on Information Theory and Applications. 2015;**22**(3):245-257

[8] Kosovskaya T. Multi-agent description of an object by means of a predicate calculus language. International Journal on Information Theories and Applications. 2016;**23**(4): 338-346

[9] Kosovskaya T. Discrete artificial intelligence problems and number of steps of their solution. International Journal on Information Theories and Applications. 2011;**18**(1):93-99

[10] Orevkov VP. The inverse method of logical derivation. In: Adamenko A, Kuchukov A, editors. Programming Logic and Visual Prolog. St. Petersburg: BHV-Petersburg; 2003. pp. 952-965. (in Russian)

[11] Kosovskaya T, Petukhova N. The inverse method for solving artificial intelligence problems in the frameworks of logic-objective approach and bounds of its number of steps. International Journal Information Models and Analyses. 2012;**1**:84-93

[12] Kosovskaya TM, Petrov DA. Extraction of a maximal common sub-formula of predicate formulas for the solving of some Artificial Intelligence problems. Series 10. Applied Mathematics. Computer Science. Control Processes. St. Petersburg: Vestnik of St. Petersburg State University; 2017. issue 3. pp. 250-263 (in Russian)

[13] Kosovskaya T. Distance between objects described by predicate formulas. In: Deza M, Petitjean M, Markov K. editors. International Book Series. Information Science and Computing. Book 25. Mathematics of Distances and Applications. Sofia, Bulgaria: ITHEA; 2012. pp. 153-159

[14] Russel SJ, Norvig P. Artificial Intelligence. A Modern Approach. New York: Pearson Education, Inc.; 2003:1132 p

[15] Kosovskaya T. Conjunctive Boolean Query as a logic-objective recognition problem. International Journal on Information Theories and Applications. 2017;**24**(3):79-82

Chapter 4

On the Computational Analysis of the Genetic Algorithm for Attitude Control of a Carrier System

Hadi Jahanshahi and Naeimeh Najafizadeh Sari

Additional information is available at the end of the chapter

http://dx.doi.org/10.5772/intechopen.74121

Abstract

This chapter intends to cover three main topics. First, a fuzzy-PID controller is designed to control the propulsion vector of a launch vehicle, accommodating a CanSaT. Then, the genetic algorithm (GA) is employed to optimize the controller's performance. Finally, through adjusting the algorithm parameters, their effect on the optimization process is examined. In this regard, the motion vector control is programmed based on the governing system's dynamic equations of motion for payload delivery in the desired altitude and flight-path angle. This utilizes one single input and one preference fuzzy inference engine, where the latter acts to avoid the system instability in high angles for the propulsion vector. The optimization objective functions include the deviations of the thrust vector and the system from the stability path, which must be met simultaneously. Parameter sensitivity analysis of the genetic algorithm involves examining nine different cases and discussing their effect on the optimization results.

Keywords: fuzzy-PID controller, CanSat, genetic algorithm, parameter sensitivity analysis

1. Introduction

Due to costly space projects, affordable flight models and test prototypes are of incomparable importance in academic and research applications, such as data acquisition and subsystems testing. In this regard, CanSat could be used as a low-cost, high-tech, and light-weight model; this makes it popular in academia. CanSat is constituted from the words "can" and "sat," which collectively means a satellite that is embeddable in a soda can [1]. In these apparatuses, an electronic payload is placed into a container dimensionally comparable to a soda can; it is then launched into space with a rocket or balloon [2]. The attained altitude is a few thousand meters, which is much lower than the altitude of sounding rockets [3].

The concept of fuzzy logic was introduced by Zadeh in 1965; it has been improved by several researchers, forming a potent tool for a variety of applications [4]. For example, Precup and Hellendoorn [5] and Larsen [6] have used fuzzy logic in controllers for various industrial and research applications. The control area has attracted the most significant studies on fuzzy systems [7–15]. Petrov et al. have used fuzzy-PID controllers to control systems with different nonlinear terms [16]. Hu and colleagues proposed a new and simple method for fuzzy-PID controller design based on fuzzy logic and GA-based optimization [17]. Juang et al. have used triangular membership functions in fuzzy inference systems along with a genetic algorithm to tune parameters or fuzzy-PID controllers [18]. Operating fuzzy-PID controllers and online adjustment of fuzzy parameters were the main output of Resnick et al. researches [19].

In 1950, Alan Turing proposed a "learning machine" which would parallel the principles of evolution [20]. Genetic algorithms (GAs) are stochastic global search and optimization methods that mimic the metaphor of natural biological evolution [21]. GAs consider the principle of survival of the fittest to produce better generations out of a population. Although genetic algorithms cannot always provide the optimal solution, it has its own advantages [22] and is a powerful tool for solving complex problems. GA is an effective strategy and had successfully been used in the offline control of systems by a number of studies. Krishnakumar and Goldberg [23] have shown the efficiency of genetic optimization methods in deriving controller structures in aerospace applications compared to traditional methods such as LQR and Powell's gain set design. Porter and Mohamed [24] have taken initiative and by the use of GA have offered a simple and applicable eigenstructure assignment solution which is applied to the design of multivariable flight-control system of an aircraft. Others have denoted how to use GA to choose control structures [25].

Heuristic methods are highly dependent on their agents and parameters. Therefore, GA properties (mainly population size and crossover ratio) are of high importance in finding optimum points which are usually found by sensitivity analysis. These parameters are defined for a better acquaintance of readers in the following.

This chapter focuses on designing a GA-based fuzzy-PID controller. A two-termed cost function containing path and thrust vector deviations is fed into GA code to be optimized. The code adjusts the parameters. Nine different combinations with relative optimality are discussed. The chapter is dissected into following sections:

- "CanSaT carrier system" which presents a simple model of the carrier system
- "Fuzzy-PID controller" that describes controller design and its parameters
- "Optimization" which describes the optimization process
- "Results and discussion" that clarify results and comparisons
- "Conclusion"
- "References"

2. CanSaT carrier system

The dynamic equations of a CanSaT carrier system is derived from the Newtonian law. It should be added that in the separation stage, the projection of satellite velocity vector must be tangent to the horizontal plane. **Figure 1** shows a simplified model of a launch vehicle in which θ is the angle of the longitudinal vector of the vehicle in the perpendicular direction (toward the ground) and φ is the angle of its propulsion with body centerline.

The dynamics of the system can be summarized in

$$\sum M_{CM} = I\alpha \tag{1}$$

in which M_{CM} is the moment around the center of mass, I is the inertial moment, and I is the angular acceleration about an axis perpendicular to the plane. Eq. (1) can be expanded to (2)

$$\frac{l}{2} \times F_n = I\ddot{\theta} \tag{2}$$

In the notation l is used for the length of the vehicle, F for the propulsion force, and F_n for its projection perpendicular to the longitudinal direction of launch vehicle. It is known that the vehicle moves along the vertical axis with acceleration of. Therefore, Newton equation for that axis is rearranged as below:

$$\sum F_z = ma \tag{3}$$

in which F_z and m are, respectively, the force along the vertical axis and the mass of the launch vehicle. Eq. (3) can be rewritten as below:

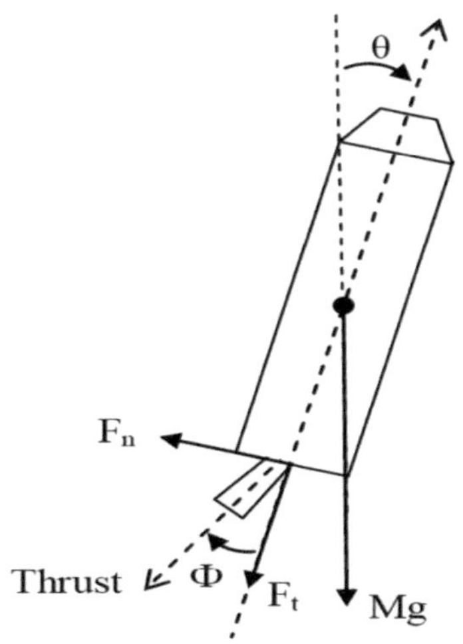

Figure 1. Carrier system scheme.

$$-mg + F_t cos\theta = ma \tag{4}$$

Meanwhile, geometric relations dictate the following equations in the vertical plane:

$$F_n = Fsin(\varphi) \tag{5}$$

$$F_t = Fcos(\varphi) \tag{6}$$

By substituting (6) in (4), we have

$$F = \frac{-m(a+g)}{\cos(\varphi)\cos(\theta)} \tag{7}$$

Insertion of (5) into (2) in a similar pattern yields to

$$\ddot{\theta} = \frac{1}{2I} lFsin(\varphi) \tag{8}$$

with considering $\theta = 0$ and substitution of (7) in (8) results in

$$\ddot{\theta} = \frac{-1}{2I} ml(a+g)\tan(\varphi) \tag{9}$$

By substituting $\frac{-1}{2I} ml(a+g)$ by b and $\tan(\varphi)$ by u_t, the dynamic equation of the system leads to

$$\ddot{\theta} = bu_t \tag{10}$$

in which u_t is the control parameter. Therefore, equations of system states take the following form:

$$\begin{aligned} \dot{x}_1(t) &= x_2(t) \\ \dot{x}_2(t) &= bu_t \\ y(t) &= x_1(t) \end{aligned} \tag{11}$$

where θ and $\dot{\theta}$ are, respectively, represented by $x_1(t)$ and $x_2(t)$. The measurable state vector is notated by $X = [x_1, x_2]^T$.

3. Fuzzy controller design

Two types of fuzzy inference motors are utilized in the proposed fuzzy controller [26]. The first type is single input fuzzy inference motor (SIFIM). The second inference motor type is the preferred fuzzy inference motor (PFIM) that represents the control priority order of each norm block output.

$$SIFIM - i \ : \ \left\{ R_i^j : if x_i = A_i^j then u_i = C_i^j \right\}_{j=1}^{m} \tag{12}$$

The $SIFIM - i$ points to single input inference motors which accepts the ith input, and R_i^j is the jth rule of the ith single input inference motor. Also, A_i^j and C_i^j are relevant membership functions. Each input item usually has a different role in the implementation of control. In order to express the different effects of implementing each input item in the system, single input fuzzy inference motor defines a dynamic importance degree (w_i^D) for each input item as (13)

$$w_i^D = w_i + B_i \times \Delta w_i \tag{13}$$

where w_i, B_i, and Δw_i are control parameters described by fuzzy rules. $SIFIM - i$ block calculates f_i as follows:

$$f_i = \frac{NB_i \times f_1 + Z_i \times f_2 + PB_i \times f_3}{NB_i + Z_i + PB_i} \tag{14}$$

The membership functions of SIFIMs are shown in **Figure 2**. As mentioned before f_1, f_2, and f_3, the *SIFIM* fuzzy rules are extracted from **Table 1**.

The other type of fuzzy inference motors (*PFIMs*) guarantees satellite control system performance using desired values in one or more axes of the coordinate system. *PFIM-i* calculates Δw_i as follows:

$$\Delta w_1 = \Delta w_2 = \Delta w_3 = \frac{w_1 \times DS + w_2 \times DM + w_3 \times DL}{DS + DM + DL} \tag{15}$$

The membership functions of PFIMs are shown in **Figure 3**, while their fuzzy rules are tabulated in **Table 2**.

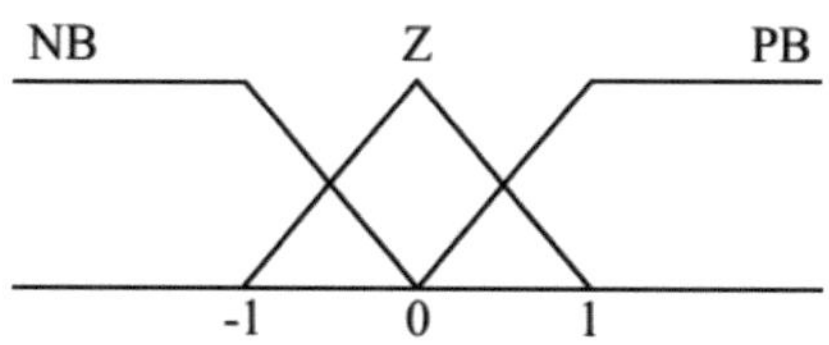

Figure 2. Membership functions of SIFIMs (note: NB = negative big; Z = zero; PB = positive big).

If	Then
NB_i	$f_1 = 1$
Z_i	$f_2 = 0$
PB_i	$f_3 = -1$

Table 1. Fuzzy rules of SIFIMs.

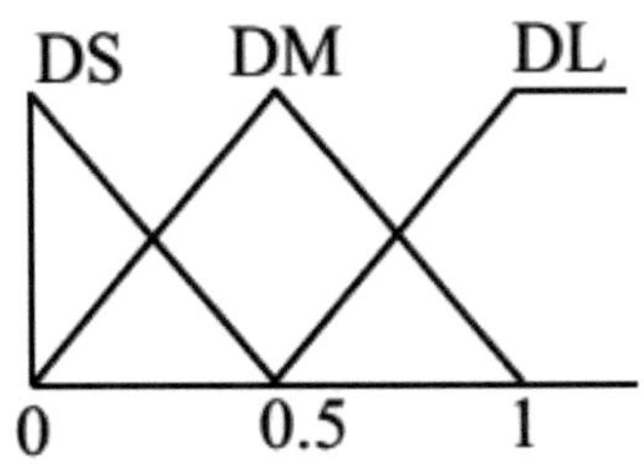

Figure 3. Membership functions of PFIM (note: DS = distance short; DM = distance medium; DL = distance long).

If		Then
$\|\theta\|$	*DS*	$w_1 = 1$
$\|\theta\|$	*DM*	$w_2 = 0.5$
$\|\theta\|$	*DL*	$w_3 = 1$

Table 2. Fuzzy rules of PFIMs.

By calculating f_i and $\Delta w_i \Delta W_i$, it is possible to define fuzzy-PID controller as (16)

$$u_{fuzzy-PID} = \widehat{K}_{i\theta} \int \widehat{\theta} dt + \widehat{K}_{p\theta} \widehat{\theta} + \widehat{K}_{d\theta} \frac{d\widehat{\theta}}{dt} \tag{16}$$

where $u_{Fuzzy-PID}$ is the control action and $\int \widehat{\theta} dt$, $\widehat{\theta}$, and $\widehat{\frac{d\theta}{dt}}$ are, respectively, the fuzzy forms of $\int \theta dt$, θ, and $\frac{d\theta}{dt}$ and should be obtained from SIFIM. In other words, we have $\int \widehat{\theta} dt = f_1$, $\widehat{\theta} = f_2$, and $\widehat{\frac{d\theta}{dt}} = f_3$. Parameters of $\widehat{K}_{i\theta}$, $\widehat{K}_{p\theta}$ and $\widehat{K}_{d\theta}$ in (7) are fuzzy variables calculated by following equations:

$$\widehat{K}_{i\theta} = K^b_{i\theta} + K^r_{i\theta} \Delta W_1 \tag{17}$$

$$\widehat{K}_{p\theta} = K^b_{p\theta} + K^r_{p\theta} \Delta W_2 \tag{18}$$

$$\widehat{K}_{d\theta} = K^b_{d\theta} + K^r_{d\theta} \Delta W_3 \tag{19}$$

in which $K^b_{i\theta}$, K^b_{θ}, and $K^b_{d\theta}$ are the base variables and $K^r_{i\theta}$, K^r_{θ}, and $K^r_{d\theta}$ are regulation variables. While it is possible to find these variables by trial and error, the best way to find them is using optimization approaches like evolutionary algorithms, especially genetic algorithm (GA).

4. Optimization

GA is an approach for solving optimization problems based on biological evolution via repeatedly modifying a population of individual solutions. At each level, individuals are chosen randomly from the current population (as parents) and then employed to produce the children for the next generation. In this chapter, the following operators are implemented for optimization of the fuzzy-PID controller:

- **Population size (PS):** Increasing the population size enables GA to search more points and thereby obtain a better result. However, the larger the population size, the longer it takes for the GA to compute each generation.
- **Crossover options:** Crossover options specify how GA combines two individuals, or parents, to form a crossover child for the next generation.
- **Crossover fraction (CF):** Crossover fraction specifies the fraction of each population, other than elite children, that are made up of crossover children.
- **Selection function:** Selection function specifies how GA chooses parents for the next generation.
- **Migration options:** Migration options determine how individuals move between subpopulations. Migration occurs if the population size is set to be a vector of length greater than 1. When migration occurs, the best individuals from one subpopulation replace the worst individuals in another subpopulation. Individuals that migrate from one subpopulation to another are copied. They are not removed from the source subpopulation.
- **Stopping criteria options:** Stopping criteria options specify the causes of terminating the algorithm.

In this chapter, the configuration of GA is set at the values given in **Table 3**.

Furthermore, the multi-objective optimization of the proposed fuzzy-PID controller is done with respect to six design variables and two objective functions (OFs). The base values

Parameter	Value
CF	0.4, 0.6, 0.8
PS	90, 200, 500
Selection function	Tournament
Mutation function	Constraint dependent
Crossover function	Intermediate
Migration direction	Forward
Migration fraction	0.2
Migration interval	20
Stopping criteria	Fitness limit to 10^{-4}

Table 3. GA configuration parameters.

$[K^b_{i\theta}, K^b_{p\theta}, K^b_{d\theta}]$ and regulation values $[K^r_{i\theta}, K^r_{p\theta}, K^r_{d\theta}]$ are the design variables. The system's angle of deviation from equilibrium point and the thrust vector's angle of deviation are, respectively, defined as OF1 and OF2:

$$OF1 = \int |\theta| dt \tag{20}$$

$$OF2 = \int |\Phi| dt \tag{21}$$

5. Results and discussion

In this section, by regarding two aforementioned OFs, the effect of two parameters of PS and CF is measured in the optimization. **Figure 4** represents Pareto fronts of these two functions after optimization. Meanwhile, **Figure 5** shows the system's position under performance of the designed controller. The angle of propulsion vector of the CanSaT carrier system is demonstrated in **Figure 6**. **Tables 4–6** display the magnitude of design variables. OF1 and OF2 are shown for optimum points of A_i, B_i, and C_i in **Tables 7–9**. The best values satisfying the two OFs with the constraints of minimum settling time and overshoot are presented. The relevant magnitude of PS and CF to each figure is brought in its legend. The points $A_i(i = 1, 2, \ldots, 9)$, $B_i(i = 1, 2, \ldots, 9)$, and $C_i(i = 1, 2, \ldots, 9)$ are, respectively, the best for the first, the second, and both OFs.

Further, as seen in **Figure 4**, points A_i and C_i are in a near proximity in which in some cases a coincidence occurs. It is mainly due to non-convergence of CanSaT carrier launch vehicle points with points far from A_i. A similar behavior is observed from Pareto fronts of the situation, angular velocity, and angle of the propulsion vector for the launch vehicle.

To analyze the effects of each parameter in GA, **Figures 7–12** are produced. **Figure 7** shows the dependency of OF1 (at points A_i) to nine different combination forms of GA parameters. The figure shows that the minimum area under "situation of launch vehicle" curve is obtainable for PS = 200 and CF = 0.8. It is also inferred that for better results, parameters PS and CF must be increased simultaneously. For low PS, increasing CF helps to improve first OF, but with more magnitudes of PS, higher CFs yield better results.

Figure 8 represents dependency of OF2 (at points A_i) to nine different forms of combinations of GA parameters. The figure shows the least area below the deviation angle of the thrust curve for CanSaT carrier system when PS = 500 and CF = 0.6. **Figures 9** and **10** propose that the smallest magnitude for the first and second OFs (pertaining to B_i) is achievable for, respectively, PS = 500 and CF = 0.6 and PS = 500 and CF = 0.4. In **Figures 11** and **12**, magnitudes of the first and second objective functions in C_i Points are represented, respectively. The first OF proposed the point C_1 with PS = 90 and CF = 0.4. Meanwhile, the second function insists on the point with PS = 90 and CF = 0.8.

http://dx.doi.org/10.5772/intechopen.74121

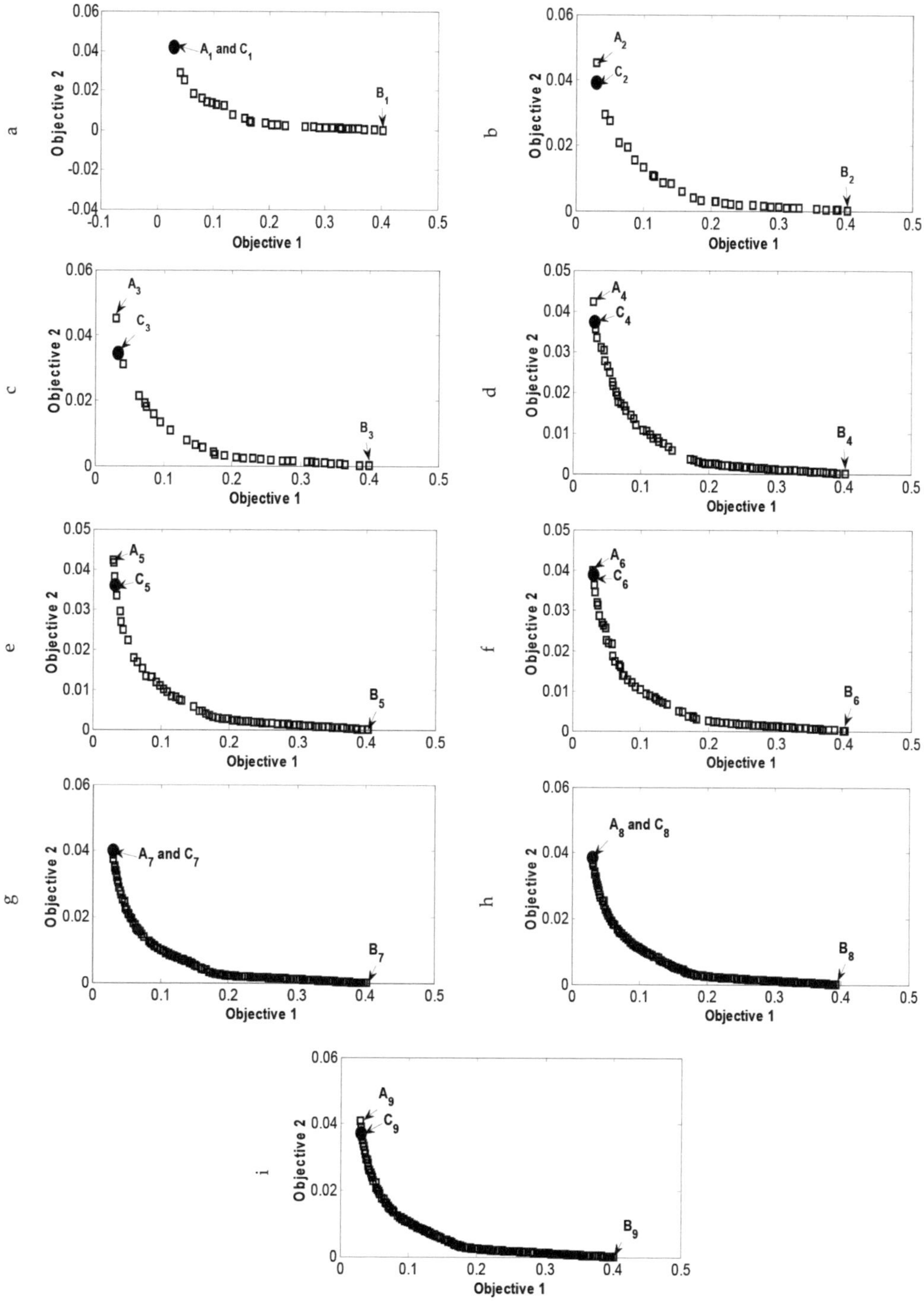

Figure 4. Pareto front by Objectives 1 and 2 corresponds to the (a) PS = 90 and CF = 0.4, (b) PS = 90 and CF = 0.6, (c) PS = 90 and CF = 0.8, (d) PS = 200 and CF = 0.4, (e) PS = 200 and CF = 0.6, (f) PS = 200 and CF = 0.8, (g) PS = 200 and CF = 0.4, (h) PS = 200 and CF = 0.6, and (i) PS = 200 and CF = 0.8.

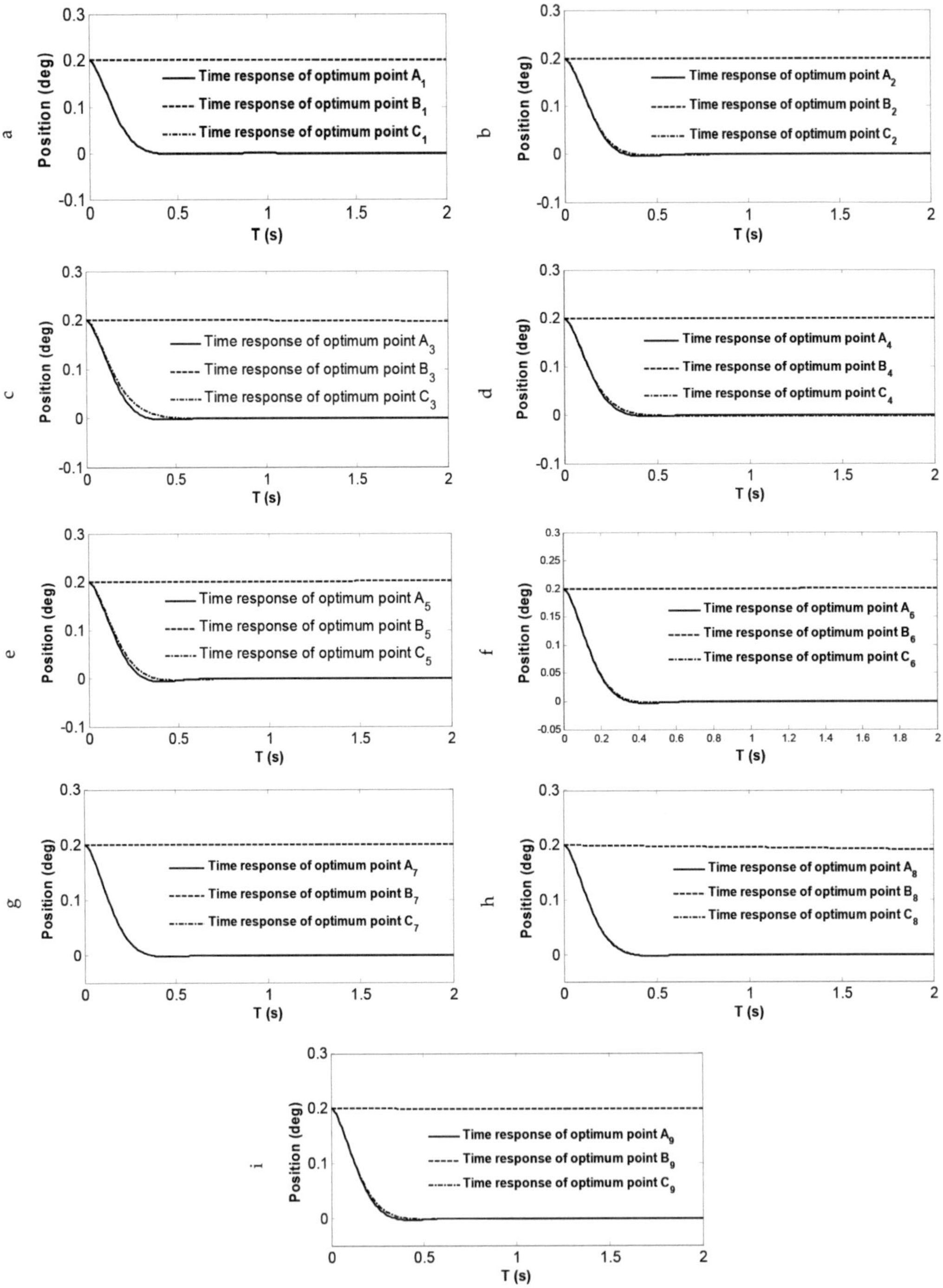

Figure 5. Time response of the CanSaT carrier system's position for (a) A_1, B_1, and C_1; (b) A_2, B_2, and C_2; (c) A_3, B_3, and C_3; (d) A_4, B_4, and C_4; (e) A_5, B_5, and C_5; (f) A_6, B_6, and C_6; (g) A_7, B_7, and C_7; (h) A_8, B_8, and C_8; and (i) A_9, B_9, and C_9 as the optimum points.

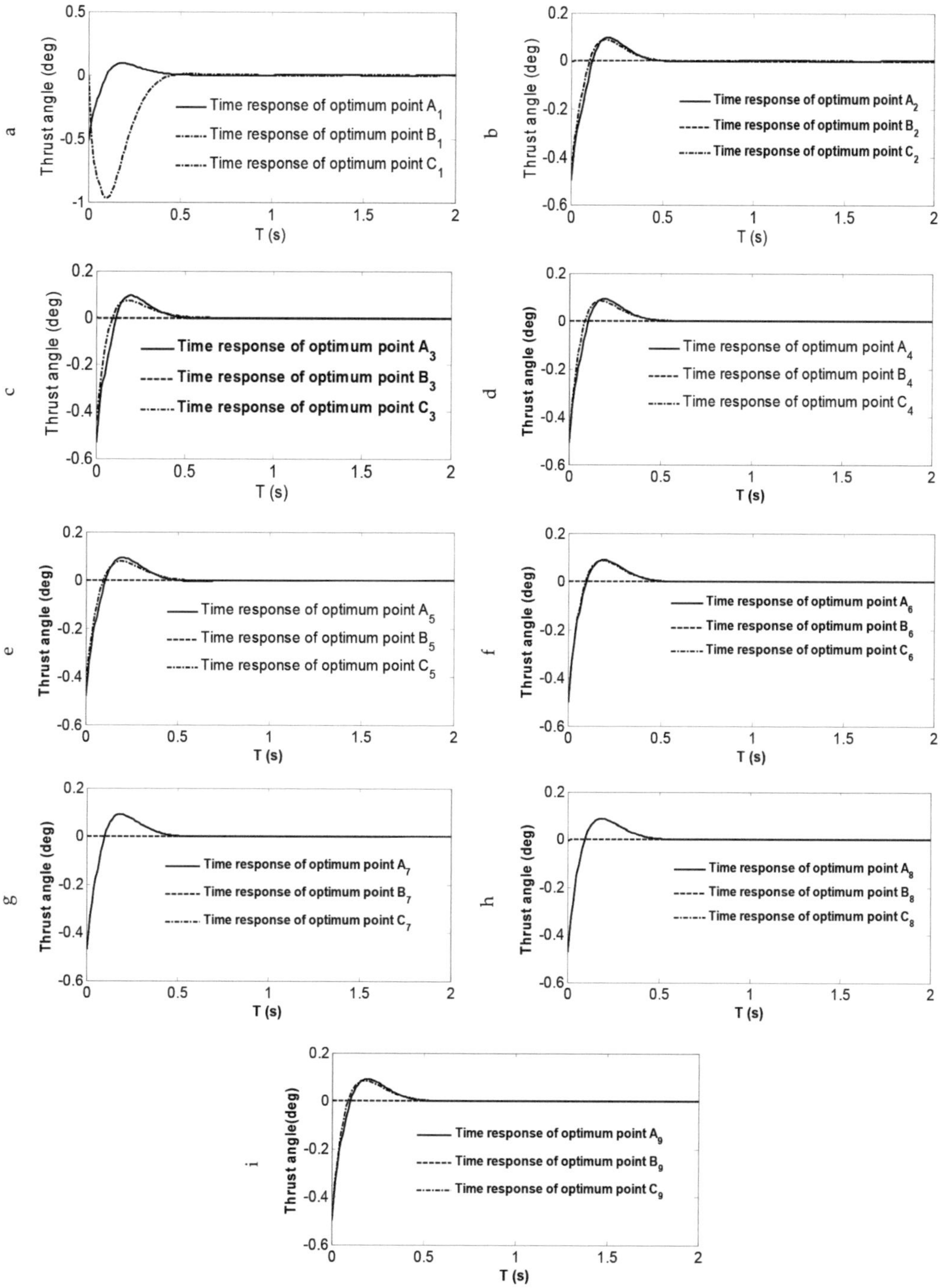

Figure 6. Time response of the thrust angle of CanSaT carrier system for (a) A_1, B_1, and C_1; (b) A_2, B_2, and C_2; (c) A_3, B_3, and C_3; (d) A_4, B_4, and C_4; (e) A_5, B_5, and C_5; (f) A_6, B_6, and C_6; (g) A_7, B_7, and C_7; (h) A_8, B_8, and C_8; and (i) A_9, B_9, and C_9 as the optimum points.

Design variable	Point PS = 90/CF = 0.4	Value	Point PS = 90/CF = 0.6	Value	Point PS = 90/CF = 0.8	Value
$K^b_{i\theta}$	A_1	−0.0094	A_2	0.0050	A_3	0.013
K^b_{θ}		2.83		2.71		2.93
$K^b_{d\theta}$		0.36		0.30		0.35
$K^r_{i\theta}$		0.36		−0.036		−0.25
K^r_{θ}		0.46		3.17		0.68
$K^r_{d\theta}$		0.95		1.94		0.83
$K^b_{i\theta}$	B_1	−0.0075	B_2	0.044	B_3	−0.039
K^b_{θ}		−0.0023		0.00019		−0.0069
$K^b_{d\theta}$		2.90		2.31		2.11
$K^r_{i\theta}$		0.022		0.021		−0.036
K^r_{θ}		−0.022		−0.26		0.39
$K^r_{d\theta}$		1.68		3.19		1.71
$K^b_{i\theta}$	C_1	−0.0094	C_2	0.033	C_3	0.036
K^b_{θ}		2.83		2.48		2.33
$K^b_{d\theta}$		0.36		0.31		0.36
$K^r_{i\theta}$		0.36		0.025		0.044
K^r_{θ}		0.46		3.083		0.34
$K^r_{d\theta}$		0.95		2.05		1.022

Table 4. Design variables for A_i, B_i, and C_i (i = 1, 2, 3).

Design variable	Point PS = 200/ CF = 0.4	Value	Point PS = 200/ CF = 0.6	Value	Point PS = 200/ CF = 0.8	Value
$K^b_{i\theta}$	A_4	0.015	A_5	−0.0025	A_6	−0.01061
K^b_{θ}		2.79		2.59		2.7385
$K^b_{d\theta}$		0.35		0.33		0.3856
$K^r_{i\theta}$		−0.60		0.13		0.4005
K^r_{θ}		1.76		0.63		0.8030
$K^r_{d\theta}$		0.92		−0.17		−1.1440
$K^b_{i\theta}$	B_4	−0.088	B_5	−0.15	B_6	0.01091
K^b_{θ}		−0.00020		0.0017		0.000345
$K^b_{d\theta}$		2.84		2.48		3.2541
$K^r_{i\theta}$		−0.0046		0.055		0.009406

Design variable	Point PS = 200/ CF = 0.4	Value	Point PS = 200/ CF = 0.6	Value	Point PS = 200/ CF = 0.8	Value
K_{θ}^{r}		0.45		0.64		−0.08872
$K_{d\theta}^{r}$		2.97		0.78		1.5818
$K_{i\theta}^{b}$	C_4	0.093	C_5	0.016	C_6	0.009348
K_{θ}^{b}		2.75		2.23		2.7109
$K_{d\theta}^{b}$		0.40		0.33		0.3817
$K_{i\theta}^{r}$		0.056		0.16		0.3722
K_{θ}^{r}		1.94		0.68		0.5992
$K_{d\theta}^{r}$		0.53		−0.055		−0.4311

Table 5. Design variables for A_i, B_i, and C_i (i = 4, 5, 6).

Design variable	Point PS = 500/ CF = 0.4	Value	Point PS = 500/ CF = 0.6	Value	Point PS = 500/ CF = 0.8	Value
$K_{i\theta}^{b}$	A_7	0.0018	A_8	−0.013	A_9	−0.014
K_{θ}^{b}		2.55		2.56		2.71
$K_{d\theta}^{b}$		0.31		0.35		0.36
$K_{i\theta}^{r}$		0.040		0.48		0.61
K_{θ}^{r}		0.52		1.30		1.29
$K_{d\theta}^{r}$		1.50		0.32		−0.57
$K_{i\theta}^{b}$	B_7	−0.011	B_8	−0.17	B_9	−0.040
K_{θ}^{b}		0.00013		0.030		0.0064
$K_{d\theta}^{b}$		2.43		1.26		0.77
$K_{i\theta}^{r}$		−0.0015		0.027		0.012
K_{θ}^{r}		0.058		0.86		0.16
$K_{d\theta}^{r}$		2.84		1.42		0.36
$K_{i\theta}^{b}$	C_7	0.0017	C_8	−0.013	C_9	−0.00073
K_{θ}^{b}		2.55		2.56		2.60
$K_{d\theta}^{b}$		0.31		0.35		0.38
$K_{i\theta}^{r}$		0.040		0.48		0.52
K_{θ}^{r}		0.52		1.30		0.54
$K_{d\theta}^{r}$		1.50		0.32		−0.45

Table 6. Design variables for A_i, B_i, and C_i (i = 7, 8, 9).

Objective function	Point PS = 90/ CF = 0.4	Value	Point PS = 90/ CF = 0.6	Value	Point PS = 90/ CF = 0.8	Value
OF1	A_1	0.029	A_2	0.030	A_3	0.030
OF2		0.042		0.045		0.045
OF1	B_1	0.40	B_2	0.40	B_3	0.40
OF2		0.000017		0.000011		0.000079
OF1	C_1	0.029	C_2	0.030	C_3	0.000079
OF2		0.042		0.039		0.034

Table 7. Objective functions for A_i, B_i, and C_i (i = 1, 2, 3).

Objective function	Point PS = 200/ CF = 0.4	Value	Point PS = 200/ CF = 0.6	Value	Point PS = 200/ CF = 0.8	Value
OF1	A_4	0.029	A_5	0.030	A_6	0.029
OF2		0.042		0.042		0.040
OF1	B_4	0.40	B_5	0.40	B_6	0.40
OF2		0.0000037		0.000035		0.0000073
OF1	C_4	0.032	C_5	0.032	C_6	0.030
OF2		0.037		0.0359		0.039

Table 8. Objective functions for A_i, B_i, and C_i (i = 4, 5, 6).

Objective function	Point PS = 500/ CF = 0.4	Value	Point PS = 500/ CF = 0.6	Value	Point PS = 500/ CF = 0.8	Value
OF1	A_7	0.030	A_8	0.030	A_9	0.029
OF2		0.040		0.038		0.041
OF1	B_7	0.40	B_8	0.39	B_9	0.40
OF2		0.0000021		0.00012		0.000065
OF1	C_7	0.030	C_8	0.030	C_9	0.030
OF2		0.040		0.038		0.037

Table 9. Objective functions for A_i, B_i, and C_i (i = 7, 8, 9).

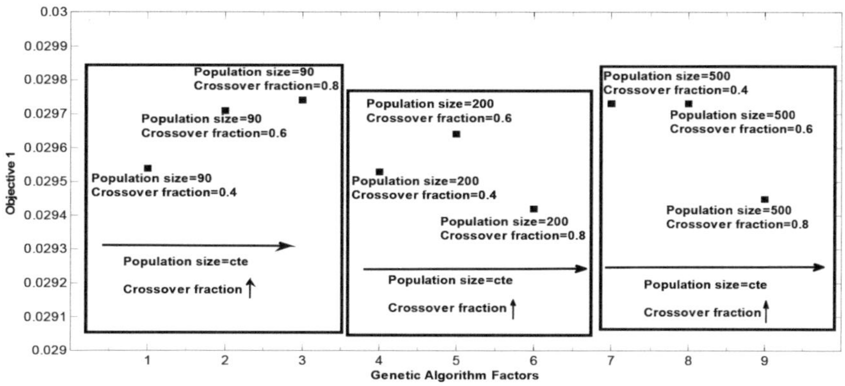

Figure 7. GA parameters versus OF1 for the best points from the viewpoint of OF1.

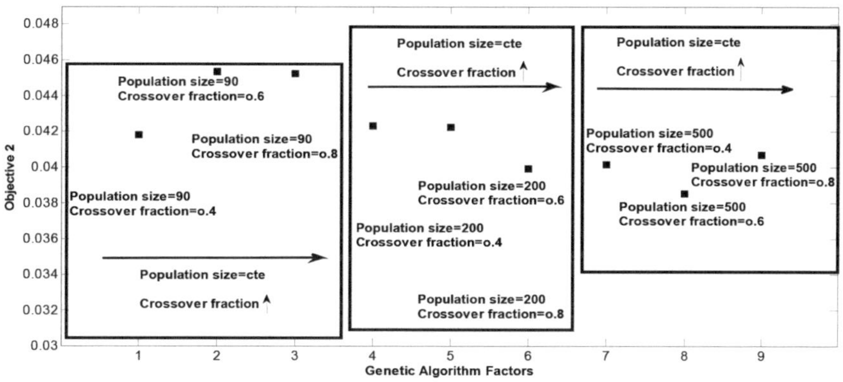

Figure 8. GA parameters versus OF2 for the best points from the viewpoint of OF1.

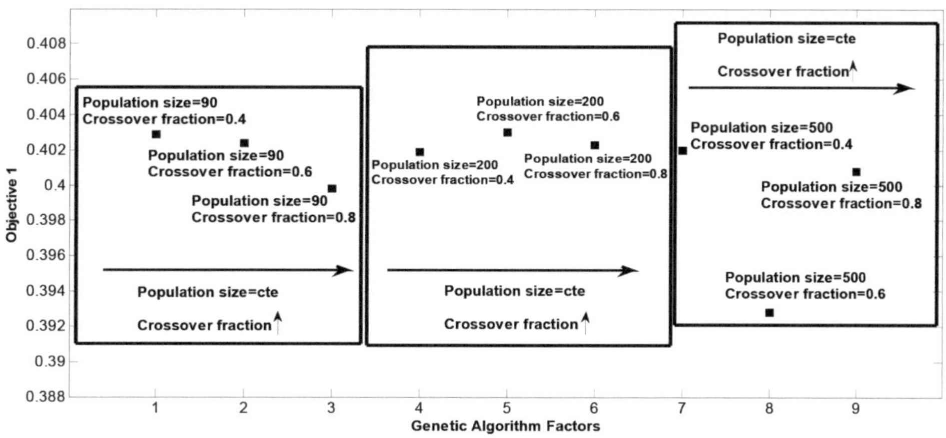

Figure 9. GA parameters versus OF1 for the best points from the viewpoint of OF2.

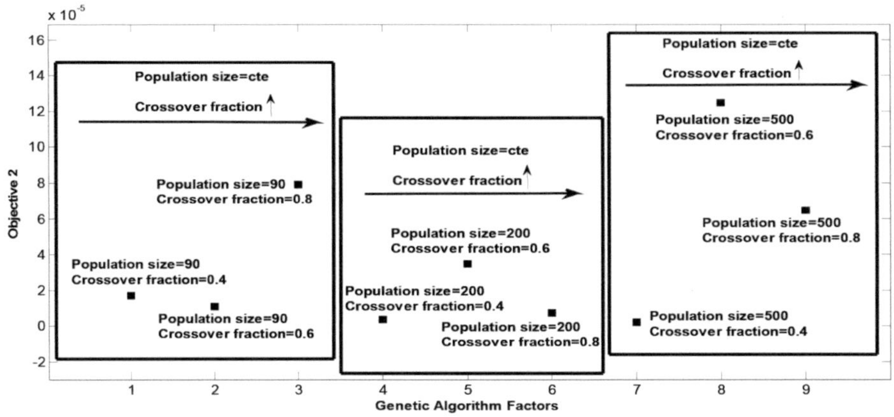

Figure 10. GA parameters versus OF2 for the best points from the viewpoint of OF2.

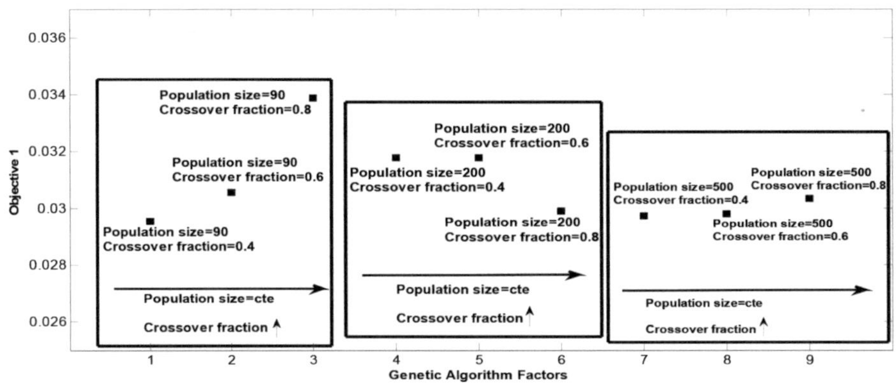

Figure 11. GA parameters versus OF1 for the best points from the viewpoint of OF1 and OF2.

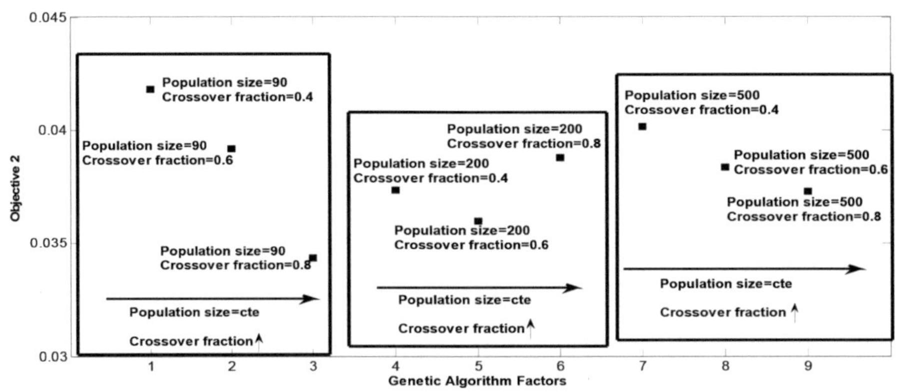

Figure 12. GA parameters versus OF2 for the best points from the viewpoint of OF1 and OF2.

6. Conclusion

This chapter represents a design of a fuzzy controller based on a GA code for the purpose of controlling propulsion vector of a launch vehicle which carries CanSaT. Minimizing the errors initiated by system deviation from equilibrium state and propulsion thrust deviation are two objectives for optimizing this controller. This is done by manipulating GA parameters in nine different combination forms to satisfy each objective function and also both of them simultaneously. Further it is examined how these parameters affect the optimal points.

By observing constraints of minimum settling time and overshoot, the results show that the optimal points proposed by the first OF are in proximity with the ones from both OFs which in some cases end in coincidence. Finally, by comparing magnitudes of OFs for various combinations of GA parameters, the optimum points and their relevant parameters are introduced.

Conflict of interest

The authors declare that there is no conflict of interest.

Author details

Hadi Jahanshahi* and Naeimeh Najafizadeh Sari

*Address all correspondence to: hadi_jahanshahi@ut.ac.ir

Deptartment of Aerospace Engineering, University of Tehran, Tehran, Iran

References

[1] Soyer S. Small space can: CanSat. In: Proc. 5th Int. Conf. Recent Adv. Sp. Technol.—RAST2011. 2011. pp. 789-793. DOI: 10.1109/RAST.2011.5966950

[2] Aly H, Sharkawy O, Nabil A, Yassin A, Tarek M, Amin SM, Ibrahim MK. Project-based space engineering education: Application to autonomous rover-back CanSat. In: 2013 6th Int. Conf. Recent Adv. Sp. Technol. 2013. pp. 1087-1092. DOI: 10.1109/RAST.2013.6581164

[3] Okninski A, Marciniak B, Bartkowiak B, Kaniewski D, Matyszewski J, Kindracki J, Wolanski P. Development of the Polish Small Sounding Rocket Program. Acta Astronautica. 2015;**108**:46-56. DOI: 10.1016/j.actaastro.2014.12.001

[4] Zadeh LA. Fuzzy sets. Information and Control. 1965;**8**:338-353. DOI: 10.1016/S0019-9958(65)90241-X

[5] Precup R-E, Hellendoorn H. A survey on industrial applications of fuzzy control. Computers in Industry. 2011;**62**:213-226. DOI: 10.1016/j.compind.2010.10.001

[6] Martin Larsen P. Industrial applications of fuzzy logic control. International Journal of Man-Machine Studies. 1980;**12**:3-10. DOI: 10.1016/S0020-7373(80)80050-2

[7] Kosari A, Jahanshahi H, Razavi SA. An optimal fuzzy PID control approach for docking maneuver of two spacecraft: Orientational motion. Engineering Science and Technology, an International Journal. 2017;**20**:293-309. DOI: 10.1016/j.jestch.2016.07.018

[8] Larimi SR, Nejad HR, Hoorfar M, Najjaran H. Control of artificial human finger using wearable device and adaptive network-based fuzzy inference system. In: 2016 IEEE Int. Conf. Syst. Man, Cybern. 2016. pp. 3754-3758. DOI: 10.1109/SMC.2016.7844818

[9] Lygouras JN, Botsaris PN, Vourvoulakis J, Kodogiannis V. Fuzzy logic controller implementation for a solar air-conditioning system. Applied Energy. 2007;**84**:1305-1318. DOI: 10.1016/j.apenergy.2006.10.002

[10] Marinaki M, Marinakis Y, Stavroulakis GE. Fuzzy control optimized by PSO for vibration suppression of beams. Control Engineering Practice. 2010;**18**:618-629. DOI: 10.1016/j.conengprac.2010.03.001

[11] Precup R-E, David R-C, Petriu EM, Rădac M-B, Preitl S, Fodor J. Evolutionary optimization-based tuning of low-cost fuzzy controllers for servo systems. Knowledge-Based Systems. 2013;**38**:74-84. DOI: 10.1016/j.knosys.2011.07.006

[12] Kosari A, Jahanshahi H, Razavi A. Optimal FPID control approach for a docking maneuver of two spacecraft: Translational motion. Journal of Aerospace Engineering. 2017;**30**: 4017011. DOI: 10.1061/(ASCE)AS.1943-5525.0000720

[13] Kosari A, Jahanshahi H, Razavi A. Design of optimal PID, fuzzy and new fuzzy-PID controller for CANSAT carrier system thrust vector. International Journal of Design and Manufacturing Technology. 2015;**8**(2). http://www.mjme.ir/index/index.php/me/article/view/938

[14] Jee S, Koren Y. Adaptive fuzzy logic controller for feed drives of a CNC machine tool. Mechatronics. 2004;**14**:299-326

[15] Ping L, Fu-Jiang JIN. Adaptive fuzzy control for unknown nonlinear systems with perturbed dead-zone inputs. Acta Automatica Sinica. 2010;**36**:573-579

[16] Petrov M, Ganchev I, Taneva A. Fuzzy PID control of nonlinear plants. Proceedings of the First International IEEE Symposium on Intelligent Systems. 2002;**1**:30-35. DOI: 10.1109/IS.2002.1044224

[17] Hu B, Mann GKI, Gosine RG. New methodology for analytical and optimal design of fuzzy PID controllers. IEEE Transactions on Fuzzy Systems. 1999;**7**:521-539. DOI: 10.1109/91.797977

[18] Juang Y-T, Chang Y-T, Huang C-P. Design of fuzzy PID controllers using modified triangular membership functions. Information Sciences (Ny). 2008;**178**:1325-1333. DOI: 10.1016/j.ins.2007.10.020

[19] Reznik L, Ghanayem O, Bourmistrov A. PID plus fuzzy controller structures as a design base for industrial applications. Engineering Applications of Artificial Intelligence. 2000; **13**:419-430. DOI: 10.1016/S0952-1976(00)00013-0

[20] Turing A. Computing machinery and intelligence. Mind. 1950;**59**:433-460

[21] Holland JH. Adaptation in Natural and Artificial Systems: An Introductory Analysis with Applications to Biology, Control and Artificial Intelligence. Cambridge, MA, USA: MIT Press; 1992

[22] Gaber J, Goncalves G, Hsu T, Lecouffe P, Toursel B. Non-numerical data parallel algorithms. In: Second Euromicro Work. Parallel Distrib. Process; Malaga, Spain; 1994. pp. 167-174. DOI: 10.1109/EMPDP.1994.592485

[23] Krishnakumar K, Goldberg DE. Control system optimization using genetic algorithms. Journal of Guidance, Control, and Dynamics. 1992;**15**:735-740. DOI: 10.2514/3.20898

[24] Porter B, Mohamed SS. Genetic design of multivariable flight-control systems using eigenstructure assignment. In: First IEEE Reg. Conf. Aerosp. Control Syst.; Westlake Village, CA, USA. 1993. pp. 435-439

[25] Varsek A, Urbancic T, Filipic B. Genetic algorithms in controller design and tuning. IEEE Transactions on Systems, Man, and Cybernetics. 1993;**23**:1330-1339. DOI: 10.1109/ 21.260663

[26] Mahmoodabadi MJ, Jahanshahi H. Multi-objective optimized fuzzy-PID controllers for fourth order nonlinear systems. Engineering Science and Technology, an International Journal. 2016;**19**:1084-1098. DOI: 10.1016/j.jestch.2016.01.010

Section 2

Developments and Advances in Intelligent Systems and Applications

Chapter 5

Multiagent Intelligent System of Convergent Sensor Data Processing for the Smart&Safe Road

Alexey Finogeev, Alexandr Bershadsky,
Anton Finogeev, Ludmila Fionova and Michael Deev

Additional information is available at the end of the chapter

http://dx.doi.org/10.5772/intechopen.73610

Abstract

The results of monitoring and analyzing traffic accidents, fixed by an intelligent monitoring system with photoradar complexes, are considered. The system works with a network of distributed photoradar vehicle detectors for road accidents, video surveillance cameras, vehicle information and communication systems, built-in car navigation equipment and mobile communication equipment. A multiagent approach developed to address the tasks of sensor data collecting and processing. The system functionality is implemented by several agents that perform data collecting, cleaning, clustering, comparing time series, retrieving data for visualization, preparing charts and reports, performing spatial and intellectual analysis, etc. Convergent approach is the convergence of cloud, fog and mobile data processing technologies. The diagnostic system is necessary for remote maintenance of photoradar equipment. The structure of the neural network is adapted to the diagnosing problems and forecasting. The tasks of intellectual analysis and forecasting traffic accidents are solved. The hybrid fuzzy neural network is synthesized. Because of the comparison of time series of traffic accidents and time series of meteorological factors, the presence of factors to become determinants for an abnormal change in the traffic situation in controlled areas is established.

Keywords: smart road environment, intelligent system, multiagent system, data mining, machine learning, convergent model, smart&safe city, decision support, wireless sensor networks, big sensor data

1. Introduction

Smart&Safe City means the development and implementation of projects such as Smart Manufacturing, Smart Houses, Smart Light, Smart Energy, Intelligent Transportation System,

Smart Road, and so on [1, 2]. The goal of Smart Technology Development & Safe City is to ensure the comfort and safety of human life in the urban infrastructure and efficient production in the industrial sector. Smart&Safe City components are integrated into a multimodal smart environment [3]. It provides interaction of cyberphysical devices, cloud computing resources and mobile communication systems. Smart Environment helps the artificial intelligence system to solve problems of automatic control or to support decision-making based on big data monitoring about the surrounding reality. It is based on the Internet of Things network platform for the collection and processing of sensor data. The platform includes the following:

1. Intelligent sensors (sensors, measuring devices, photo and video fixation devices).
2. Telecommunication networks of broadband data transmission (fiber-optic and wireless) and mobile communication systems.
3. Satellite navigation systems.

The paradigm of an intelligent multimodal environment includes three basic concepts such as ubiquitous (pervasive) computing and networking [4]; intellectual assistance (ambient intelligence) [5] and smart environments [6].

The creation of smart road environment (SRE) is an important direction in the Smart&Safe City concept [7]. Environment is needed for the interaction of satellite vehicle monitoring systems, intelligent transport systems (ITS) [8], unmanned vehicles, intelligent road infrastructure components and mobile communication users. SRE includes a built-in intelligent functionality in the vehicles, objects of road transport infrastructure and intelligent system for monitoring and traffic management. It is based on the methods of monitoring and managing traffic flows [9], provides information and safety to road users. Research in this area relates to the creation of traffic monitoring systems [10], for example, using radio tags [11] or embedded monitoring complexes [12]. Monitoring technology includes stream sensor data processing (photos, video streams, telemetry data, user information), data mining, machine learning, forecasting, multiagent processing [13] and the convergence of computing models (clouds, fog and mobile computing) [14]. The monitoring tasks are as follows: monitoring the condition of the pavement, meteorological monitoring, monitoring of traffic flows and monitoring violations of traffic rules.

Modern road transport infrastructure consists of a system of satellite navigation, traffic signal control, regulation of cargo transportation, information boards, detection systems of car numbers, registration of traffic accidents and violations. The intellectualization of the road transport infrastructure is to develop intelligent systems for monitoring and surveillance, parking management system, decision-making systems for traffic flows regulation, intelligent transport systems, and so on. The purpose of the SRE elements is to influence the behavior of cars, drivers and pedestrians in terms of optimizing transport routes and passenger flows, reducing security risks by preventing emergency situations.

The main elements of the SRE are as follows:

1. Intelligent real-time monitoring system
2. Real-time traffic information system for alerting and warning road users
3. System of accounting and analysis of road users' social reactions [15]
4. Interactive journey planner system
5. Intelligent traffic lights systems
6. Intelligent signaling system
7. Surveillance cameras (CCTV) and photoradar complexes
8. Satellite systems of transport monitoring
9. Parking and loading areas information systems
10. Sensor systems for the movement of unmanned vehicles
11. Intelligent vehicle transport systems
12. Electronic payment systems for road services

An important element of SRE is an intelligent monitoring system for decision-making on the management of the road infrastructure objects. The system works with a network of spatially distributed photoradar vehicle detectors for road accidents, video surveillance cameras, vehicle information and communication systems (VICS), built-in car navigation equipment and mobile communication equipment. It is designed for the collection and sensor data processing. The monitoring objectives are analysis, assessment and forecast of changes in traffic situations to control the behavior of vehicles and road users and to alert police, emergency services, ambulance, maintenance and other services.

2. Photoradar complexes for data collection in SRE

Monitoring of objects and incidents in the road infrastructure is carried out on the basis of the collection and sensor data processing obtained from ground platforms, aerial and space surveillance facilities. The main ground platforms in SRE are CCTV cameras and photoradar vehicle detector complexes (**Figure 1**).

Photoradar complexes allow in an automatic mode to fix incidents on objects of road transport infrastructure, to collect and accumulate sensor data [16]. A lot of complexes receive a huge amount of data, which cannot be processed by a person in real time. Complexes can recognize objects in photos and in a video stream, measure the speed of vehicles in the control zone,

Figure 1. CCTV cameras and photoradar vehicle detector complexes.

automatically capture and save photos of violators, recognize license plates, collect and transfer data to the data center. However, the complexes do not have the capabilities of intellectual analysis and forecasting in real-time mode.

Creation of a heterogeneous transport environment is required for the interaction of the complexes and the transfer of sensor data to the data center. The trend in the field of telecommunications consists of replacing wired networks with wireless channels for monitoring distributed objects [17]. A wireless network is necessary for the interaction of mobile and fixed elements of the SRE. It includes a segment of the Internet of Things for the data exchange between complexes, intelligent transport systems, surveillance systems, a segment of the cellular network for data exchange between users and a segment of the satellite navigation system. The heterogeneous network is realized through technologies of wireless sensor networks (WSN) [18], cellular networks, Wi-Fi networks and satellite networks.

3. Convergent model for sensor data processing in the smart road environment

Modern approaches to distributed computing and storage of sensor data are based on the concept of convergence [19]. Convergence is defined as the interlinking of computing and storage technologies such as media, content and communication networks. Convergence in relation to network technologies means the process of telecommunication technologies' convergence with the appearance of similar characteristics in network equipment, communication channels, network standards and protocols and data transfer processes. For example, the technology integration of mobile and cloud computing is the result of the convergence [20]. Another example is the convergence of cloud and fog computing models in a wireless sensor network [21], which is proposed to create a computing platform for distributed sensor data processing in the SRE. The convergent model of cloud, fog and mobile computing (**Figure 2**) is designed for sensor data processing, obtained from spatially distributed photoradar complexes, a video surveillance camera, navigation equipment, intelligent transport systems and mobile equipment.

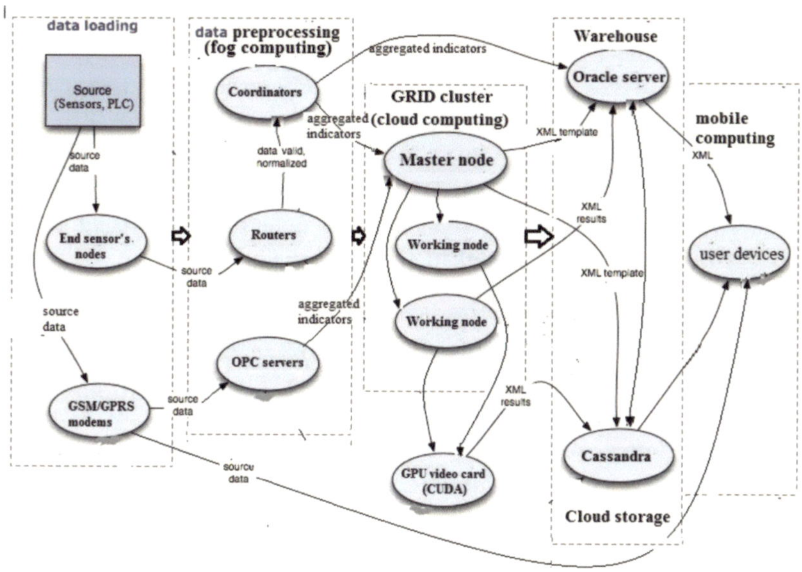

Figure 2. The data flow diagram of convergence model.

The convergence network platform may include some hardware and software levels that are as follows:

1. The sensor nodes are associated with industrial controllers and sensors, directly implementing fog computing.
2. Clusters network segments with coordinators, cellular modems, router, which collects and transfers sensor data into the data warehouse.
3. Cloud computing clusters.
4. Warehouse of sensor data and monitoring results.
5. The user mobile devices for the organization of access to computing and information resources.

The first level of the platform is a fog computing model. It provides the collection and sensor data processing on distributed nodes of the sensor network, in measuring devices and automation devices. Fog computing model is also the platform for data storage services on end-terminal devices and network services for data transmission. Computation is performed by terminal devices with limited computing and energy resources, including WSN nodes, controllers, industrial equipment, household appliances with microprocessors equipment and sensor network nodes. Modern WSN nodes have sufficient processing power to organize distributed computing [22]. The fog computing model is the basis of the Internet of Things [23]. Fog computing platform is necessary for realization of multiagent processing of sensor data and consolidated storage of calculated results on sensor network nodes [24, 25].

The second level of the convergent platform is implemented on the basis of the cloud computing model. Cloud platforms are now used in almost all areas of activity [26]. It is used for the ubiquitous network for access to a common pool of configurable resources (software, server, information, platform, etc.) at any time. The user uses the technology of "thin" client as a means of access to applications and data. The infrastructure of the information system is located at the provider of cloud services. The information is stored in cloud storage on the servers of the network. It is temporarily cached by the analytical processing [27]. The trend is the creation of distributed storage for BigData processing [28].

The third level of the convergent platform is related to the data processing on smart phones and tablets for presentation of monitoring results to users with the visualizing events and making decisions to reduce road incidents [29]. Mobile computing model is the platform for human-computer interaction. It involves mobile communication, mobile hardware and software. Communication issues include ad hoc networks and infrastructure networks as well as communication properties, protocols, data formats and mobile technologies.

4. Multiagent data collection, data mining and forecasting

Monitoring of road infrastructure includes procedures that are as follows:

1. Vehicle detection and identification in a controlled section of the road with the measurement of its speed
2. Photography and video fixation of traffic rules violations
3. Collect data on the traffic flow parameters in all monitored areas and transfer to the data processing center via communication channels
4. Vehicle detection on demand and tracking them with visualization of routes of their movements on a cartographic basis
5. Photographs and video materials processing about violations
6. Accumulation and statistical data processing on offenses for periods of time to identify and analyze the dependencies of changes in violations and road accidents from the influence of various factors (weather conditions, traffic volume, repair work, city events, time of day, seasonal factors, etc.)
7. Spatial analysis of offenses to identify critical areas and "bottlenecks" in the road transport infrastructure and their dependence on changes in traffic conditions with visualization on the map
8. Intellectual data mining and forecasting of road traffic situations for making decisions to improve traffic safety

Multiagent approach is advisable for the implementation of monitoring procedures. It involves the use of software agents for data collection, data mining and forecasting, as well as to alert road users about road traffic situation via mobile and navigation equipment [30]. The data collection and initial data processing are realized in the fog computing layer by means of agents loaded into sensor nodes. Sensor units are connected to the photoradar complexes. Agents interact with server components of the monitoring system.

The hypervisor is used to manage agents. It is consolidated computing resources for distributed data processing. Software agents are operated on the sensor nodes. Agents respond to requests, decide on the selection of data processing functions, clone and migrate to other network nodes. A feature of the agents is the behavior realization. The behavior is determined by the mathematical function, which implements the steps of sensor data processing. Other options determine the agent behavior in case of certain kinds of situations. The model of brokers is offered to agent interaction with server applications at the data center. Broker is an agent that runs on routers and realizes the storage, data protection, transmission and warehouse loading functions.

The multiagent system includes the following software agents:

1. Agent for the synthesis and control of the photoradar devices queue for inquiry.

2. Agent for creating threads for asynchronous device polling.

3. Agents of data polling from devices, separated by geographic zones and by types (devices Cordon-Temp, KrisP, Parkon, etc.). The data polling from device sensors is carried out by the agents from different zones using the SNMP protocol.

4. Agents that keep event logs directly on the complexes. Each complex maintains a local database, recording events in the log files. A lot of local databases represent a distributed hierarchical data warehouse. Agents keep a log file of vehicle passages, a log file of traffic violations, a log file of telemetry parameters for device diagnostics, and so on.

5. Agents for uploading data from device logs to central storage. Agents work through the web interface and generate a lot of files in XML format. One file contains the data of one violation and is associated with a digital signature file and violation pictures.

6. Agent for aggregating data about recorded violations for a period of time. This agent generates a comma separated values (CSV) file containing rows with parameters of all violations for a given period. It is an element of a distributed fog database. A lot of CSV files on different devices form a distributed hypertable of summary data on violations over a period of time.

7. Agent for aggregating the values of the complex parameters over a period of time. This agent creates a CSV file containing rows with the values of the complex parameters. It is also an element of a distributed database. A lot of CSV files with parameters of different devices form a hypertable for their diagnosis over a period of time.

8. Agent for parsing the files with violation parameters and parameters of the complexes for loading data into the central cloud storage.

9. Data mining agents for the analysis of data violations. This group of agents analyzes the time series of the uploaded violations data over a time period to identify the dependencies of growth or to reduce violations from various factors.

10. Data mining agents for the analysis of device parameter. This group performs analysis of time series of device parameters to detect parameter deviations from the required and reference values (benchmarking). The tools include data visualization agent, data aggregation agent, data selection agent, data mining agent and data analyze agent [31, 32].

11. Agents for forecasting violations of traffic rules and agents for forecasting failures and errors in the operation of complexes. Forecasting is performed using the technique of deep machine learning based on the synthesis of a fuzzy neural network, its training and forecasting changes in the operating parameters of the complex.

12. Agents for data visualization on computers in the data center and on mobile units. A variety of agents form a distributed content management system. Agents are downloadable php and js scripts. They allow in standard browsers to present historical, current and forecast data in the form of graphs, tables and dashboards. The data correspond to the polling time and geographical coordinates of the complex location.

The data aggregation agent is needed to support the technology of work with database in the aggregation mode for the selection and visualization of hypertable data mart. When the mode is setup, the user should define a set of object properties (columns of values) that will be shown in the hypertable. Available properties can be selected from the drop-down list.

The visualization agent allows to see information in the hypertable data mart. The hypertable is a nonstandard user interface for data visualization. It combines the functionality of a classic table with a tree structure. Elements of the hypertable can be located on distributed sensory nodes. Elements allow to view the dynamic changes of the values changes in real time. The data are grouped according to the parameters and levels of aggregation. A distinctive feature of the hypertable is that the number of rows is not a static value, a row character and functionality are not equal and some of them are the aggregates. The aggregates are nodal and show summary information on the relevant columns of the lower-level aggregation rows. The actual number of the hypertable rows varies dynamically, depending on the grouping of rows. Another feature of the hypertable is the ability to view quickly and analyze changes. The user can view hypertable change of any selected index for the period, as well as the predicted values for the specified forecast horizon. An example of data visualization, photoradar complex parameters, is shown in **Figure 3**.

The data analyze agent allows choosing the data needed for the analysis of a concrete situation. The data marts selection criteria can be quite complex. For this purpose, the system uses multilevel queries and filters that limit the data choice. The agent allows the personnel easily create queries to choose the right information.

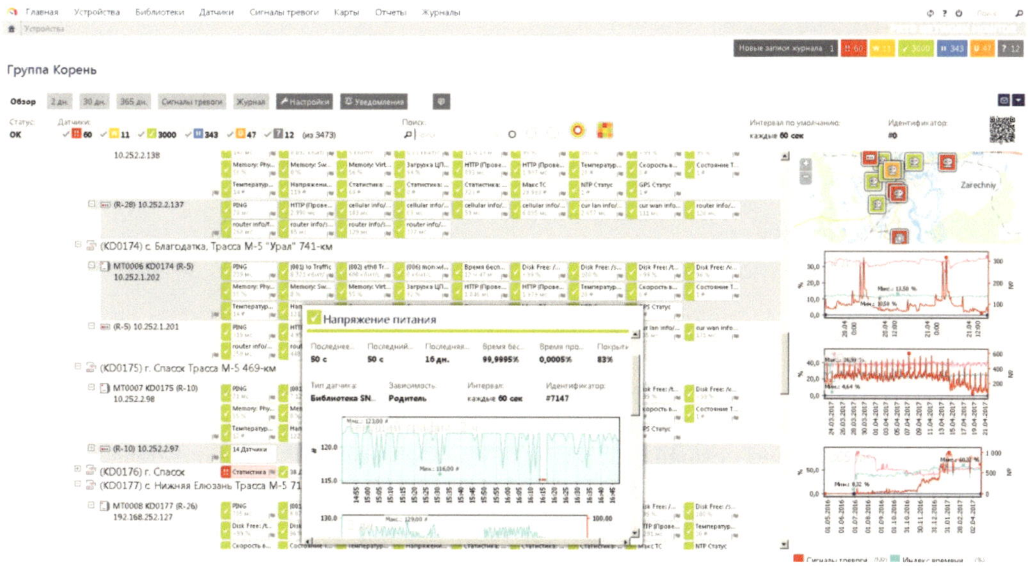

Figure 3. The diagnostic data of the complex.

5. Prognostic models and machine learning methods for multiagent diagnostics of photoradar complexes and road incidents

The diagnostic system is necessary for remote maintenance of photoradar equipment. The system should monitor the complex parameters, transmit telemetric information, predict possible malfunctions and automatically report about failures. The complex has a set of parameters such as supply voltage, response time, housing temperature, ambient temperature, and so on. Since the complexes are distributed over a large area, a multiagent remote diagnostic system is being developed to monitor their operation. Key element of a diagnostic system is the mechanism of forecasting a change, depending on its current parameters, level of external indignations and the influences. The data mining tasks and failures' forecasting tasks are solved using deep machine learning and fuzzy neural networks based on the analysis of time series of complex parameters. The monitoring task for the equipment is determined by the high requirements for the uninterrupted operation of devices. In the event of emergency situations, the minimum time is allocated to correct the malfunctions. For a short time, it is necessary to determine the order of repair work and the required amount of resources such as the working time of specialists, the need to operate machinery and the required spare modules. The evaluation of the reliability of the complex is based on the data analysis on the device state at times and data analysis on the violations in the complex operations. Data for assessing the reliability of the complex include the following:

a. The work time of complex for the reporting data

b. The uninterrupted work time of complex

c. The time of fixing traffic accidents

d. The number of fixed objects

e. The number of recorded traffic accidents

f. The complex downtime for failure

g. The failure frequency

h. The cost of repairs

i. The number of errors in fixing traffic accidents

The purpose of the analysis is to identify the deviations of the complex parameters and to detect errors and malfunctions. The deviations of the parameters are exceeding thresholds, deviation of values from normative and normalized previous data. The results of forecasting are used to plan an unscheduled repair work in order to prevent possible failures. The work schedule depends on the following parameters: location of the complex; density of traffic on the repair location; availability of spare parts; nature of the malfunction; types of repair work carried out earlier with the device; frequency of malfunctions and required resources to restore functionality.

We consider the system of forecasting of a qualitative condition of the photoradar complex on the basis of indistinct implication [33]. In case of N variables, rules of a conclusion have generally the following appearance: if x_1 is A_1 and x_2 is A_2 .... and x_N is A_N, then, y is B, where A and B are the linguistic values identified in the indistinct way through the corresponding functions. The x_1, x_2,... x_N variables form an N-dimensional entrance vector x, the making argument of a condition in which A_1, A_2,..., A_N and B designate sizes of the corresponding function of accessories $\mu_A(x_i)$ ($i = 1\ldots N$) and $\mu_B(y)$, the function of Gauss defined in this case:

$$\mu_A(x) = \frac{1}{1 + \left(\frac{x-c}{\sigma}\right)^{2b}} \tag{1}$$

where c, σ and b are the parameters of the function of Gauss defining its center, width and form, respectively.

If to consider that is available M-rules (and M-functions of accessory), the matrix of values of functions of accessory of the $N \times M$ size is formed:

Rule 1: If $x_1^{(1)}$ is $A_1^{(1)}$ and $x_2^{(1)}$ is $A_2^{(1)}$ .... and $x_N^{(1)}$ is $A_N^{(1)}$, then, $y^{(1)}$ is $B^{(1)}$,

Rule 2: If $x_1^{(2)}$ is $A_1^{(2)}$ and $x_2^{(2)}$ is $A_2^{(2)}$ .... and $x_N^{(2)}$ is $A_N^{(2)}$, then, $y^{(2)}$ is $B^{(2)}$,

...

Rule M: If $x_1^{(M)}$ is $A_1^{(M)}$ and $x_2^{(M)}$ is $A_2^{(M)}$ .... and $x_N^{(M)}$ is $A_N^{(M)}$, then, $y^{(M)}$ is $B^{(M)}$.

We present further sequences of the functioning of the diagnostics system of photoradar complexes with a conclusion of Mamdani-Zade in the form of the following stages:

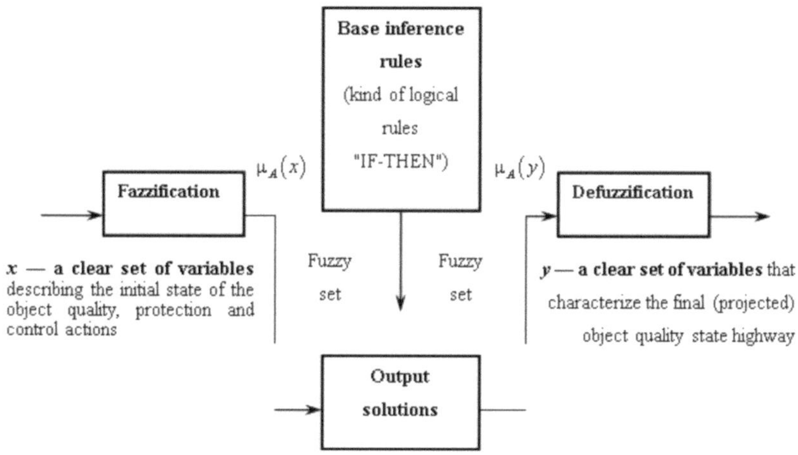

Figure 4. Defuzzificator transforms an indistinct set to a completely determined exact decision y, representing the predicted condition of the photoradar complex.

The first stage is the aggregation of the reasons for failures in the systems: The arriving value of the function $\mu_A(x)$ are aggregated in the algebraic form:

$$\mu_A(x) = \prod_{i=1}^{N} \mu_A(x_i). \tag{2}$$

The second stage is the aggregation effects of disruption of complexes: Each implication of the unique value of function $\mu_{A \to B}$ is attributed. This operation is also carried out with the use of operation of algebraic work:

$$\mu_{A \to B} = \mu_A(x) \times \mu_B(y). \tag{3}$$

The third stage is the aggregation of results: At this stage, the operator of the sum is applied to aggregation of results of implication of many rules.

In final part of the conclusion of Mamdani-Zade, the procedure of a defuzzification allowing to receive accurate value of an output variable—the predicted condition of photoradar complex is carried out (**Figure 4**).

Since $\mu_A^{(k)}(x) = \prod_{i=1}^{N} \mu_A^{(k)}(x_i)$ for $M-$rules of defuzzification procedure can be written as:

$$y = \frac{\sum_{k=1}^{M} y^{(k)} \left[\prod_{i=1}^{N} \mu_A^{(k)}(x_i) \right]}{\sum_{k=1}^{M} \left[\prod_{i=1}^{N} \mu_A^{(k)}(x_i) \right]}. \tag{4}$$

The main weak spot in an implication method with a conclusion of Mamdani-Zade is subjectivity of the creation of a grid of rules and functions of accessory. This defect method can be eliminated by creation of the hybrid computing mechanism where implication of Mamdani-Zade is mediated by work of the neural network (NN), with the training mechanism inherent in it. Forecasting is the process of making predictions of the future based on past and present data. Forecasting accuracy is constantly being improved with the continual introduction of machine learning techniques. Time series sensor data are any data set that collects telemetry information regularly over a period of time. The fundamental problem for machine learning and time series is the same: to predict new outcomes based on previously known results. Time series and machine learning can be combined together in order to give the benefits of each approach. Time series does a good job at decomposing data into trended and seasonal elements. This analysis can then be used as an input for an NN model, which can incorporate the trend and seasonal information into its algorithm. The NN represents the parallel computing system consisting of a large number of elementary units of information processing—the neurons, accumulating experimental knowledge and providing them for the subsequent processing. The term "training" is understood as ability of NN to receive reasonable results on the basis of the data, which were not found in the course of training. The sequence of training on the basis of procedure of the return distribution is presented in **Figure 5**.

This property is used at realization of hybrid indistinct neural network (HINN). We consider the sequence of functioning of HINN (**Figure 6**).

On the first layer, the fuzzification is carried out. The formula of a fuzzifikation looks as follows:

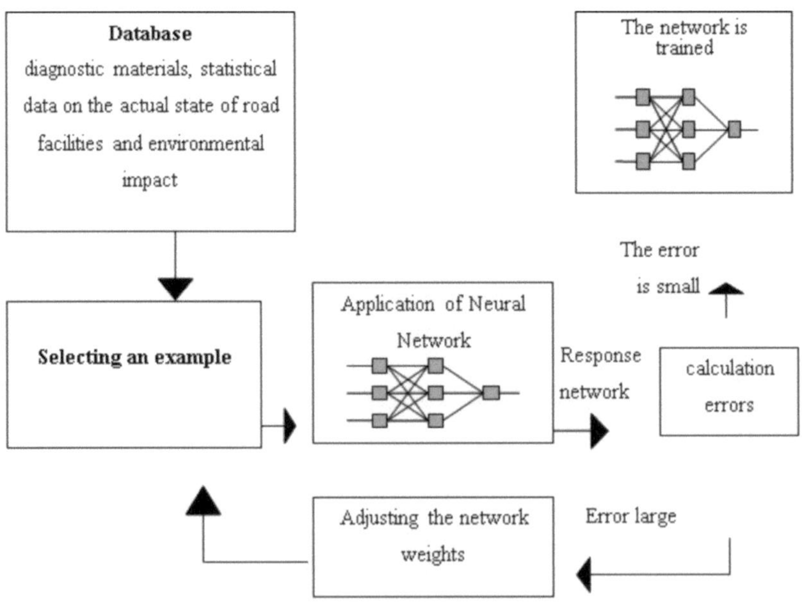

Figure 5. The scheme of HINN training for forecasting the complex state.

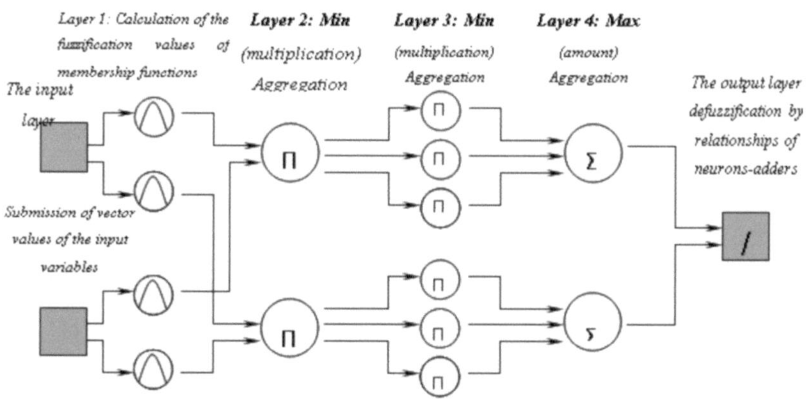

Figure 6. The general structure of NN-mediating work of indistinct implication on forecasting with the indication of neuron minimizers and neuron adders.

$$\mu_A^{(k)}(x_i) = \frac{1}{1 + \left(\frac{x_i - c_j^{(k)}}{\sigma_j^{(k)}}\right)^{2b_j^{(k)}}}. \tag{5}$$

where k is the quantity of functions of accessory ($k = 1\ldots M$); j is the quantity of variables ($j = 1\ldots N$); $c_j^{(k)}, \sigma_j^{(k)}, b_j^{(k)}$ – are the parameters of the center, which determine the width and form of the k functions of accessory jth variable, respectively.

It is necessary to consider that generally, the number of functions of accessory does not coincide with the number of rules. Therefore, if each x_i variable has m functions of accessory, the maximum quantity of rules, which can be created at their combination, will make $M = m^N$.

In the second layer, the aggregation of values of the x_i variables is carried out:

$$w_k = \prod_{j=1}^{N} \left(\frac{1}{1 + \left(\frac{x_i - c_j^{(k)}}{\sigma_j^{(k)}}\right)^{2b_j^{(k)}}} \right). \tag{6}$$

Thus, the calculated parameters w_k ($k = 1\ldots M$) at the same time move further in the third layer (for multiplication on weight) and in the fourth layer for calculation of their sum in f_2 neuron.

The third layer when using a conclusion of Mamdani-Zade calculates the centers for k-rules for a formula: $y_k = p_{k0}$, where p_{k0} can be considered as the center of the function of accessory of c_k in the Mamdani-Zade model.

After that aggregation of a consequence with the use of operation of algebraic work is carried out: $w_k \times y_k(x)$.

The fourth layer is presented by two neurons f_1 and f_2, which are carrying out results:

$$f_1 = \sum_{k=1}^{M} w_k \times y_k(x) = \sum_{k=1}^{M} \left[\left(\prod_{j=1}^{N} \mu_A^{(k)}(x_j) \right) \times c_k \right],$$
$$f_2 = \sum_{k=1}^{M} w_k = \sum_{k=1}^{M} \left[\prod_{j=1}^{N} \mu_A^{(k)}(x_j) \right]. \tag{7}$$

The fifth layer is presented by the unique neuron, which is carrying out a defuzzification:

$$y(x) = \frac{f_1}{f_2} = \frac{\sum_{k=1}^{M} w_k \times y_k(x)}{\sum_{k=1}^{M} w_k} = \frac{\sum_{k=1}^{M} \left[\left(\prod_{j=1}^{N} \mu_A^{(k)}(x_j) \right) \times c_k \right]}{\sum_{k=1}^{M} \left[\prod_{j=1}^{N} \mu_A^{(k)}(x_j) \right]}. \tag{8}$$

The algorithm of HINN training can conditionally be shared into two stages. At the first stage, parameters of the center of output functions of accessory in the third layer are subject to training. For this purpose, parameters of scales for the fixing of parameters of functions of accessory on the first layer (center, width and form) were determined as:

$$y(x) = \sum_{k=1}^{M} w_k' p_{k0}.$$

It should be noted that output signals y HINN replace with reference signals d from p of the training selections (the training examples $x^{(l)}$, $d^{(l)}$), where $l = 1 \ldots p$. Then: $wp = d$, where w is the matrix A simplified as a result of replacement of a polynom.

Further, the decision of system of the equations is carried out on the basis of pseudo-inversion of matrixes: $Ap = d$ from $p = A^{+}d$, where A^{+} is the pseudo-return matrix A.

At the second stage, after fixing of values of linear parameters $y_k = p_{k0}$ calculated the actual exits of HINN $y(i)$ for $i = 1 \ldots p$ and a vector of a mistake $\varepsilon = y - d$. Further, applying a method of the fastest descent, formulas for adjustment of parameters of functions of accessory are used:

$$c_j^{(k)}(n+1) = c_j^{(k)}(n) - \eta \frac{\partial E(n)}{\partial c_j^{(k)}},$$
$$\sigma_j^{(k)}(n+1) = \sigma_j^{(k)}(n) - \eta \frac{\partial E(n)}{\partial \sigma_j^{(k)}}, \tag{9}$$
$$b_j^{(k)}(n+1) = b_j^{(k)}(n) - \eta \frac{\partial E(n)}{\partial b_j^{(k)}}.$$

where n is the number of iteration and η is the training speed parameter.

http://dx.doi.org/10.5772/intechopen.73610

6. The results of the intellectual analysis

This method was also used to forecast traffic accidents, based on the processing of accident statistics on controlled road sections. A method for forecasting road accidents was implemented depending on three factors: the amount of traffic flow per unit of time, the number of road accidents and the temperature indicators in the control areas. Before we begin to analyze how to conduct traffic accident inference with location and time information, a proper data structure is needed. When analyzing such spatial and temporal data, the use of matrix is widely accepted as the first choice. For temporal dimension, in order to match the time interval of traffic accident data, we select 1 hour as the time interval and divide 1 day into 24 slices. For spatial dimension, we mesh location into Δd latitude and Δd longitude. To guarantee each region in an approximate 500 m × 500 m square, which is a proper area for traffic accident analysis, we select Δd latitude = 0.004 and Δd longitude = 0.005 on a Penza region map (Russia). Therefore, we have a time index t and region index r for each element in the matrix. In this way, we have obtained grid data, if traffic accident happened n times in region r at time t, we define the risk level. Seventeen areas for traffic accident analysis were chosen for the prediction with installed photoradar complexes (**Figure 7**).

To accumulate the statistics, their spatial and intellectual analysis, synthesis of graphs and reports to support decision-making, the system employs a special agent for remote polling of photo-video fixing complexes and automatic unloading of data on driver offenses and road accidents. Statistical data are presented in the form of time series or function graphs (**Figure 8**) of incidents, changes in speed and density of the flow of vehicles in controlled areas, ambient temperatures and are input parameters for training the neural network.

In the process of analyzing time series with the moments of road incidents, time intervals were chosen in which the number of incidents deviated from the average indicators. As an example, we present graphs of statistics on incidents collected from six complexes during the month (**Figure 9**).

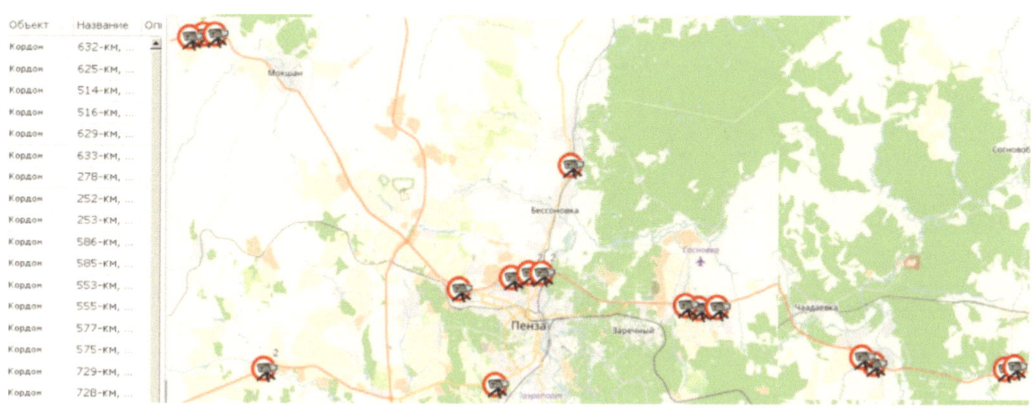

Figure 7. Road area with photo-video fixing complexes.

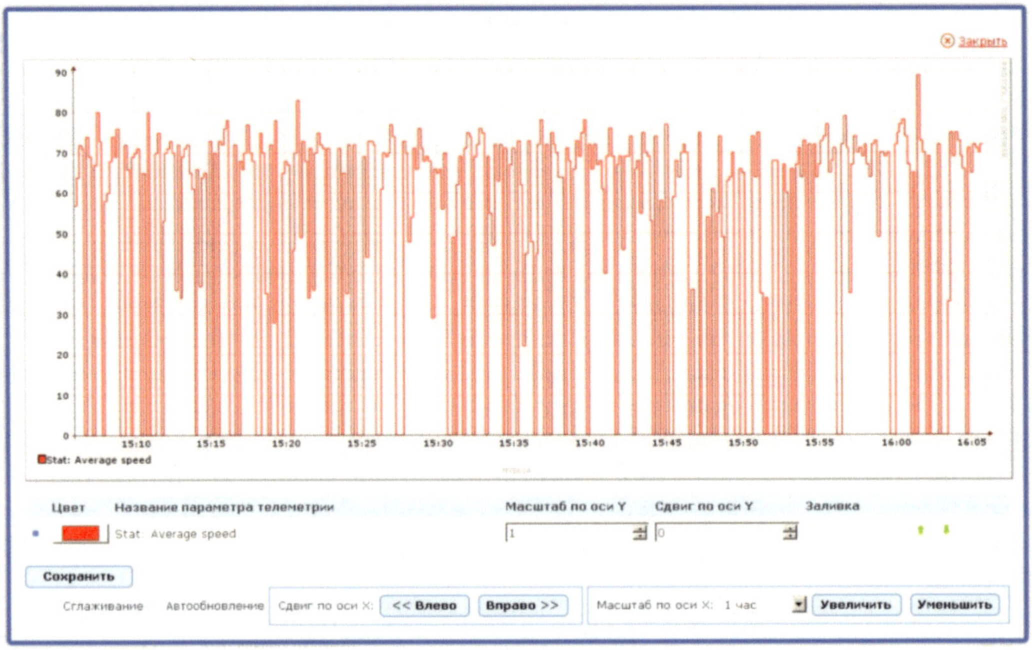

Figure 8. An example of a graphical representation of the average transport speed.

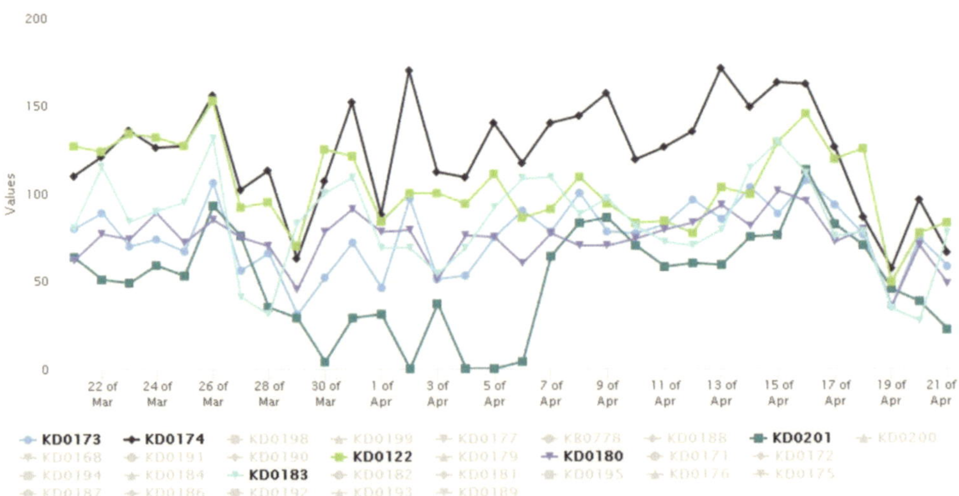

Figure 9. Graphs of the road incidents dynamics at six complexes (22 March–22 April 2017).

Analysis of the data presented in the graphs showed anomalies. It is seen that for a month on five complexes (KD0173, KD0174, KD0183, KD0122 and KD0180) that the number of road incidents is fixed, which on the average is about 60–70 units with the exception of the KD0201 complex. However, after April 17, there is a decrease in the number of road incidents simultaneously on all the complexes.

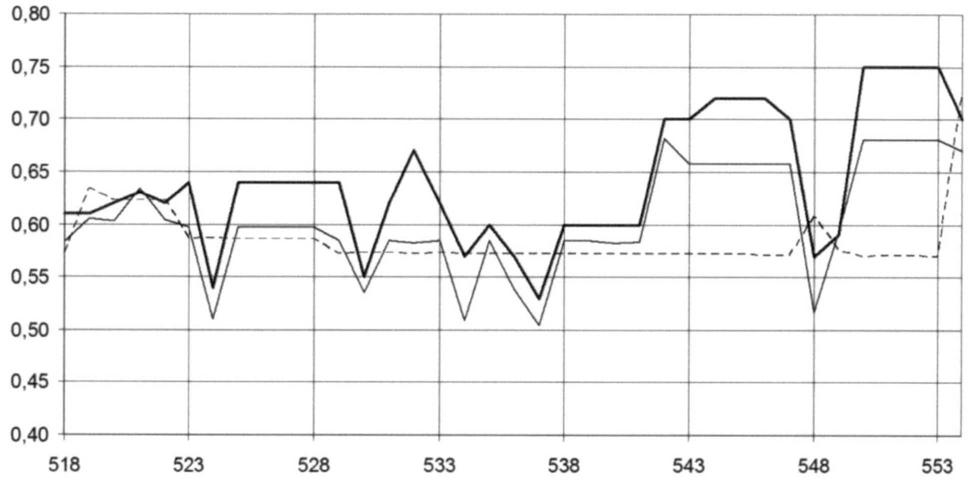

Figure 10. Results of forecasting the number of road accidents (bold line indicates fact, dashed line indicates forecast before training and fine line indicates forecast after training).

To determine the causes of anomalies and the forecast of incidents, meteorological data (temperatures, atmospheric pressure and precipitation) were collected at anomalous areas at similar time intervals.

Indicators in the form of the number of incidents, temperature values and traffic density values have become input parameters for training the neural network. The number of neurons of the first layer of the network was set to 18 and the number of rules as 9. After training the network, a forecast was made for road accidents (**Figure 10**).

The results of the network showed an acceptable error in the forecast of an average of 13%. The model made it possible to determine the dependence of the number of incidents on the changes in traffic and on the temperature regime in the controlled sections of the road. In particular, the prognostic model showed the dependence of the level of incidents recorded by the Kordon-Temp complexes on the M-5 (Ural, Russia) route from changes in temperature and precipitation. It can be concluded that the neural network and the prediction system provide sufficient accuracy for the prediction model.

7. Conclusion

The results of monitoring and analysis of traffic accidents, fixed by an intelligent monitoring system with photoradar complexes, are considered. A multiagent approach was developed to address the tasks of collecting and processing sensor data. Functionality of agents and brokers is defined as a mathematical function that determines the action to sensor data processing and the selection of behaviors to respond to emerging events. The system functionality is implemented by several agents that perform data collecting, cleaning, clustering, comparing time series, retrieving data for visualization in the dynamic hypertable form, preparing charts and reports, performing spatial and intellectual analysis, generating push notifications to mobile client, and so on. To accumulate the statistics, their spatial and intellectual analysis, synthesis of graphs and reports to support decision-making, the system employs special agents for remote polling of photo-video fixing complexes and automatic upload of data. The agent collects and downloads multimedia data such as photos and frames from the video stream, as well as various sensor data on traffic parameters.

Convergent approach is the convergence of distributed data processing technologies (cloud, fog and mobile computing). The model is designed for the collection, processing and integration of sensor data obtained in the process of monitoring and control of spatially distributed objects and processes. Convergent model of distributed computing includes three levels of data processing. The first level is fog computing. Here, processing and aggregation of sensor data is realized by migrating software agents in heterogenic sensor networks. At the next level (cloud computing), sensor data and aggregates are implemented in the server cluster. The cluster includes the main server to control the hypervisor and network servers at local network. The third level is implemented on mobile systems, where agents are to retrieve and visualize the results of monitoring and intellectual analysis with geo-information technologies.

The tasks of intellectual analysis and forecasting using methods of deep machine learning are solved. As a prognostic model, a hybrid fuzzy neural network was synthesized and its training was performed. The structure of the neural network is adapted to the problems of diagnosing and forecasting the operation of photoradar complexes, as well as for analysis and prediction of road accidents. As an example, consider the results of the intellectual analysis of unloading data collected from complexes in a month's time in comparison with meteorological data in order to reveal the patterns of variation in the number and severity of road incidents. In the process of spatial analysis, similar sections of the road and transport infrastructure are identified by the number and type of traffic accidents. Clustering of such areas allows to define the most emergency areas. In the process of intellectual analysis of time series, time intervals are determined, in which an abnormal deviation of the incidents number from average indicators are occurred. A comparison of the time series of road accidents and time series of meteorological factors has shown that changes in the traffic situation in controlled areas are strongly dependent on weather conditions.

Acknowledgements

The reported study was funded by Russian Foundation for Basic Research (RFBR) according to the research projects № 18-07-00975, 16-07-00031, 17-307-50010, 17-37-50033.

Author details

Alexey Finogeev*, Alexandr Bershadsky, Anton Finogeev, Ludmila Fionova and Michael Deev

*Address all correspondence to: alexeyfinogeev@gmail.com

Penza State University, Penza, Russia

References

[1] Batty M, Axhausen KW, Giannotti F, et al. Smart Cities of the Future. 2013. Available from: http://www.complexcity.info/files/2013/08/BATTY-EPJST-2012.pdf [Accessed: 2017–11-01]

[2] Ouzounis G, Portugali Y. Smart cities of the future. The European Physical Journal Special Topics. 2012;**214**(1):481-518

[3] Deakin M, Al Waer H. From intelligent to smart cities. Journal of Intelligent Buildings International. Taylor and Francis: 2012;**3**(3):95 p. DOI: 10.1080/17508975.2011.586671

[4] Cook D, Das S. Smart Environments. Technologies, Protocols and Applications. Hoboken, NJ: Wiley-Interscience; 2005. 432p

[5] Nakashima H, Aghajan H, Augusto JC. Handbook of Ambient Intelligence and Smart Environments. New York: Springer; 2010. 413p

[6] Hernandez-Muñoz JM et al. Smart cities at the forefront of the future internet. In: Proceedings of the Future Internet Assembly: Achievements and Technological Promises. Heidelberg, Berlin: Springer; 2011:447-462

[7] Scott M. Kozel Roads to the Future. Available from: http://www.roadstothefuture.com/main.html [Accessed: 2017–11-01]

[8] Nowacki G. Development and standardization of intelligent transport systems. International Journal on Marine Navigation and Safety of Sea Transportation. 2012;**6**(3): 403-411

[9] Praba DM. Smart Monitoring Infrastructure on the Smart Road System. Available from: http://lib.ui.ac.id/abstrakpdfdetail.jsp?id=20350225&lokasi=lokal [Accessed: 2017–11-01]

[10] Pandit A, Talreja J, Mundra A. RFID tracking system for vehicles (RTSV). In: Proceedings of the First International Conference on Computational Intelligence, Communication Systems and Networks. 2009. pp. 160-165

[11] Fritz E. RFID in Vehicles. Louisville, Kentucky: NetWorld Alliance LLC. 2012;143 p. Available from: http://www.KioskMarketplace.com [Accessed: 2017-11-01]

[12] Ma H-J, Hu Y-H, Yuan H-B, Guo W. Design and analysis of embedded GPS/DR vehicle integrated navigation system. In: Proceedings of the The 2008 International Conference on Embedded Software and Systems Symposia. 2008

[13] Finogeev AG, Parygin DS, Finogeev AA, et al. Multi-agent approach to distributed processing of big sensor data based on fog computing model for the monitoring of the urban infrastructure systems. In: Proceedings of the 5th International Conference on System Modeling & Advancement in Research Trends. 2016;**1**:305-310

[14] Finogeev AG, Parygin DS, Finogeev AA. The convergence computing model for big sensor data mining and knowledge discovery. Human-Centric Computing and Information Sciences. 2017;**7**:11. DOI: 10.1186/s13673-017-0092-7

[15] Sadovnikova NP, Finogeev AG, Parygin DS, et al. Monitoring of social reactions to support decision making on issues of urban territory management. In: Proceedings of the 5th International Young Scientist Conference on Computational Science. 2017;**101**: 243-252

[16] Finogeev A, Finogeev A, Shevchenko S. Monitoring of road transport infrastructure for the intelligent environment «smart road». In: Kravets A, Shcherbakov M, Kultsova M, Groumpos P, editors. Creativity in Intelligent Technologies and Data Science. (CIT&DS 2017). Communications in Computer and Information Science, Springer, Cham. 2017;**754**: 655-668

[17] Lorincz K, Malan D, Fulford-Jones TRF, Nawoj A, Clavel A, Shnayder V, Mainland G, Welsh M, Moulton S. Sensor networks for emergency response: Challenges and opportunities. IEEE Pervasive Computing. 2004;**3**(4):16-23

[18] Bielsa A. Smart Roads – Wireless Sensor Networks for Smart Infrastructures: A Billion Dollar Business Opportunity. 2013. Available from: http://www.libelium.com/smart_roads_wsn_smart_infrastructures/ [Accessed: 2017-11-01]

[19] Roco M, Bainbridge W, editors. Converging Technologies for Improving Human Performance: Nanotechnology, Biotechnology, Information Technology and Cognitive Science. Arlington: Kluwer Academic Publisher; 2004. 482 p

[20] Fernando N, Loke SW, Rahayu W. Mobile cloud computing: A survey. Proceedings of the Future Generation Computer Systems. 2013;**29**(1):84-106

[21] Finogeev AG, Parygin DS, Finogeev AA, et al. A convergent model for distributed processing of big sensor data in urban engineering networks. Journal of Physics: Conference Series: In Proceedings of the International Conference on Information Technologies in Business and Industry. 2017;**803**:1-6

[22] Dargie W, Poellabauer C. Fundamentals of Wireless Sensor Networks: Theory and Practice. John Wiley and Sons; 2010

[23] Stojmenovic I, Wen S. The fog computing paradigm: Scenarios and security issues. In Proceedings of the Federated Conference on Computer Science and Information Systems (ACSIS). 2014;**2**:1-8

[24] Bonomi F, Milito R, Zhu J, Addepalli S. Fog computing and its role in the internet of things. In: Proceedings of the First Edition of the MCC Workshop on Mobile Cloud Computing, Ser. MCC'12. ACM. 2012. pp. 13-16

[25] Al-Karaki JN, Ul-Mustafa R, Kamal AE. Data aggregation in wireless sensor networks—Exact and approximate algorithms. In: Proceedings of IEEE Workshop on High Performance Switching and Routing (HPSR) IEEE. Phoenix, USA. 2004

[26] Armbrust M, Fox A, Griffith R, Joseph AD, Katz R, Konwinski A, Lee G, Patterson D, Rabkin A, Stoica I, Zaharia M. A view of cloud computing. Communications of the ACM. 2010;**53**(4):50-58

[27] Lee B, Tim G, Patt-Corner R, Jeff V. Cloud Computing Synopsis and Recommendations. Gaithersburg, US: National Institute of Standards and Technology (NIST) Special Publication 800-146. 2012:81 p

[28] Google Cloud Platform. BigQuery. A fast, economical and fully managed data warehouse for large-scale data analytics. Available from: https://cloud.google.com/bigquery [Accessed: 2017-11-01]

[29] Sadovnikova NP, Finogeev AG, Parygin DS, Finogeev AA, et al. Visualization of data about events in the urban environment for the decision support of the city services actions coordination. In: Proceedings of the 5th International Conference on System Modeling & Advancement in Research Trends. 2016;**1**:283-290

[30] Botvinkin PV, Kamaev VA, Nefedova IS, Finogeev AG. On information of security risk management for GPS/GLONASS-based ground transportation monitoring and supervisory control automated navigation systems. The Social Sciences (Medwell Journals). 2015; **10**(2):201-205

[31] Alexey F, Valery K, Ludmila F, Anton F, Egor F, Thang MN. Tools for data mining and secure transfer in the WSN for energy management. Journal of Applied Engineering Research. 2015;**10**(15):35373-35381

[32] Kamaev V, Finogeev A, Finogeev A, Shevchenko S. Knowledge discovery in the SCADA databases used for the municipal power supply system. In: Proceeding of the Knowledge-Based Software Engineering (JCKBSE-14). 2014. pp. 1-15

[33] Finogeev AG, Skorobogatchenko DA, Trung DT, Kamaev VA. Application of indistinct neural networks for solving forecasting problems in the road complex. ARPN Journal of Engineering and Applied Sciences. 2016;**11**(16):9646-9653

Chapter 6

An Expert System Based on Computer Vision and Statistical Modelling to Support the Analysis of Collagen Degradation

Yaroslava Robles-Bykbaev, Salvador Naya,
Silvia Díaz Prado, Daniel Calle-López,
Vladimir Robles-Bykbaev, Luis Garzón-Muñóz,
Clara Sanjurjo Rodríguez and Javier Tarrío Saavedra

Additional information is available at the end of the chapter

http://dx.doi.org/10.5772/intechopen.72982

Abstract

The poly(DL-lactide-co-glycolide) (PDLGA) copolymers have been specifically designed and performed as biomaterials, taking into account their biodegradability and biocompatibility properties. One of the applications of statistical degradation models in material engineering is the estimation of the materials degradation level and reliability. In some reliability studies, as the present case, it is possible to measure physical degradation (mass loss, water absorbance, pH) depending on time. To this aim, we propose an expert system able to provide support in collagen degradation analysis through computer vision methods and statistical modelling techniques. On this base, the researchers can determine which statistical model describes in a better way the biomaterial behaviour. The expert system was trained and evaluated with a corpus of 63 images (2D photographs obtained by electron microscopy) of human mesenchymal stem cells (CMMh-3A6) cultivated in a laboratory experiment lasting 44 days. The collagen type-1 sponges were arranged in 3 groups of 21 samples (each image was obtained in intervals of 72 hours).

Keywords: computer vision, collagen degradation, statistical modelling, long short-term neural networks

1. Introduction

The statistical analysis (almost classical) of data collected through techniques like segmentation of images of biomaterials focuses their attention on a descriptive analysis and an implication analysis or quasi-implication analysis. This approach can cause the loss of the study of possible influences of variables relative to the experiment of cell seed over biomaterials like type I collagen.

However, there are alternatives to classical statistical analysis based on classification methods, descriptive statistics, implication statistics and quasi-implication statistics, among others. One of them is the hybrid methodology based on the application of neural networks, image segmentation and statistical modelling of the probable relation of variables that affect biomaterials degradation like type I collagen in the mesenchymal stromal cell culture over those biomaterials. This hybrid system becomes a robust system with high complexity and low computational cost. On the one hand, it allows a reliable analysis of experimental data relative to the seeding of those cells, that is, to establish if there is any possible relationship between the medium of cell culture and the degradation of the biomaterial where the named cell lineage is seeded. On the other hand, the system enables the making of decisions taking into account into the acquired data after the application of the analytical model.

Meanwhile, image segmentation allows the improvement of images to use them later and the following data collection to analyse this data statistically. While neural networks are capable of improving data prediction [1], the statistical modelling allows identifying and explaining possible relationships among variables (predictor ones) that could influence in the degradation of type I collagen as regards time (in vitro one). Therefore, the hybrid system encompasses several data analysis systems. In addition to the cluster analysis, the system includes an alternative statistic for improving the method to examine the experimental results of the cell culture over biomaterials.

The growing requirement for making new materials compatible with life implies not only their design and tests, but it also involves the statistical study of the relationship between the type of biomaterial and the cells seeded in it. This analysis is necessary due to the following experimental phases that depend upon it. Some examples of this kind of studies are:

- Statistical analysis devoted to determining the biomaterials degradation. This kind of studies allows a better identification of the effects of the variables under investigation like the type of biomaterial, the cell group, the culture medium, the time of cell growth and the degradation of the biomaterial as regards time [2–5].
- Chen et al. developed a numeric model taking into account the stochastic hydrolysis and the transportation of mass to simulate the biomaterials degradation process and their erosion [2].
- Hoque et al. have modelled the loss of mass using an exponential expression. They made it, supposing that water diffusion and water hydrolysis are the leading causes of the degradation processes of the biomaterials under analysis [3].
- To our purpose, we applied statistical learning tools (field related to the interrelation between statistics and informatics) relative to complex data for modelling tends of degradation and reliability regarding the studied materials [6].

The above research shows up the need for modelling statistically not only the mechanical, physical or rheological phenomes of biomaterials like type I collagen, as well as the requirement to model the degradation degree for this biomaterial in cell cultures. But also, it is necessary to statistically model the cell growth and cell distinction. All these studies establish robust methods to analyse these degradation processes thanks to the contribution with additional information about the variables effects. The analysis of these variables is usually unknown with the application of just descriptive statistical methods.

The current proposal focuses their attention on a smart model that combines segmentation and analysis of images to get databases, which can be analysed later with a statistical model. Additionally, the intelligent system applies neural networks to the previously obtained data for improving the capacity of prediction processes. Namely, the smart system is a methodological proposal that allows predicting and understanding the behaviour of experimental data of biological populations.

2. Baseline methodologies for the system development

The objective of this proposal is to determine the relationship among the degradation of type I collagen where we seeded mesenchymal stromal cells. This deterioration was conditioned by the time (period) of study we made the observation.

The experiment was done through the statistical modelling of the type I collagen degradation degree. Additionally; we did a previous segmentation analysis (particle identification and particle detachment) of images acquired by an optical microscope and coloured with haematoxylin-eosin techniques.

This intelligent system allows the improvement of making decisions and conclusions because its methodology is more precise thanks to the system that applies data arithmetic analysis. Thus, decision-making is made according to a robust statistical analysis of the relationship between the type I collagen degradation and the presence of possible influent variables in that degradation.

As is depicted in **Figure 1**, below we describe all methodologies used to make up our proposal.

2.1. Generalised linear models (GLM)

Regarding the statistical modelling of experiments relative to the cell culture, that is, modelling the biological behaviour, we applied GLM because this kind of models allows some degree of flexibility for this type of data. Nelder and Wedderburn used GLM for the first time in 1972. These models let variables to follow an exponential probability distribution and not just a normal distribution [7].

Concerning the summary of the GLM function, this last one does not produce a p-value to the model nor an R^2. The maximum verisimilitude estimation is the base for estimation and inference with GLM, even though, maximisation of probability requires an iterative method for the least-squares approach [8].

GLM capacity to adjust the mean of the data μ, instead of the data, is the base to choose these models. In a GLM context, a reasonable approach would be to select among models considering their capacity to maximise log-likelihood $l(\beta; \mu)$ instead of $l(\beta; y)$. But, to apply this focusing,

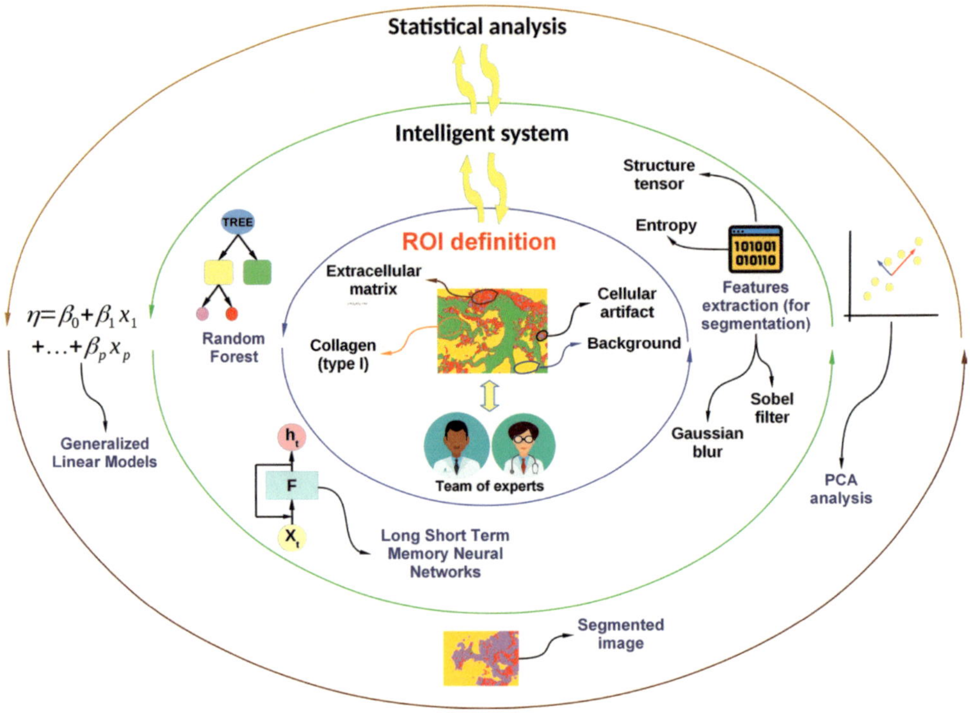

Figure 1. General architecture of the proposed approach.

it is necessary to estimate l (β; μ) first. Likewise, it is essential to select the model with the lowest value of Akaike information criterion (AIC) [8].

In GLM models, the linear predictor is

$$n = \beta_0 + \beta_1 x_1 + \beta_2 x_2 + \ldots + \beta_p x_p \tag{1}$$

where

$h(\mu) = \eta$

h = link function

η = nonadditive lineal predictor

2.1.1. *Predictive values*

Predictive values communicate what the value of result would be expected according to the observed pattern between the co-variables and the outcome. At least three different values are essential for us, which can be calculated by regression adjustment:

1. Values adjusted to representative or particular values of X
2. Values adjusted to the mean of X
3. Values adjusted to the arithmetic mean [8]

2.2. Computer vision in decision-making for cell differentiation

Nowadays, the computer vision allows us determining the cells' biological behaviour such as the growth and cell differentiation as well as the biomaterials degradation (collagen type I). In this line, the image segmentation is an important methodology used to achieve this objective: "a central problem in many studies, and often considered as the cornerstone of image analysis, is its segmentation" [9]. That is why "the type and quality of the acquired images influence the success of cell segmentation (identification and separation of objects)" [10].

In the same line, although segmentation seems a process with a certain degree of complexity and "although the segmentation is conceptually simple, it lacks generality and, therefore, cannot be implemented reliably and effortlessly in all cell lines, modalities of image and densities of cells without pre-processing images" [11].

The limitations such as the specific needs related to the research, the type of objects to be treated in the image, the objectives pursued by the research and the restricted knowledge of the technician in charge of the segmentation process lead to the need to create specialised proposals for the treatment and image analysis. The absence of a universal image segmentation procedure is no surprise; however, it is now possible to analyse the 2D images of the behaviour of stem cells in vivo, such as sequential growth and differentiation with time using various techniques [11]. The most commonly used segmentation and image processing techniques include colour threshold, region growth, edge detection and Markov random fields (MRF) [12].

2.2.1. Random forest classifier

Using the extracted descriptors from the images, it is possible to apply any classifier to perform the image segmentation by pixels (a division of the image into different segments or groups of pixels that share certain characteristics). In this research, we have used a classifier that allows operating on modular attributes avoiding the overfitting of certain classes and has an optimised computational cost.

In recent years, decision forests have established themselves as one of the most promising techniques in machine learning, computer vision and medical image analysis [13].

The random forests operate by constructing several decision trees (predictive processes that map observations on an article to conclusions about the objective value of the article) in the training phase, to then result in class fashion (by its nature as a classifier) for each tree.

In order to train the classifier, it is necessary to define attributes, so it is necessary to extract the following information for each region of interest (ROI) in the training images:

- Structure tensor

A structure tensor is a matrix representation of the image partial derivatives defined as the second-order symmetric positive matrix **J**:

$$J = \begin{bmatrix} < f_x, f_x > w & < f_x, f_y > w \\ < f_x, f_y > w & < f_y, f_y > w \end{bmatrix} \tag{2}$$

where f_x and f_y are the images of the partial spatial derivatives, ∂f/∂x and ∂f/∂y, respectively [14].

From this matrix, all major and minor eigenvalues are separated for each pixel and channel in the image:

$$T(v) = \lambda v \quad (3)$$

- Entropy

Draws a circle of radius **r** around each pixel, obtains the histogram of that separated circle as fragments of binarised image and then calculates the entropy as $\sum_{pin\ histogram} -p * log_2(p)$ for each particle, where **p** is the probability of each chunk in the histogram of each channel of the image, in both RGB and HSB.

- Gaussian blur

In order to obtain the features related with the Gaussian blur, we perform circumvolutions with a Gaussian function to smooth; for this we define the following values:

- σ represents the decay radius exp(−0.5)~61%. For example, the standard deviation σ of the Gaussian.
- Scale units represents that the value of σ is not in pixels but in units defined by the scale of the image size.

Then, for the process of extracting attributes, we perform **n** individual circumvolutions with Gaussian nuclei with **n** normal variations of **σ**. The larger the radius, the more unfocused the image will be until it reaches the point where the pixels are homogeneous [15]:

$$\boldsymbol{\sigma}_{min}, 2\,\boldsymbol{\sigma}_{min}, 4\,\boldsymbol{\sigma}_{min}, \ldots, 2^{n-1}\,\boldsymbol{\sigma}_{min} \quad (4)$$

where $2^{n-1}\,\boldsymbol{\sigma}_{min} \leq \boldsymbol{\sigma}_{max}$.

It should be noted that for all convolution operations, the pixels that are outside the image are assigned the value of the pixel corresponding to the nearest edge. This gives more weight to the pixels at the edge of the image with respect to the central ones and greater weight to the pixels of the corners than to the non-corners [16].

- Sobel filter

The Sobel operator, sometimes called the "Sobel-Feldman operator" or "Sobel filter", is used in image processing and computer vision, particularly in edge detection algorithms where images are generated with sharp edges. This operator makes a measurement of the spatial gradient of an image in order to highlight areas with high spatial frequency that corresponds to the edges. The numerical analysis shows that for certain kinds of surfaces, an even better estimate can be obtained by using the average weights of three such central differences [17].

For the extraction of attributes related to this filter, an approximation of the gradient of the intensity of each pixel in the image is calculated. Prior to the application of the filter, Gaussian blurs are applied varying the value of σ.

Based on the identification of the components of the training images, the intelligent system will be in charge of receiving the pertinent attributes to said classes, to later classify each pixel of all the images of the corpus. The correct identification of these classes allows generating probability maps [15] for each object class of CMMh3A6 cells and extracting attributes such as the area for further analysis. With the probability maps assembled, we proceeded to segment the images and extract several interesting features (physical features) such as area, mean, ratios, etc.

2.3. Long short-term memory neural networks as forecasting support tools

In addition to the statistical modelling techniques that were applied to model the level of degradation of type I collagen, a long short-term memory neural network (LSTM NN) was implemented. A network of this type is characterised by being able to learn long-term dependencies, an aspect that makes them an ideal strategy to carry out prediction processes based on previously viewed values. Traditional recurrent neural networks (RNNs) work with predetermined time lags in order to learn the processing of temporal sequences. This aspect makes it inappropriate to use an RNN for the problem described in this chapter, since the time periods in which the laboratory samples that are taken could be variable. When using an NTS LTSM, we have two important advantages over traditional RNNs: (i) it is feasible to take a long number of samples to train the system, and (ii) the optimal time window size can be variable [18].

Figure 2 presents the general architecture of the LSTM NN used. The basic unit of this network is the block of memory that contains one or more memory cells and a pair of adaptive, multiplicative gather units which gate input and output to all cells in the block. Memory blocks allow cells to share the same gates in order to reduce the number of adaptive parameters. Each memory cell has a linear unit called Constant Error Carousel (CEC) connected to it. This unit allows that when there is no new input or error signals sent to the cell, the local value of the error (CEC) remains constant [18, 19].

In this line, we have used in this research a LSTM NN with the aim of forecasting intermediate values of the collagen type I degradation. Originally, the laboratory samples were taken each day (21 samples), whereas with the neural network, we can generate around 180 projection values (for every variable such as area, perimeter, diameter, eccentricity or roundness, mean intensity, centroid (x, y), skew and kurtosis, with respect to time). To this aim, the neural network was trained with the 21 original samples, and posteriorly, it predicted the rest of the values according to intervals of 0.25* day (6 hours).

2.4. Principal component analysis (PCA)

During the last decades, some techniques such as the Fourier-transform infrared spectroscopy (FTIR) has shown their high potential carrying out some genetic studies as well as providing support as a complementary tool for immunohistochemical methods. The great development that experimented several techniques of molecular biology aimed at the study of cell differentiation has shown that implementing alternative approaches to perform the analysis of an important set of data that can be obtained from in vivo or in vitro tests is necessary [20].

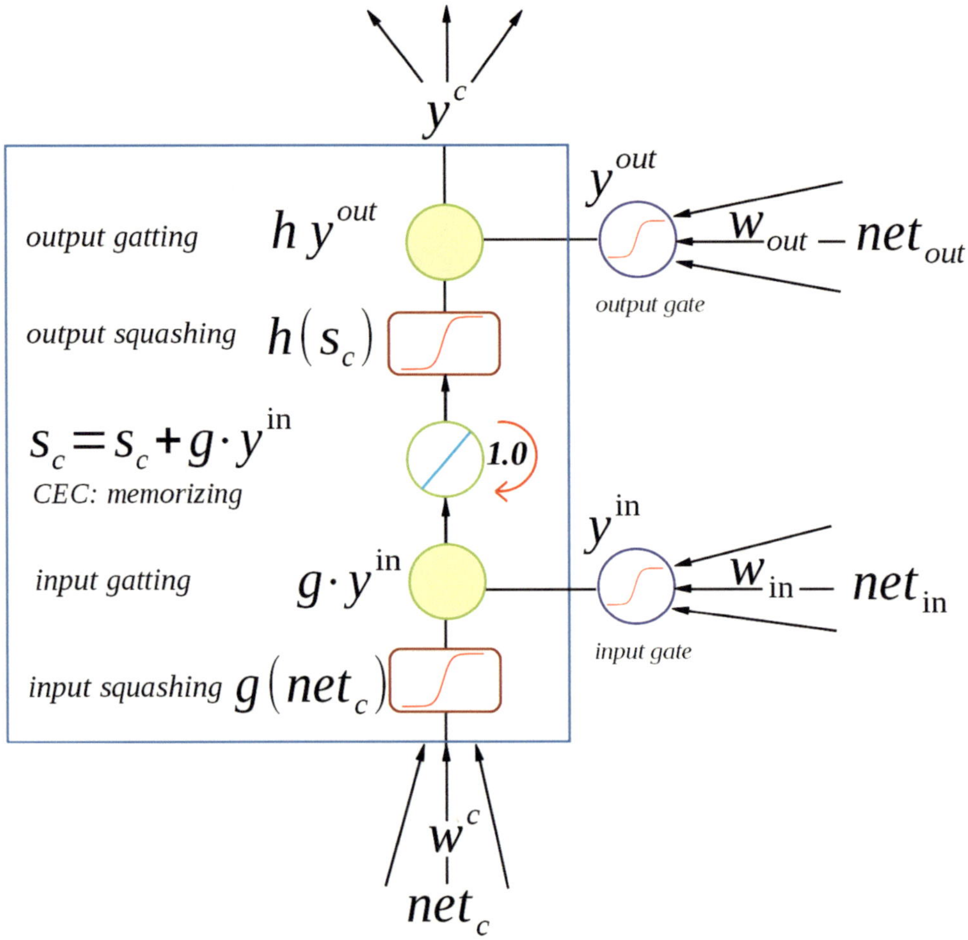

Figure 2. General architecture of a LSTM NN [19].

The principal component analysis (PCA) is a statistical method that has been widely used in several types of research of different scientific areas. Given a set data obtained experimentally, this method allows selecting the most representative variables and, consequently, reducing the dimensionality. For example, nowadays this method is used to perform different tasks such as X-ray fluorescence image analysis [21, 22] to identify objects; classify and extract features from gastric cancer images [23]; determine complex interrelations between patients, diseases and the best treatments for lung cancer [24]; or analyse sets of data obtained from brain magnetic resonance imaging (MRI) [25].

3. Experiment: Materials and samples getting

Biomaterials are considered like mechanically, functionally and physiologically acceptable products used to replicate the function of living tissues in biological systems securely. These products are implanted temporarily or permanently inside a body to try the restoration of the existent effect and, in some cases, tissue regeneration [26].

We cultivated human mesenchymal stem cells 3A6 (CMMh-3A6); it means a lineage of immortalised mesenchymal stem cells, which were given by the Department of Medical Research & Education and Orthopaedics & Traumatology, Veterans General Hospital, Taipei, Taiwan.

We cultivated 4'200.000 CMMh-3A6 cells from x + passages. We made two changes in culture medium and one subcell culture (passage2 or overseeding) per week. These changes were made due to the observed plaques by the inverted microscope; we saw a great confluence (90%) in a relatively short period (approximately between 3 and 4 days).

The biomaterial type I collagen (trade house) was obtained by using a biopsy punch and cutting the biomaterial in shape of 8 mm diameter discs. We arrange Col I sponges in 3 groups of 21 samples each of them. For technical purposes, we call group #1, #2 and #3 like CCO, CCT and CO, respectively.

The 21 samples of group No. 1 (CCO) were type I collagen, CMMh-3A6 cells and commercial osteogenic cell culture medium: hMSC Osteogenic Differentiation BulletKit™ Medium (Lonza, España). The group No. 2 (CCT) had 21 samples formed by CMMh-3A6 cells, type I collagen and cell culture medium DMEM (Dulbecco's modified essential medium). These cells had 1 g/L D-glucose and pyruvate (Gibco, Estados Unidos), 5% glutamax (Gibco) and 10% foetal bovine serum (Gibco). This cell culture medium was seeded over type I collagen biomaterial. Finally, the group N° 3 (CO) had only 21 samples with type I collagen and commercial osteogenic cell culture medium—hMSC Osteogenic Differentiation BulletKit™ Medium (Lonza, España)—but without cells. Therefore, the last group was the group of control.

The experiment lasted 44 days in total, and it was under conditions to replicate human organism (culture oven): pH = 7.4, temperature = 37°C and 5% of CO2. The samples were sent to histomorphology to embed them in paraffin. After that, paraffin was removed from the samples (de-paraffinisation, de-waxing). Later, we stain the samples with haematoxylin and eosin. Finally, we took 2D photographs with electronic microscopy. The result was 60 photos, which were segmented through machine learning algorithms for each group of analysis with a set of binary features. The classification takes into account according to the following characteristics: type I collagen, extracellular matrix, image artefacts and background.

That process requires extraction of attributes to train the system, characteristics that are the base for the learning process. Then, we extract a set of binary images (one per each segmentable attribute), and from these pictures, we get relevant information for detecting these characteristics in any photo.

4. Results

We segmented the images of the three experimental groups (group #1 CCO, group #2 CCT and group #3 CO). The group of control was group #3 because it had only type I collagen and commercial osteogenic cell culture medium without cells: hMSC Osteogenic Differentiation

BulletKit™ Medium (Lonza, España). Groups #2 and #1 contained not only cell culture medium (osteogenic and non-osteogenic, respectively), but also they had mesenchymal stromal cells. Besides, each group had 21 samples. Then, the results we got from the image segmentation with and without the use of a neural network and after the application of generalised linear models (GLM) to the database are:

4.1. Generalised linear models (GLM) without the neural network

In this section, we show up the results we got from the statistical modelling of the data group that was acquired from the image segmentation and before the application of a neural network.

GLM modelling: collagen degradation as regards time + cell culture group—time effects and cell group in the degradation of type I collagen.

With this model, where $\eta = \mu_x = \beta_0 + \beta_1 x_1 \, (Time) + \beta_2 x_2 \, (group)$, μ_x follows a normal distribution. The variance proportion explained in the model (residual deviance) was apparently small (4.0879e-05), and the AIC was 1454.2.

To test $H0{:}\beta_0 = 0$, we use $z = 2.049 \; (p-value = 2.70e-08)$. Consequently, the cell culture group, as regards time, seems to have a meaningful impact on the probability of the type I collagen degradation after time goes (i.e., once the model includes that variable "glm.without.network"). Namely, that model has the best p-value for time and the group and the smallest values for AIC and residual deviance compared to the other proposed models (see **Table 1**).

Next, we display the graphic diagnosis of the model (see **Figure 3**):

The normal QQ-plot shows normalised standard waste. Waste for predicted values is in the left panel. This waste presents a tendency to the mean; therefore, the error independence condition is fulfilled. It means the lower left panel exhibits that collagen degradation (pixels) has a tendency.

The right panel displays how the waste values of the model "glm.without.network" adjust to the regression line of the model, and there are atypical values. Probably, these atypical results belong to the error allowed in this type of experiment, as it is complicated to control shifts that occur due to the intrinsic activity of the cell samples under culture.

To determine the waste normality, we applied the Shapiro–Wilk test, where:

- HO: this sample comes from a normal distribution.
- H1: this sample does not come from a normal distribution.

Coefficients	P-value
(Intercept)	<2e-16***
Time	2.70e-08***
Group	0.0453*

Table 1. Statistical significance of the time and group co-variables in the results of the model without neural network.

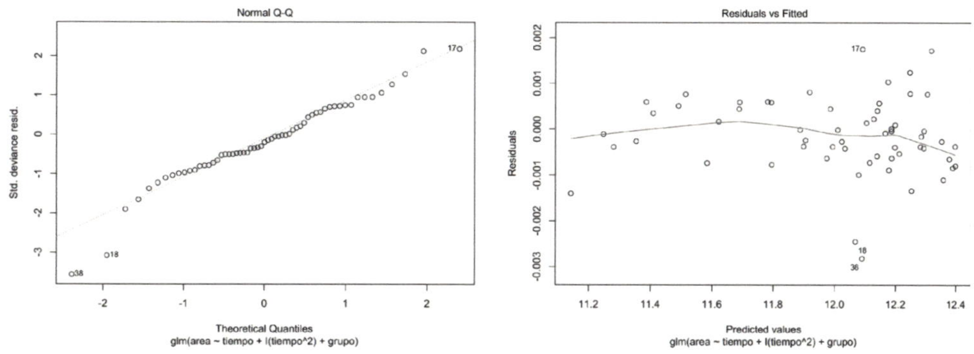

Figure 3. Images of primary control (diagnosis) to the model "glm.Without.Network" of the type I collagen degradation as regards time and cell culture group.

As the obtained p-value (0.0006396) is less than 0.05, we cannot deny that the distribution is normal (**Figure 4**).

Violet tone, as result of haematoxylin and eosin stain, depicts how collagen gradually degrades by time. This colour shows up according to the pixel intensity (from 0 to 255 values) or to the initial amount of collagen. (See **Figure 3**, these images display how the collagen has

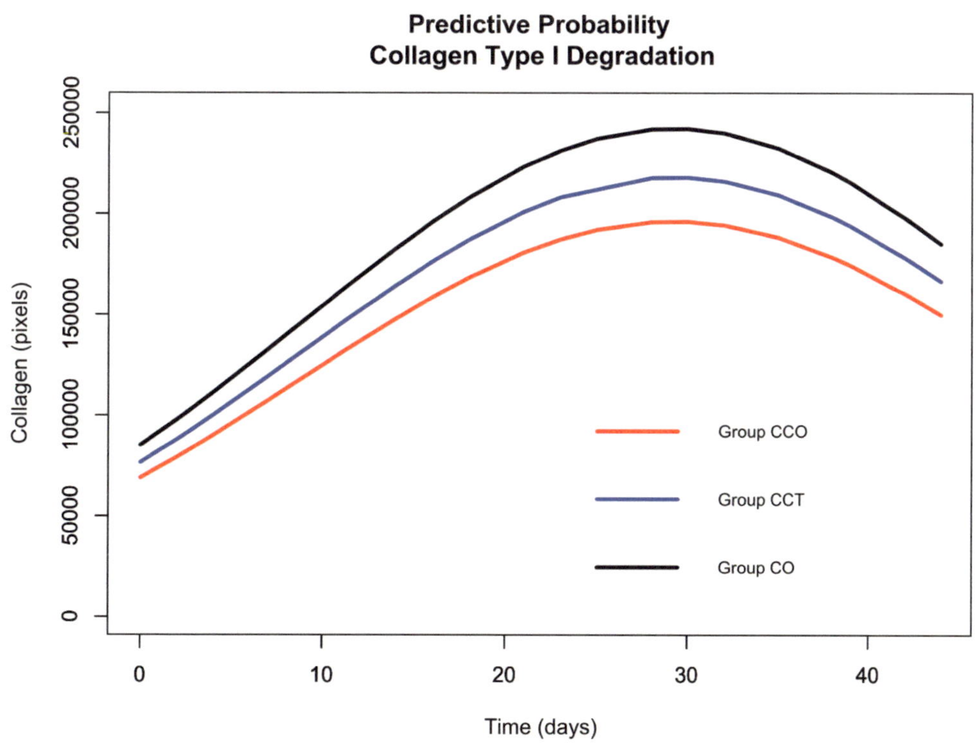

Figure 4. Adjustment of type I collagen degradation according to time and the group through the use of the model "glm.Without.Network" without the neural network. The image displays the prediction of this model for collagen degradation as regards time and according to each group of cell culture (CCO, CCT and CO).

more colour at the beginning and less intensity at the end. Also, the graphics show how the part of the extracellular matrix is more stained than the beginning.) As white is predominant, then the value of pixels is close to 255 (this is the maximum colour for pixels: white). In such manner, this variance of intensity from violet hue to palest hue can be understood as indirect degradation of collagen in pixels as regards time and influenced by it. Then, this figure of the model predictions illustrates, in a particular manner, how this model adjusts better to type I collagen degradation as regards time and the cell culture group.

However, the fall of the curve, in the graphic, points out that after time, the cell activity produces an extracellular matrix (biologic cell activity). This matrix has a colouration darker than the collagen during the degradation process; therefore, it tends to the initial values. To understand this process, see **Figure 5** that depicts the three groups of the sample cells in culture (CCO, CCT and CO) and their colour change. This figure presents the cells at the beginning (T0) and the end (T40) of the experiment and exhibits how the intensity of colour diminishes in the collagen but increases in the extracellular matrix.

To calculate how the probability of collagen degradation changes as regards time and the group, we computed the odds ratio for time (1.074290e+00), the odds ratio for the group (1.111437e+00) and the corresponding intervals of confidence. As the interval of confidence is from 1.051247 to 1.097838e+00 and odds ratio for time is 1.074290e+00, then this value is inside the range. It means if the group variable is included in the model "glm.without.network", then the probabilities of collagen degradation, regarding the time, will increase by 11.6% (0.111).

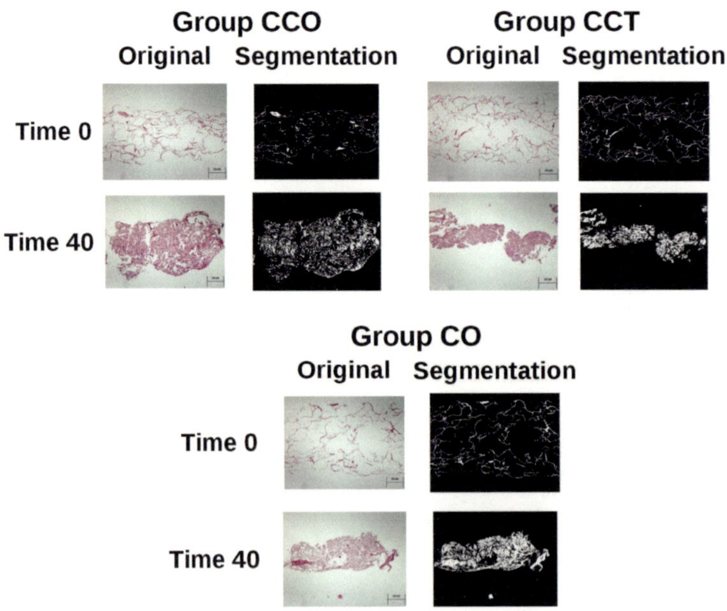

Figure 5. The difference of the colour of type I collagen between time 0 and 40 for the three cell culture groups is shown. Notice how the intensity of haematoxylin-eosin for collagen diminishes, while the tone for extracellular matrix begins to increase. The scale of all images is 300 μm.

http://dx.doi.org/10.5772/intechopen.72982

Therefore, when we include the group in the model "glm.without.network", the time of collagen degradation is associated with an increase of 11.1% in the mean of probabilities for the collagen degradation.

4.2. Generalised linear models (GLM) with the neural network

GLM modelling: collagen degradation as regards time + a group of cell culture—time effects and cell group in the degradation of type I collagen.

With this model, where $\eta = \mu_x = \beta_0 + \beta_1\, x_1\ (Time) + \beta_2\, x_2\ (group)$, μ_x follows a normal distribution. The variance proportion explained in the model (residual deviance) was apparently small (0.00006353), and the AIC was 12,200.

To test $H0{:}\beta_2 = 0$, we use $z = 38.035\ (p-value = 2e-16)$. Consequently, the cell culture group, as regards time, seems to have a meaningful impact on the probability of type I collagen degradation after time goes (i.e., once the model includes that variable "glm.with.network"). Namely, that model has the best p-value for time and the group, and the smallest values for AIC and residual deviance compared to the other proposed models.

Then, the following image shows the graphic diagnosis of the model (see **Figure 6**).

The normal QQ-plot shows normalised standard waste. Waste for predicted values is in the left panel. This waste presents a tendency to the mean; therefore, the error independence condition is fulfilled. Thus, collagen degradation (pixels) has a tendency.

The right panel displays how the waste values of the model "glm.with.network" adjust to the regression line of the model, and there are atypical values. Probably, these atypical results, same as the model without red, could be due to the error allowed in this type the experiment. As we explained previously, it is complicated to control shifts that occur due to the intrinsic activity of the cell samples under culture.

To determine the waste normality, we applied the Shapiro–Wilk test, where:

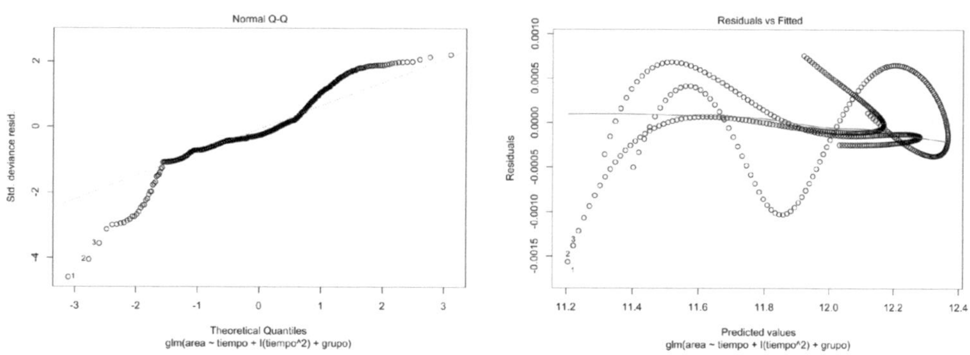

Figure 6. Graphics of primary control (diagnosis) to the model "glm.With.Network" for type I collagen degradation as regards time and cell culture group.

- HO: this sample comes from a normal distribution.
- H1: this sample does not come from a normal distribution.

As the obtained p-value (3.414e-14) is less than 0.05, we cannot deny that the distribution is normal.

Figure 7 shows how the model with the neural network, as **Figure 3** does with the model without the neural network, represents the prediction of collagen degradation as regards time and the group. **Figure 7** depicts a softer behaviour about the recovering of violet tone that belongs to the colour of extracellular matrix that is produced by cell culture in their last days as we explained with **Figure 4**. It means the colour shows up according to the intensity of the values of pixels (0–255) or to the initial value of collagen. Then, the violet tone, as a result of haematoxylin and eosin stain, shows how collagen gradually degrades by time (see **Figure 7**; these images display how the collagen has more colour at the beginning and less intensity at the end. Also, the graphics show how the part of the extracellular matrix is more stained than the beginning). As white is predominant, then the value of pixels is close to 255 (this is the maximum colour for pixels: white). In such manner, this variance of intensity from violet hue to palest hue can be understood as indirect degradation of collagen in pixels as regards time and influenced by it. Then, this figure of the model predictions illustrates, in a particular manner, how this model adjusts better to type I collagen degradation as regards time and the cell culture group.

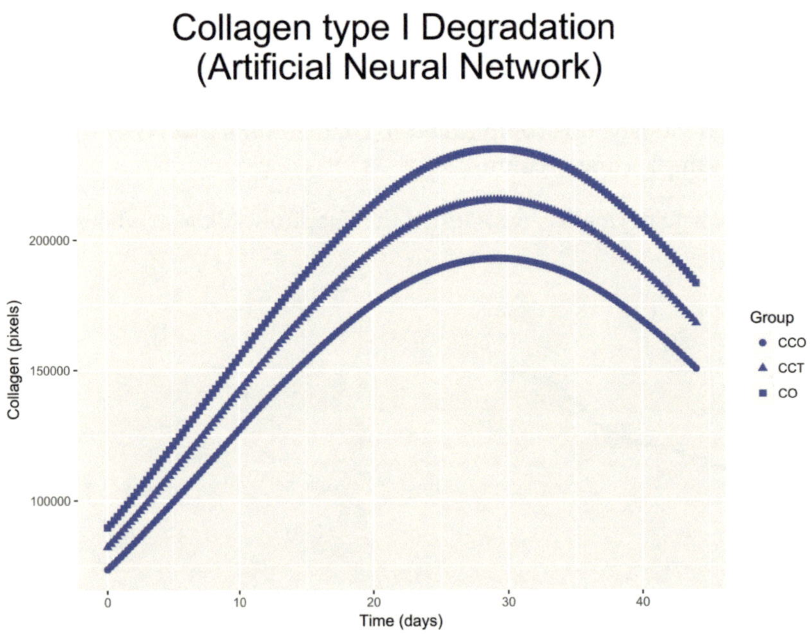

Figure 7. Adjustment of type I collagen degradation according to time and the group through the use of model "glm. With.Network" with the neural network. The image displays the prediction of this model for collagen degradation as regards time and in function of each cell culture group (CCO, CCT and CO).

Nonetheless, as we stated before, the biological behaviour of the cell culture is the same. This conduct means the fallen of the curve, in the graphic, shows up that after time and the cell activity produces an extracellular matrix (biologic cell activity). This matrix has a colouration darker than the collagen during the degradation process; therefore, it tends to the initial values. To understand this process, see **Figure 7** that depicts the three groups of sample cells in culture (CCO, CCT and CO) and their colour change. This figure presents the cells at the beginning (T0) and the end (T40) of the experiment and exhibits how the intensity of colour diminishes in the collagen but increases in the extracellular matrix.

To calculate how the probability of collagen degradation changes as regards time and the group, we computed the odds ratio for time (1.068284e+00), the odds ratio for the group (1.116472e+00) and the corresponding intervals of confidence. As the interval of confidence is from 1.064654e+00 to 1.071926e+00 and odds ratio for time is 1.074290e+00, then this value is inside the range. The odds ratio for the group is 1.116472e+00, value that is also inside the interval of confidence (1.085327e+00, 1.148511e+00). It means if the group variable is included in the model "glm.with.network", then the probabilities of collagen degradation, regarding the time, will increase by 11.6% (0.111).

Hence, when we include the group in the model "glm.with.network", the time of collagen degradation is associated with an increase of 11.6% in the mean of probabilities for the collagen degradation.

4.3. PCA applied to a set of images acquired by means of optical microscopy

In this section, we will describe the strategy followed with the aim of determining the relations among variables or descriptors obtained through optical microscopy from the calibrated images. For our study, we have worked with the following variables (descriptors): area, perimeter, diameter, eccentricity or roundness, mean intensity, centroid (x,y), skew and kurtosis. Each of the aforementioned variables can be related to physical variables in the statistical models. In our case, with the support of the PCA method, we want to determine how the area varies with respect to time, considering that several groups of study with specific characteristics exist.

In order to establish points of comparison for the descriptors, we used on each group of images the machine learning approach described in Section 2. The mathematical backgrounds as well as the details of the method followed (PCA) are described in several researches published in the last years [27–30].

In this analysis, we have established three groups of study, where the collagen is present in each of them. Through the image analysis and machine learning approach are followed, we were able to define regions of interest and extract the corresponding descriptor for each value of time. In this way, the information matrix of each group of images is defined as follows:

a. Cells + collagen + osteogenic culture medium (CCO).

b. Cells + collagen + non-osteogenic medium (CCT).

c. Collagen + osteogenic culture medium, (CO), has no cells (control group).

With the aim of applying the PCA analysis, we started from the hypothesis of time dependence (0–40 days) in which determining the area variation is possible. The area "variation" in which determining aspects such as presence of extracellular matrix due to the collagen degradation, the change of pixel intensity as time goes by or the geometric shape that adopts the group in study according to time is possible is part of the analysis proposal as well as of the statistical model to interpret the images according to the group and time. Likewise, as a complementary part, we propose that groups in the analysis have a relevant weight in the collagen degradation.

The following analysis shows how the area classified according to the groups CO, CCT and CCO changes. We have used labels with the following structure: **XX_T**, where **XX** represents the group and **T** the time. For example, the label **CO_14** is the label for group **CO** and for the day (time variable) **14**.

From the principal components extracted in the CO group, we selected the three most representative that have a cumulative variance of 80.60%. In **Figure 8**, the weights of the components selected are represented, and it is possible to see that the variables of the right side have a positive correlation. However, the variables standard deviation (StdDeev) and Round have a negative weight (negative correlation). In this line, it is possible to establish that a positive correlation between time and the descriptors of the right side of the figure exists. This means that area grows when the variables of the right side grow.

Figure 9 shows a graphic dispersion (biplot) of the data obtained for the groups CO, CCO and CCT in the 40 days of experimentation (two principal components). Likewise, it is possible to see small groups far from the centre.

Figure 8 presents the groups under study and the corresponding descriptors. In the same way, in **Figures 9** and **10**, it is possible to see how the first two components explain the 68.4% of data. The standard deviation is in the region of control groups during the first 3 days. On the other hand, all the variables placed on the right side of the principal component are positively correlated. In the same way, the groups that can be observed are those of control CO_T, with values greater than 30 days, CCO with values greater than 20 days and CCT with values greater than 15 days.

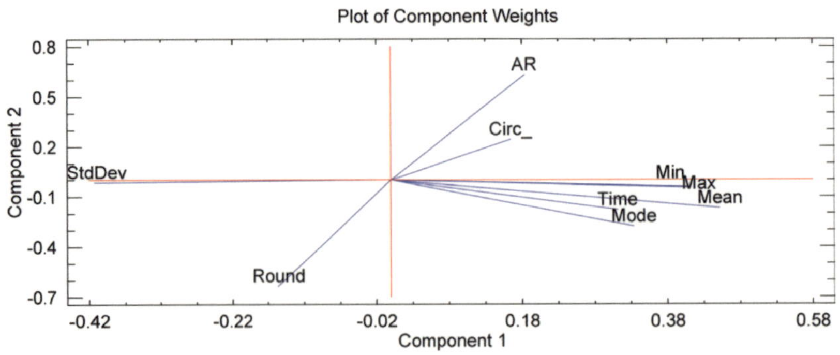

Figure 8. Plot of component weights obtained for CO control group.

http://dx.doi.org/10.5772/intechopen.72982

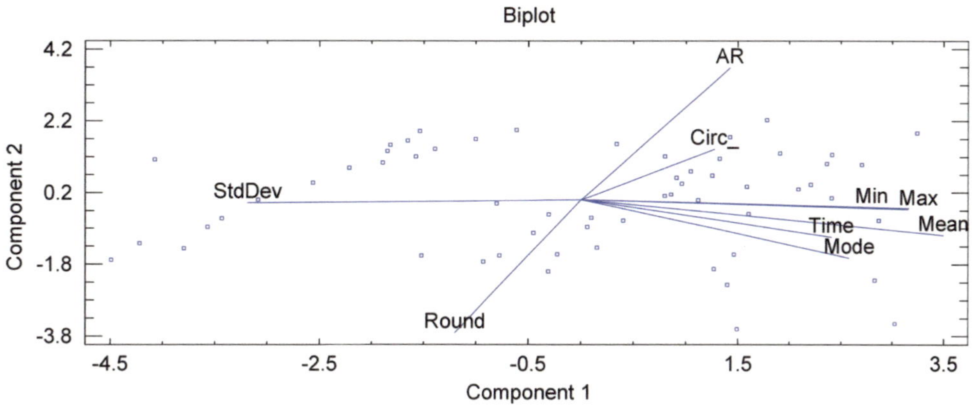

Figure 9. Biplot for descriptors and dispersion values.

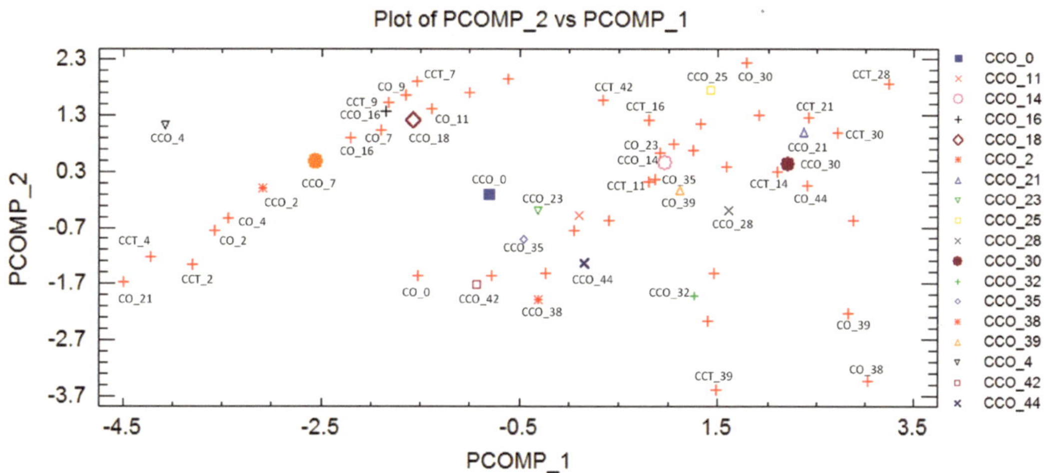

Figure 10. Plot of principal components enhances CO, CCO and CCT groups.

5. Conclusions

GLM models allow greater flexibility in the statistical modelling. Namely, we can observe how neural networks support the improvement of p-values both for group co-variables like for the time. Neural networks also enhance probabilities of collagen degradation (see **Tables 2–5**) as it changes from 11.1% when a neural network is not applied to 11.6%. In the same manner, waste of the model is presumably smaller 4.0879e-05 than 0.00006353 without the neural network. It is necessary to point out that the AIC value is slightly sacrificed when the neural network is applied. However, this loss is part of this implementation; and despite this, in a general view, the use of a neural network has allowed a better adjust of the model.

Variables	IC	
	2.5%	97.5%
(Intercept)	47839.657556	8.052878e+04
Time	1.051247	1.097838e+00
Group	1.004596	1.229641e+00

Table 2. Confidence intervals to the parameters of the model "glm.Without.Network".

Coefficients	P-value
(Intercept)	<2e-16***
Time	<2e-16***
Group	1.09e-13*

Table 3. Statistical significance of the time and group co-variables in the results of the model with neural network.

Variables	IC	
	2.5%	97.5%
(Intercept)	7.115130e+04	7.591534e+04
Time	1.064654e+00	1.071926e+00
Group	1.085327e+00	1.148511e+00

Table 4. Confidence ranges to the parameters of the model "glm.With.Network".

Coefficients	GLM without neural network		GLM with neural network	
	P-value	Odds ratio	P-value	Odds ratio
(Intercept)	<2e-16	6.206826e+04	<2e-16	7.349473e+04
Time	2.70e-08	1.074290e+00	<2e-16	1.068284e+00
Group	0.0453	1.111437e+00	1.09e-13	1.116472e+00
AIC	0.00006353		4.0879e-05	
Residual deviance	0 12,200		1454.2	

Table 5. Comparison for goodness of fit of parameters between GLM with and without the application of a neural network.

The proposal that was established about the dependence of the area with respect to time, the study group and the descriptors obtained through image analysis will help to establish a mathematical model to explain the variation of the area. In the method used, we observed groupings that allow us to interpret similarities and highly positive or negative correlations with respect to time and the study group. An important aspect to take into account when deciding what type of neural network and the types of filters to use can both define the thresholds in the images and eliminate information that is not representative.

On the other hand, the LSTM neural network allows predicting a presumptive value of the level of collagen degradation for those instants of time for which information is not available (features, measurements, etc.). All this is feasible since the neural network has a recurrent structure and a short-term memory, whereby can infer better what are the possible values that will have to increase the time. Similarly, we have observed in this work that neural networks of this type can work with a long number of samples to train the system and also support optimal time window size variables.

Acknowledgements

This project was partially funded by the "Ministerio de Educación y Ciencia MTM2014-59543-P"; also by the "Secretaría Nacional de Educación Superior, Ciencia, Tecnología e Innovación del Ecuador (SENESCYT)"; by the "Catedra UNESCO UPS Cuenca-Ecuador, Grupo de Investigación en Inteligencia Artificial y Tecnologías de Asistencia (GIATA) Cuenca-Ecuador"; and by the "Grupo de Investigación en Materiales (GiMaT) Universidad Politéncia Salesiana, Cuenca-Ecuador".

Author details

Yaroslava Robles-Bykbaev[1,2], Salvador Naya[3], Silvia Díaz Prado[1], Daniel Calle-López[4], Vladimir Robles-Bykbaev[4*], Luis Garzón-Muñóz[5], Clara Sanjurjo Rodríguez[1] and Javier Tarrío Saavedra[3]

*Address all correspondence to: vrobles@ups.edu.ec

1 Grupo de Investigación en Terapia Celular y Medicina Regenerativa (TCMR), Departamento de Medicina, PROTERM, MODES, Universidade da Coruña, España

2 GI-IATa, Universidad Politécnica Salesiana, Cuenca, Ecuador

3 Departamento de Matemáticas, Grupo MODES, Universidad de la Coruña, Ferrol, La Coruña, Spain

4 GI-IATa, Cátedra UNESCO Tecnologías de apoyo para la Inclusión Educativa, Universidad Politécnica Salesiana, Cuenca, Ecuador

5 GI-MAT, Grupo de Investigación en Nuevos Materiales y Procesos de Transformación, Universidad Politécnica Salesiana, Cuenca, Ecuador

References

[1] Santana J. Predicción de series temporales con redes neuronales: una aplicación a la inflación colombiana. Revista Colombiana de Estadística. 2006;**29**(1):77-92

[2] Chen Y, Zhou S, Li Q. Mathematical modeling of degradation for bulk-erosive polymers: Applications in tissue engineering scaffolds and drug delivery systems. Acta Biomaterialia. 2011;**7**(3):1140-1149. DOI: 10.1016/j.actbio.2010.09.038

[3] Hoque ME, Yong LC, Ian P. Mathematical modeling on degradation of 3d tissue engineering scaffold materials. Regenerative Research. 2012;**1**(1):58-59

[4] Pitt CG, Zhong-wei G. Modification of the rates of chain cleavage of poly (ϵ-caprolactone) and related polyesters in the solid state. Journal of Controlled Release. 1987;**4**(4):283-292. DOI: 10.1016/0168-3659(87)90020-4

[5] Sandino C, Planell JA, Lacroix D. A finite element study of mechanical stimuli in scaffolds for bone tissue engineering. Journal of Biomechanics. 2008;**41**(5):1005-1014. DOI: 10.1016/j.jbiomech.2007.12.011

[6] Hastie T, Tibshirani R, Friedman J. The elements of statistical learning: Data mining, inference, and prediction. Biometrics. 2002

[7] Bocanegra G, Domínguez J. Modelos lineales generalizadas en el contexto de diseño robusto. In: Instituto Nacional de Estadística, Geografía e Informática, editors. Memorias XX Foro Nacional de Estadística. México:2006

[8] Wood S. Generalized Additive Models: An Introduction with R. CRC Press; 2006

[9] Meijering E. Cell segmentation: 50 years down the road [life sciences]. IEEE Signal Processing Magazine. 2012;**29**(5):140-145. DOI: 10.1109/MSP.2012.2204190

[10] Kasprowicz R, Suman R, O'Toole P. Characterising live cell behaviour: Traditional label-free and quantitative phase imaging approaches. The International Journal of Biochemistry & Cell Biology. 2017;**84**:89-95. DOI: 10.1016/j.biocel.2017.01.004

[11] Alanazi H, Canul AJ, Garman A, Quimby J, Vasdekis AE. Robust microbial cell segmentation by optical-phase thresholding with minimal processing requirements. Cytometry Part A. 2017;**91**(5):443-449. DOI: 10.1002/cyto.a.23099

[12] Grys BT, Lo DS, Sahin N, Kraus OZ, Morris Q, Boone C, Andrews BJ. Machine learning and computer vision approaches for phenotypic profiling. Journal of Cell Biology. 2016. jcb-201610026. DOI: 10.1083/jcb.201610026

[13] Criminisi A, Shotton J, Konukoglu E. Decision forests: A unified framework for classification, regression, density estimation, manifold learning and semi-supervised learning. Foundations and Trends® in Computer Graphics and Vision. 2012;**7**(2-3):81-227. DOI: 10.1561/0600000035

[14] Budde MD, Frank JA. Examining brain microstructure using structure tensor analysis of histological sections. NeuroImage. 2012;**63**(1):1-10. DOI: 10.1016/j.neuroimage.2012.06.042

[15] Arganda-Carreras I, Kaynig V, Rueden C, Eliceiri KW, Schindelin J, Cardona A, Sebastian Seung H. Trainable Weka Segmentation: A machine learning tool for microscopy pixel classification. Bioinformatics. 2017;btx180. DOI: 10.1093/bioinformatics/btx180

[16] Schindelin J, Rueden CT, Hiner MC, Eliceiri KW. The ImageJ ecosystem: An open platform for biomedical image analysis. Molecular Reproduction and Development. 2015;**82**(7-8):518-529. DOI: 10.1002/mrd.22489

[17] Sobel I. An isotropic 3×3 image gradient operator. Machine vision for three-dimensional scenes. 1990:376-379

[18] Ma X, Tao Z, Wang Y, Yu H, Wang Y. Long short-term memory neural network for traffic speed prediction using remote microwave sensor data. Transportation Research Part C: Emerging Technologies. 2015;**54**:187-197. DOI: 10.1016/j.trc.2015.03.014

[19] Gers F. Long Short-Term Memory in Recurrent Neural Networks. Unpublished PhD dissertation. Lausanne, Switzerland: Ecole Polytechnique Fédérale de Lausanne; 2001

[20] Cao J, Ng ES, McNaughton D, Stanley EG, Elefanty AG, Tobin MJ, Heraud P. The characterisation of pluripotent and multipotent stem cells using Fourier transform infrared microspectroscopy. International Journal of Molecular Sciences. 2013;**14**(9):17453-17456. DOI: 10.3390/ijms140917453

[21] Aida S, Matsuno T, Hasegawa T, Tsuji K. Application of principal component analysis for improvement of X-ray fluorescence images obtained by polycapillary-based micro-XRF technique. Nuclear Instruments and Methods in Physics Research Section B: Beam Interactions with Materials and Atoms. 2017. DOI: 10.1016/j.nimb.2017.03.123

[22] Egan CK, Jacques SDM, Cernik RJ. Multivariate analysis of hyperspectral hard X-ray images. X-Ray Spectrometry. 2013;**42**(3):151-157. DOI: 10.1002/xrs.2448

[23] Gan L, Lv W, Zhang X, Meng X. Improved PCA+ LDA applies to gastric cancer image classification process. Physics Procedia. 2012;**24**:1689-1695. DOI: 10.1016/j.phpro.2012.02.249

[24] Juma K, He M, Zhao Y. Lung cancer detection and analysis using data mining techniques, principal component analysis and artificial neural network. American Scientific Research Journal for Engineering, Technology, and Sciences (ASRJETS). 2016;**26**(3):254-265

[25] Smith SM, Hyvärinen A, Varoquaux G, Miller KL, Beckmann CF. Group-PCA for very large fMRI datasets. NeuroImage. 2014;**101**:738-749. DOI: 10.1016/j.neuroimage.2014.07.051

[26] Ballester A, Sueiro-Fernández J, editors. Biomateriales y Sustitutos Óseos en Traumatología y Cirugía Ortopédica. 1st ed. Cádiz: Universidad de Cádiz; 2011

[27] Hervé A, Williams LJ. Principal component analysis. Wiley Interdisciplinary Reviews: Computational Statistics. 2010;**2**(4):433-459

[28] Ghosh A, Barman S. Application of Euclidean distance measurement and principal component analysis for gene identification. Gene. 2016;**583**:112-120

[29] Godoy JL, Vega JR, Marchetti JL. Relationships between PCA and PLS-regression. Chemometrics and Intelligent Laboratory Systems. 2014;**130**:182-191

[30] Han Y, Feng X-C, Baciu G. Variational and PCA based natural image segmentation. Pattern Recognition. 2013;**46**:1971-1984

Chapter 7

Neural Network Configurations Analysis for Multilevel Speech Pattern Recognition System with Mixture of Experts

Washington Luis Santos Silva,
Priscila Lima Rocha and
Allan Kardec Duailibe Barros Filho

Additional information is available at the end of the chapter

http://dx.doi.org/10.5772/intechopen.72575

Abstract

This chapter proposes to analyze two configurations of neural networks to compose the expert set in the development of a multilevel speech signal pattern recognition system of 30 commands in the Brazilian Portuguese language. Then, multilayer perceptron (MLP) and learning vector quantization (LVQ) networks have their performances verified during the training, validation and test stages in the speech signal recognition, whose patterns are given by two-dimensional time matrices, result from mel-cepstral coefficients coding by the discrete cosine transform (DCT). In order to avoid the pattern separability problem, the patterns are modified by a nonlinear transformation to a high-dimensional space through a suitable set of Gaussian radial base functions (GRBF). The performance of MLP and LVQ experts is improved and configurations are trained with few examples of each modified pattern. Several combinations were performed for the neural network topologies and algorithms previously established to determine the network structures with the best hit and generalization results.

Keywords: automatic speech recognition, neural network, DCT models, multilayer perceptron, learning vector quantization, Gaussian radial basis function, mixture of experts, multiclass task

1. Introduction

The human ability to recognize patterns involves the sophisticated neural and cognitive systems that, from the accumulation of experience on a given environment, can extract the relevant characteristics that shape a given situation and store that information for using when there is a need. This ability makes the decision-making process much faster. Thus, many researchers work to understand the biological pattern recognition mechanism of human for the development of computational algorithms for learning machines that are increasingly robust for use in practical applications [1, 2].

Pattern recognition is a scientific area that aims to classify patterns, also called instances or examples, according to their characteristics that form a multidimensional space (space of characteristics) in distinct sets, which are called classes or labels or categories so that an action can subsequently be better performed according to each category. Since pattern examples are needed to obtain the distinct sets, the pattern recognition process involves a statistical analysis to obtain the models, as well as the insertion or not of the expert knowledge in the application domain, which can characterize a supervised or unsupervised classification, respectively.

The task of speech signals recognition is challenging, since the signals obtained in the speech production process are highly variable, due to the great amount of attributes of the human speech, besides the specific characteristics involved in speech, such as environment noise and the properties of each language. The development of systems based on speech signal pattern recognition is one of the practical applications in using pattern classification. Indeed, speech is the most natural and expressive mode in human communication, and thus methodologies for analysis and recognition of speech signal have been developed and influenced by the knowledge of how this task is solved by humans [1, 2].

Currently, speech recognition system applications cover a wide area of domains such as dictation tools in text editors, automatic answering services in telephone exchanges, hands-free car-based systems, people with motor disabilities, mobile interface via speech, ticket reservation applications in airlines, security systems by speech identification, and so on. Then, the pattern recognition task involves different steps and its efficient execution guarantees greater accuracy. The development stages required of a pattern recognition system are as follows [3–5]: data acquisition, preprocessing and extraction of the most relevant characteristics; data representation and definition of the classifier for decision-making.

The techniques of digital signal processing and digital signal coding are the tools that support the representation of the patterns. Advances in digital speech processing methodologies allow the maximum use of speech signal attributes for use in the speaker or speech recognition, depending on the application [6, 7]. In addition to the need of good attributes extraction that represents the patterns to be recognized, it is also important that they are coded in a reduced number of parameters. Indeed, the more information you add to the system, the greater the probability of good results. However, this relationship must be taken with caution because this increase in data expands configuration complexity and computational cost of the system. For this reason, appropriate digital signal coding techniques contribute significantly to determine the equilibrium between number of parameters and computational cost [8].

After speech signal coding process and obtainment of representative patterns, the recognition task can be performed efficiently using algorithms of patterns identification, according to the third step mentioned. These algorithms (also called classifiers) develop models that generalize each category or class belonging to the system from patterns set (called training set). The classification algorithm is responsible for establishing relationship between patterns and their respective categories. Then, in testing stage, the classifier can determine to which category the new pattern belongs. A crucial point for classifiers is to determine the decision boundaries between each class, that is, to specify the model that allows the identification of new data. It becomes more complex as the number of classes increases. However, many of classification methodologies were developed based on solving the problem of two classes, because of the dichotomy algorithms (called binary classifiers). In reality, it shows that classification problems require solution for more than two classes (multiclass) [9, 10].

The use of only one compact structure classifier to solve multiclass task can increase computational cost and generalization capacity of the classifier. Overcoming this problem and from the principle of *divide and conquer*, the ensemble method aims to fragment the characteristics space so that a set of simpler topology classifiers learn the specificities of each subspace. Finally, the classification result is given by individual results or by choice from result of one of the classifiers topology, according to a certain rule hence, the result of the multiclass task is obtained from simpler classifiers [11, 12].

Among patterns identification algorithms that can be used in the approach of ensembles, the neural networks configure as high potential classifiers. Neural networks are intelligent computational algorithms that simulate the behavior of biological neurons. It results in a robust system with low rate of recognition errors. The robustness provided in the classification task is a result of the inherent adaptive characteristic of neural networks, allowing them to be able to learn complex patterns and trends present in the set of data available for identification, changing rapidly to modifications in the environment in which is inserted [13–15]. The neural networks have several configurations for solution of the most problems and among such configurations with the best results in solving pattern classification problems are multilayer perceptron (MLP) and the learning vector quantization (LVQ) [16, 17].

2. Theoretical fundamentals

2.1. Multiclass learning

Bayes' statistic decision theory or Bayes' decision theory is the classic fundament for mathematically defining the task of pattern recognition. This approach expresses the problem solution in probabilistic terms. Classifiers projected from Bayes' decision theory constitute optimum classifiers, in which new classification approaches can take them as a reference for comparison of results. The classification rule based on Bayes' theory can be better understood when it is analyzed to make a decision between two classes. This definition can be generalized for multiclass task solution. Then, it is possible for calculating a posteriori probability of class γ_i to occurring when input vector x is presented through Bayes' formula given by Eq. (1):

$$P(\gamma_i \mid x) = \frac{p(x \mid \gamma_i)P(\gamma_i)}{p(x)} \tag{1}$$

where, γ_i is ith class defined in problem; $P(\gamma_i \mid x)$ is *a posteriori* probability of γ_i class; $p(x \mid \gamma_i)$ is the joint distribution of pattern x into γ_i class; $P(\gamma_i)$ is the *priori* probability of γ_i class; $p(x)$ is the probability density function. Considering the classification in more than two classes, that is, when the objective is to discriminate the feature vector x in one of C classes in set $\zeta = \{\gamma_1, \ldots, \gamma_C\}$, the conditional probability of each class is obtained by the Bayes' formula (2):

$$P(\gamma \mid \boldsymbol{x}) = \{P(\gamma_1 \mid \boldsymbol{x}), \ldots, P(\gamma_C \mid \boldsymbol{x})\} \tag{2}$$

Then, according to general Bayes decision rule, the vector x is allocated to the most probability class, given by (3):

$$\hat{\gamma} = \underset{\gamma_i \in \zeta}{argmax}\ \hat{P}(\gamma_i \mid \boldsymbol{x}) \tag{3}$$

Despite Bayesian mathematical formalism, there is a great difficulty in practical applications due to estimation of the quantities on right side of Eq. (1). This difficulty increases when the number of estimates in a multiclass problem must be defined simultaneously with high accuracy, since the boundaries among different classes may not be well defined. Thus, new methodologies are proposed to obtain more robust results in multiclass tasks [7, 18].

2.2. Speech recognition systems

Speech recognition systems extract significant characteristics of the speech signal to obtain a pattern that represents this signal and classify it into a class target space defined in recognition project. A class is a group of patterns that have similar characteristics. The purpose of speech recognition allows that these systems are divided into three ways: speaker recognition, language identification and word recognition. Speaker recognition systems are those whose focus is the recognition of the speaker who pronounced a certain word or sentence among different individuals. For identification of language, the purpose of the recognition system is to determine in which language that word or sentence is pronounced. Finally, the word recognition has the interest in identify which word or sentence was pronounced. It has the division into two different forms when the objective of the speech recognition system is to distinguish the spoken word or sentence: speaker-dependent word recognition and speaker-independent word recognition. The first one, it has the trained system to identify the word that was spoken by a specific individual. In the second case, the system identifies word or sentence spoken by people different from those used during the training because it is not important who spoke the word. Besides question of speaker dependence or not, word recognition can be accomplished through isolated words or continuous speech. In first case, it is necessary to have an interval between each word. This is done to have a clear distinction from start to finish of the word, avoiding effect of the coarticulation that causes change in the way of pronouncing the sounds. For continuous speech case, the speaker pronounces on natural way, and consequently, it is difficult to distinguish the beginning and end of the word, causing word concatenation. Continuous speech recognition is more complex because there is no pause between one word and another, generating a single sound. Systems that work with this form of recognition are based on smaller units of the word, such as syllables, phonemes, diphones, triphones, and so on [19, 20].

2.3. Radial basis function

Radial basis functions are important tools in modeling of classification and prediction tasks. They comprise a particular class of functions that have a monotonically increase or decrease response with distance from the origin or a central point, such that $\Phi(x) = \Phi(\|x\|)$ or $\Phi(x, \mu) = \Phi(\|x - \mu\|)$, respectively. In general, the norm used in radial basis functions is the Euclidean distance, but other distance functions may be used. Mathematically, a function Φ: $\mathbb{R}^s \rightarrow \mathbb{R}$ is said radial if there is a univariate function, φ: $[0, \infty) \rightarrow \mathbb{R}$ such that (4):

$$\Phi(x) = \varphi(r) \tag{4}$$

where $r = \|x - \mu\|$ and $\|\cdot\|$ is some norm in $\mathbb{R}^S$; Euclidean norm is usually used. Gaussian radial basis function is the most function used among radial functions, computed as (5):

$$\varphi(r) = e^{-\frac{r^2}{2\sigma^2}} \tag{5}$$

This function is defined by c parameter that defines Gaussian center and σ^2 represents the variance, which characterizes the base widening of the curve and indicates how dispersed a vector x in analysis is in relation to center μ. These parameters may be obtained from the data that belong to the problem to be modeled. Radial basis functions are used to make nonlinear mapping between two feature spaces. Thus, in pattern classification problems, for example, given a set χ of N patterns, $x = \{x_1, x_2, \ldots, x_N\}$ of m_0-dimension, where each one of these vectors is assigned to one of two classes, χ_1 and χ_2, if these patterns cannot be linearly separated in the original dimensional space, a set of radial basis functions can be used to map in a space that allows this separation. Then, each pattern x of the set χ is defined as new vector, where each element is represented by response of radial basis function set $\{\varphi_i(x) \mid i = 1, 2, \ldots, m_1\}$, applied to vector x as (6):

$$\Phi(x) = \left[\varphi_1(x), \varphi_2(x), \ldots, \varphi_{m_1}(x)\right]^T \tag{6}$$

The vector $\Phi(x)$ maps the vectors from m_0-dimensional input space into a new m_1-dimensional space. For the classification of complex patterns, the increase in radial basis function number creates a space of high dimensionality that increases the probability of data linear separation in this new space, making classification problem simpler. This property is supported by Cover's separability theorem that demonstrate how pattern classification problem in a high-dimensional space is more probable to be linearly separable than in low-dimensional space [21].

2.4. Neural networks

Artificial neural networks (ANNs) are systems whose computational structure is based on how the human brain processes information from environment. Also known as a connectionist model or distributed parallel processing, the ANNs arose after presentation of the simplified neuron by McCulloch and Pitts in 1943 [14, 15]. ANNs constitute distributed parallel systems composed of simple processing units (neurons) that calculate certain mathematical (usually nonlinear) functions. These units are arranged in one or more layers and interconnected by a large number of connections, usually unidirectional. In most models, these connections are associated with weights, which store the knowledge represented in the model and weighted the information received from inputs to each neuron in the network [22]. Among attractions for the use of ANNs in problem solutions, the main ones are their ability to learn through examples presented to them and to generalize the information learned. Other characteristics that further enhance its use are: possibility of considering the nonlinear behavior of the physical phenomena responsible for generating the input data, requirement for few statistical knowledge about the environment which the network is inserted and knowledge represented by ANN structure itself and by its activation state [23].

2.5. Ensemble methods

Based on *divide and conquer* principle widely used in engineering, the ensemble method partitions a problem in subspaces, where each subspace is designated for simple expert algorithm to learn the characteristics of each partition. This way, the individual response of each expert contributes to final response of the problem, reducing the learning algorithm complexity. Also called multiclass system, this approach uses classifiers with simpler topologies and few adjustable parameters than if a single classify structure was used to solve the same task. Another advantage presented by this method is the decrease in the training time, since the training time of a large topological structure will be probably greater than the training time of several experts in parallel. The simplicity in expert structure also avoids super adjustment of data because when it has a large number of free parameters to be adjusted in relation to training set size, the risk of over fitting increases. The most common architecture of ensemble method has a classifiers set that learns the training data characteristics and they represent classifier base. Several learning algorithms, such as neural networks, can form this base. Normally, the base is formed by only one type of classifier, keeping the ensemble structure homogeneous; despite that, other methodologies may adopt different classifiers to form the base, that is, the ensemble become heterogeneous. There are three variations of ensemble approach and expert mixture is mostly used in neural networks area. Expert mix strategy uses simple sets of parametric model that learns task subspaces and the definition of decision rules that provide a general solution. In pattern classification tasks, a new sample may be classified by ensemble method in two ways: (1) it combines classifier outputs, according to certain procedure to obtain the final response in classification stage and (2) only the response of one classifier is taken as the final response, according to some selection criterion [24, 25].

3. Analysis methodology

In face of the theoretical fundamentals described, it is presented a multilevel classification approach using radial basis functions and artificial neural networks expert set for multiclass task solution represented by locutions in the Brazilian Portuguese language from following commands: "zero" (zero), "um" (one), "dois" (two), "três" (three), "quatro" (four), "cinco" (five), "seis" (six), "sete" (seven), "oito" (eight), "nove" (nine), "abaixo" (below), "abrir" (open), "acima" (up), "aumentar" (increase), "desligar" (turn off), "diminuir" (decrease), "direita" (right), "esquerda" (left), "fechar" (close), "finalizar" (finish), "iniciar" (start), "ligar" (turn on), "máximo" (maximum), médio" (medium), "mínimo" (minimum), "para trás" (back), "para frente" (forward), "parar" (stop), "repousar" (rest) and "salvar" (save).

Speech signal coding, which uses the mel-cepstral coefficients and the discrete cosine transform (DCT), provides patterns consisting of a reduced number of parameters obtained in speech signal preprocessing step by generating two-dimensional time matrices of order 2, 3 and 4. These matrices reproduce the global and local speech signal variations in time as well as the spectral envelope. Then, the original feature space is formed from two-dimensional time matrices transformed to column vectors, maintaining the alignment time of the extracted mel-cepstral coefficients.

A set of 30 Gaussian radial basis functions were modeled properly to transforming the primary feature space in a new high dimensional nonlinear space in order to increase the probability of linear separation of categories. This strategy makes easier the classification process, according to Cover's theorem. Gaussian radial basis functions were modeled by centroid and variance parameters extracted from training patterns that compose the different classes. Afterwards, each pattern obtained through DCT two-dimensional time matrix was mapped into 30-dimensional space by 30 Gaussian radial basis functions properly parameterized. Because the Gaussian radial basis functions are parameterized with center and variance characteristics of each class, in this space of high dimensionality, it is expected that there will be adequate clustering of these patterns. Therefore, vectors of 30 elements form the training set applied during classifier learning process, where each element represents the RBF's outputs when pattern from two-dimensional DCT time matrix is applied.

Once the training set is finalized, the design and definition recognizer is carried out through performance analysis of two neural network configurations widely used in the literature: multilayer perceptron (MLP) and learning vector quantization (LVQ). The proposed multilevel classifier uses a set of 15 neural networks and each of them is expert in each predefined partition of the mapped feature space by the RBFs. This division of feature space reduces the topological complexity of MLP and LVQ configurations, training time and generalization capacity.

The performance analysis of the multilevel classifier is carried out in two phases: training, validation and individual test process of the experts and final test process. In this first procedure, predetermined topological elements and training algorithms for MLP and LVQ network configurations are combined to define the best characteristics of the 15 experts, where each one of them is responsible for learning the specificities of two classes. Thus, it is possible to verify the behavior of the MLP and LVQ networks and to select the expert topologies that presented the greatest global validation hit. These selected experts are tested individually to check the level of generalization for the classes they were assigned. Because of this, the level of accuracy is determined for each expert and these levels are part of the rules defined in the final classification stage. So, the expert topologies that obtained the highest accuracy are selected for the final test step. This step consists of the definition of rules for selection of the expert that will provide the final solution of the classification.

A new pattern generated by the DCT two-dimensional time matrix, different from those used in the training step, are used as inputs to the 30 Gaussian radial basis functions parameterized with the characteristics of each problem class. In addition to mapping the DCT pattern to a high dimensionality space, the outputs of each RBF provide a measure of input pattern probability belonging to a given class. The RBF outputs provide a preclassification rule in the multilevel recognition system, and their responses direct the appropriate expert to complete the classification. In order to ensure that the preclassification stage by the RBF selects the correct expert, a second selection rule is adopted. The final classification result given by the neural network chosen is compared to the accuracy result of the same class verified in the individual test step. The LVQ neural network performance study as expert in this work provides an alternative approach to the classifier, since the MLP configuration is the most executed neural network in pattern recognition problems.

3.1. Speech signal preprocessing

The locutions used in this work were recorded at sampling frequency $f_a = 22{,}050$ Hz, with 16-bit resolution. The speech signal preprocessing step was carried out through samples obtained from three different voice banks. After that, characteristics of each class were extracted to constitute feature space. Signal preprocessing step consists of segmenting and windowing speech signal from database. For this proposed work, it was defined windowing of the segments through Hamming function to speech signal preprocessing algorithm. The overlap between the windows was 50%. The window size on samples was calculated by multiplying the window duration $T_\omega = 20$ ms by the sampling frequency f_a.

3.2. Extraction of the mel-cepstral coefficients from speech signal

The coefficients are attributes extracted from the speech signal. These coefficients have vocal tract characteristics that are important information for speech recognition. In addition, its formulation makes analog to perception of sounds by humans. Then, a filter bank spaced in the mel scale was developed to obtain the mel-cepstral coefficients from speech signal samples. This filter bank covers the range of 0–4600 Hz. The bank is distributed in 20 filters, in which up to limit frequency for uniform segmentation, given by Fu = 1 kHz, filters are distributed in 10 uniform intervals. The mel-cepstral coefficients were obtained using the energy calculated for each frequency band, according to Eq. (7):

$$mfcc[k] = \sum_{i=1}^{N_F} E[i] \cos\left[\frac{i(k-0.5)\pi}{N_F}\right] \qquad (7)$$

where $k = 1, 2, \cdots, K$ is the number of mel-cepstral coefficients, N_F is the number of filters used and $E[i]$ is the energy log output of the ith band.

3.3. Generation of DCT two-dimensional time matrix

After obtaining the mel-cepstral coefficients from speech signal, the coding was performed through discrete cosine transform (DCT), which allows synthesizing the long-term variations of the spectral envelope of the speech signal [26]. The result of this coding was the generation of a DCT two-dimensional time matrix that was obtained according to Eq. (8):

$$C_k(n, T) = \frac{1}{N} \sum_{t=1}^{T} mfcc_k(t) \cos\left[\frac{(2t-1)n\pi}{2T}\right] \qquad (8)$$

where k, which varies from $1 \le k \le K$, is the kth component line of the ith segment of the matrix; K is the number of mel-cepstral coefficients; n, which varies from $1 \le n \le N$, is the nth column. n is the order of the DCT matrix; T is the number of observation vectors of the mel-cepstral coefficients in the time axis; $mfcck(t)$ represents mel-cepstral coefficients. Each locution of **D** digit has a DCT two-dimensional time matrix C_{kn}^{jm}, where $j = 1, 2, 3, \ldots, 30$ represents the class of commands to be recognized and $m = 1, 2, 3, \ldots, 20$ represents the example taken for each command. Each two-dimensional time matrix was transformed into column vector called C_N^{jm}, that preserve the time alignment of the mel-cepstral coefficients and they are given by (9):

$$C_N^{jm} = \left[c_{11}^{jm}, c_{12}^{jm}, \ldots, c_{1n}^{jm}, c_{21}^{jm}, c_{22}^{jm}, \ldots, c_{2n}^{jm}, \ldots, c_{kn}^{jm}\right]', \quad j = 1, 2, \ldots, 30 \mid m = 1, 2, \ldots, 20 \tag{9}$$

The vectors C_N^{jm} were used to form original training set or original feature space. So, DCT two-dimensional time matrices C_{kn}^{jm} of order $n = 2$, 3 and 4 were generated in order to compare the multilevel classifier performance when the number of parameters that compose primary speech patterns is increased. Thus, as a result, patterns represented by C_N^{jm} were obtained, where $N = k \times n = 4, 9, 16$, respectively.

3.4. Structuring of the multilevel speech recognition system with mixture of expert neural networks

After speech signal coding to generate command patterns used by recognizer, parameters of the Gaussian radial basis function set and topology design of expert neural networks were started. Radial basis functions and neural networks integrate the multilevel speech recognition system. The parameters required to model each RBFs are obtained from patterns generated by the DCT two-dimensional time matrix. These RBFs are responsible for the change of the feature space and for the preclassification stage of the multilevel system. The design of the expert neural networks set is carried out through simulations and based on results obtained in other similar pattern classification works. Two neural network configurations, MLP and LVQ are analyzed to constitute the experts in the proposed system. The choice for analyzing these two configurations in this chapter is justified because they are neural networks with great applicability and good results in pattern recognition field [14, 15, 22, 23]. According to presented methodology of this chapter, MLP and LVQ networks were analyzed for their performance in the pattern classification through two distinct steps. The analysis procedures of each step for integration between Gaussian RBFs and MLP and LVQ experts were carried out using the patterns from DCT two-dimensional time matrices of order 2, 3 and 4, and it was observed the multilevel system behavior under study. A block diagram of training step is shown in **Figure 1**.

The RBF's modeling and MLP and LVQ neural network training were carried out with speech signal patterns from locutions obtained by EPUSP (Polytechnic School of the University of São Paulo), INATEL (National Institute of Telecommunications) and IFMA (Federal Institute of Maranhão) banks. The training set $\Omega_{NL}^{Tr} = \{C_N^{11}, C_N^{12}, \ldots, C_N^{jm}\}$ is composed of 600 locution with 20 examples of each command to be recognized (m = 20), where $N = \{4, 9, 16\}$ represents the parameter number of patterns; L is total number of locutions and Tr indicates that set is training. The used training set is balanced type, that is, all classes have the same quantitative of examples, which avoid bias of the classifier. The training set was partitioned into the estimation subset Ω_N^E, which contains 80% of the training patterns, and into the validation set Ω_N^V, representing the remaining 20% of the training set $\Omega_{N600}^{Tr} = \{\Omega_N^E \cup \Omega_N^V\}$. The test phase is done using set Ω_{NL}^T consisting of 40 speakers, where 20 speakers are male (Ω_{NL}^{TM}) and 20 speakers are female (Ω_{NL}^{TF}). All speakers belong to IFMA voice bank, but they are speakers who did not participate in pronunciations for training set. Then, test set available to verify the generalization of the multilevel recognition system has 6000 samples in total $(\Omega_{N6000}^T = \{\Omega_{N3000}^{TM} \cup \Omega_{N3000}^{TF}\})$.

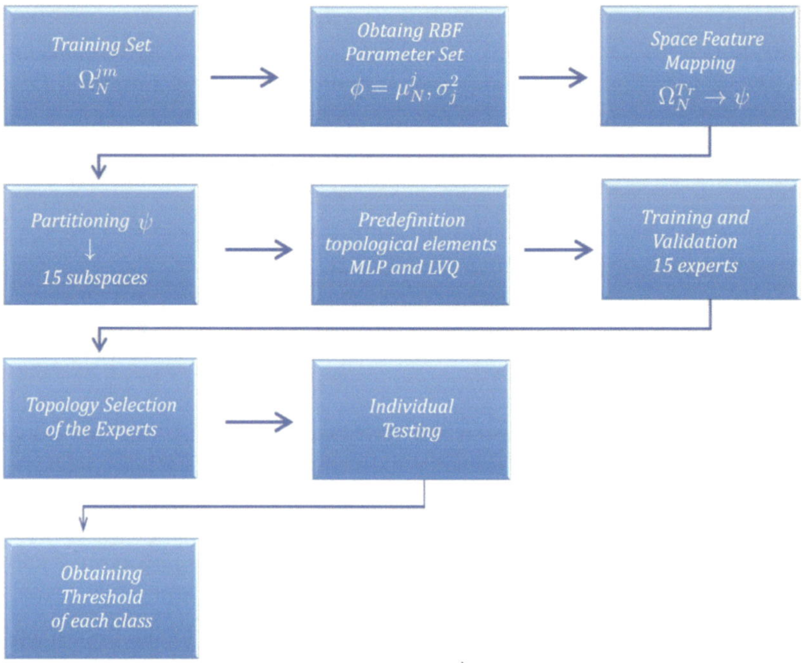

Figure 1. Block diagram of training step.

3.4.1. Parameterization Gaussian radial basis functions

The multilevel speech recognition system with mixture of experts use a set of 30 Gaussian radial basis functions that have two purposes in proposed system: the first of them, in training step, is to mapping the patterns C_N^{Jm} into a new high-dimensional nonlinear space to making easier the separability of the patterns. The second goal in testing step is to providing a preclassification rule for speech signal sample, in addition to mapping this sample into high-dimensional space. The number of chosen Gaussian radial basis functions is related to number of problem classes. Thus, the centroid parameters $\boldsymbol{\mu}_j$ and variances σ_j^2 of each class j were determined through training set Ω_{NL}^{Tr}. A suitable method for this purpose, called *k-means* [24], was used to obtain the 30 RBF centroids, whose purpose is interactively position the *k*-Gaussian centers in regions where the input patterns will tend to cluster. The training set Ω_{NL}^{Tr} was applied to *k-means* algorithm, where *k* was defined as 30, as shown in **Figure 2**.

The variance σ_j^2 was determined by criterion of the average quadratic distance. The variance σ_j^2 is expressed as:

$$\sigma_j^2 = \frac{1}{m^{(j)}} \sum_{x^{(n)} \in \Omega_j} \sum_{i=1}^{n_1} \left(x_i^{(n)} - c_j\right)^2 \tag{10}$$

Therefore, at the end of these procedures, all vectors C_N^{Jm} from training set Ω_{NL}^{Tr} are mapped into a nonlinear 30-dimensional space by radial basis functions set $\Phi(x) = \{\varphi_1, \varphi_2, \ldots, \varphi_{30}\}$ duly modeled with characteristics of the classes.

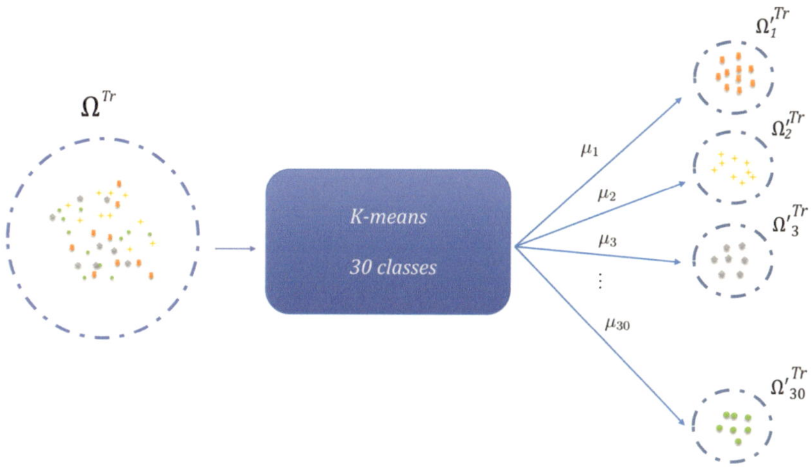

Figure 2. Schematization of the *k-means* algorithm.

3.4.2. Expert neural network design

The distribution of each 30 classes among the defined experts is shown in **Table 1**, both for LVQ and MLP configuration.

It is necessary to specify the best structure for characteristics learning of each class of training set Ω^{Tr}_{NL}. Thus, for the 15 expert neural networks, both MLP and LVQ configurations, the topological elements and training algorithms were combined during the training step. Next, it is shown how the LVQ and MLP configurations were specified in the training step [27].

3.4.2.1. LVQ experts

For the structure of the LVQ neural network, it was necessary to define the η learning rate and the *n* number of neurons of the competitive layer. The defined values in η set are often used in the specialized literature [17, 18, 26] and the *n* set was specified considering that the number of neurons in hidden layer should be greater than the number of inputs and greater than the number of neural network outputs. Because the vectors C^{lm}_{N}, where $N = \{4, 9, 16\}$ are mapped into a 30-dimensional space, the input of 15 LVQ experts is a set with 30 source nodes. The number of classes that integrate each specified subset gives the output number of each expert. Due to recognition problem of this work has partitioned the Ω^{Tr}_{NL} set into 15 subsets, the output of each expert should have two neurons, that is, one neuron for each class. It was defined a neuron set represented by multiple numbers of neural network inputs, starting with 60 neurons as the smallest number of neurons in hidden layer. The increase of neurons in hidden layer until neuron maximum value of *n* set allows to observe the network behavior in relation to increase the number of neurons in hidden layer.

It is summarized in **Table 2**, the topology elements and training algorithm for the simulations of the LVQ expert neural networks.

Classes	Experts	Classes	Experts	Classes	Experts
'ZERO'	1	'ABAIXO'	6	'INICIAR'	11
'UM'		'ABRIR'		'LIGAR'	
'DOIS'	2	'ACIMA'	7	'MAXIMO'	12
'TRÊS'		'AUMENTAR'		'MÉDIO'	
'QUATRO'	3	'DESLIGAR'	8	'MINIMO'	13
'CINCO'		'DIMINNUIR'		'PARA TRÁS'	
'SEIS'	4	'DIREITA'	9	'PARA FRENTE'	14
'SETE'		'ESQUERDA'		'PARAR'	
'OITO'	5	'FECHAR'	10	'REPOUSAR'	15
'NOVE'		'FINALIZAR'		'SALVAR'	

Table 1. Division of classes among experts.

Elements	Symbol
No. of neurons	$n = \{60, 90, 120, 150\}$
Learning rate	$\eta = 0.01$
No. of epoch	Epoch = 1000
Training algorithm	LVQ-1

Table 2. LVQ neural network elements.

3.4.2.2. *MLP experts*

The MLP neural network structure is defined by some variable elements that, properly chosen, allow a good performance of the neural network in solution of the proposed problem. It is presented in **Table 3**, these variable elements that are combined in some simulations to define the best topology.

In addition to defining the network topological elements, four different training algorithms were used in MLP network. This way, it can be verified the algorithm that presents better results to pattern set presented to network. The chosen training algorithms were: gradient descendent (GD); gradient descendent with momentum (GDM); resilient propagation (RP); Levenberg-Marquardt (LM). The simulated number of hidden layers was defined by fact that, for pattern classification problems, the use of up to two layers is sufficient for this application. The η set and the n set were defined according to same criteria of LVQ configuration. For simulations involving MLP networks of two hidden layers, it was defined that second hidden layer presents 30 neurons. This value was specified because it is a smaller number than all those belonging to n set and greater than number of neural network outputs. This value is fixed for all combinations with n set. The used activation function in all neurons is the hyperbolic tangent function. For each combination of training algorithm "versus" number of layers "*versus*" number of neurons "*versus*" learning rate were carried out in 100 training algorithms. Each of them used different initializations of the weights, made over a random uniform distribution between the values [−0.01, 0.01]. This interval of random initialization of weights is justified by the fact that it is smaller than the range of values that comprise the parameters of the training set patterns,

Elements	Symbol	Typical range
No. of hidden layers	Θ	1 e 2
No. of hidden neurons 1° layer	n	60, 90, 120, 150
No. of hidden neurons 2° layer	n_1	30
Learning rate	η	0.01, 0.1 ,0.5, 0.9
Momentum constant	α	0.8

Table 3. Variable elements of the multilayer perceptron.

avoiding the saturation of activation function that prevent the convergence of the neural network [28]. So, it was possible to observe the neural network behavior in relation to training time and generalization capacity, since an adequate set of initial weights allows reduction in training time and high probability of reaching the global minimum of function error. Moreover, this set can significantly improve performance in generalization. Simulated topologies are trained using $\Omega_{4L}{}^{Tr}, \Omega_{9L}{}^{Tr}, \Omega_{16L}{}^{Tr}$ sets and this way, it is verified MLP network response to parameter number increment of the speech signal patterns presented in the original feature space.

4. Experimental results

4.1. Training and validation of LVQ experts

It is shown in **Figure 3(a)** and **(b)**, respectively, the global hit result (in percentage) of the commands in training and validation in relation to the n neuron set simulated to original training set Ω_{NL}^{Tr} with $N = 16$. It was observed that, by using the patterns C_{16}^{jm}, the mean of global training hit increased over the experiments using patterns with four and nine parameters, reaching 97.5%. The result of global validation hit mean for this experiment was 91.45%.

4.2. Individual test of the LVQ experts

In view of these results of training and validation, the topologies for each expert that presented global validation hit greater than 80% were tested. Besides the criterion of the value of the global validation hit for the application of the tests, the choice of a simple topology with the acceptable validation error is also necessary. Consequently, through the training and validation results, the LVQ expert neural networks with 60 neurons in the competitive layer were chosen for the individual test step. The individual test step has the objective of verifying the expert networks generalization capacity for classes that they were trained. From the results achieved in this step, a classification threshold for outputs of each expert was defined. The information of classification threshold is part of the decision rules of the multilevel speech recognition system with mixture expert neural networks. The established criteria for choice of the best topology were applied for each experiment carried out in the training step. The test sets $\Omega_{N3000}{}^{TM}$ and $\Omega_{N3000}{}^{TF}$ with $N = \{4, 9, 16\}$ were applied to the topologies in the three experiments performed. The individual classification results tests applied to topologies that presented global validation hit above 80% and lower topological complexity (60 neurons) for the training sets using the original patterns $C_4{}^{jm}$, $C_9{}^{jm}$ and $C_{16}{}^{jm}$ are shown in **Table 4**, where it is observed the results of global hit for each expert,

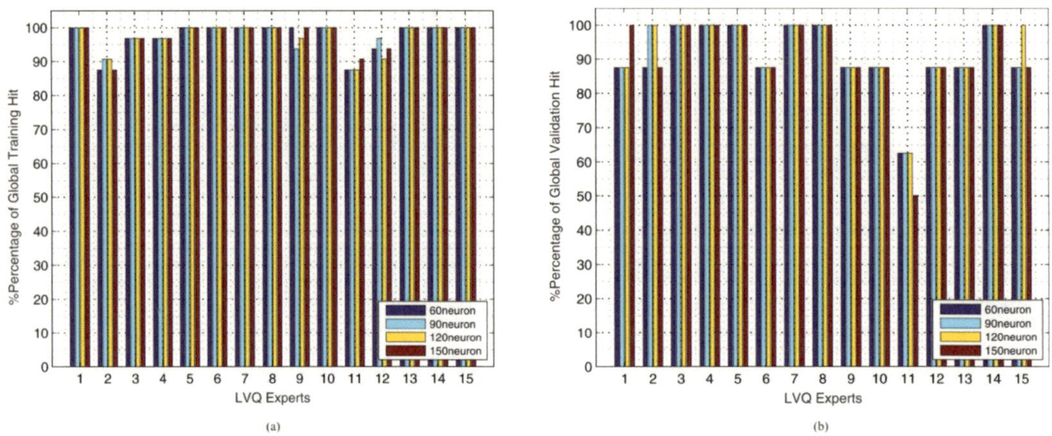

Figure 3. LVQ experts C_{16}^{jm}: result of global training and validation hit.

Experts	C_4^{jm}			C_9^{jm}			C_{16}^{jm}		
	% Global Hit	% Hit Output Class 1	% Hit Output Class 2	% Global Hit	% Hit Output Class 1	% Hit Output Class 2	% Global Hit	% Hit Output Class 1	% Hit Output Class 2
1	82.1	85.3	78.9	95.8	93.2	98.4	90.3	85.3	95.3
2	79.5	88.9	70.0	91.6	93.7	89.5	86.1	94.7	77.4
3	99.2	98.9	99.5	99.5	100	98.9	100	100	100
4	91.1	83.2	98.9	94.5	94.2	94.7	94.2	93.2	95.3
5	91.8	91.6	92.1	95.5	95.3	95.8	97.1	94.2	100
6	88.9	85.8	92.1	87.4	93.2	81.6	82.4	87.9	76.88
7	93.2	88.9	97.4	94.2	90	98.4	99.5	100	98.9
8	97.1	96.3	97.9	97.1	95.3	98.9	99.7	99.5	100
9	77.9	70.0	85.8	72.4	71.6	73.2	93.9	96.3	91.6
10	82.9	75.3	90.5	85.8	93.7	77.9	92.4	92.1	92.6
11	75.0	90.0	60.0	73.4	86.8	60	72.1	65.8	78.4
12	82.1	76.3	87.9	73.7	54.2	93.2	73.4	69.5	77.4
13	99.2	98.4	100	99.5	98.9	100	99.7	99.5	100
14	97.1	98.9	95.3	97.6	97.9	97.4	95.8	96.8	94.7
15	75.8	72.1	79.5	67.9	60.5	75.3	71.3	62.1	80.5

Table 4. Individual test of the expert LVQ with 60 neurons.

as well as individual results of their classes. It is assumed that the values % Hit Output Class 1 and % Hit Output Class 2 constitute the classification threshold for each command

4.3. Training and validation of MLP experts

At the end of all simulations that combine topological elements and training algorithms and number of hidden layers, it can be observed the behavior of the proposed topologies and

http://dx.doi.org/10.5772/intechopen.72575

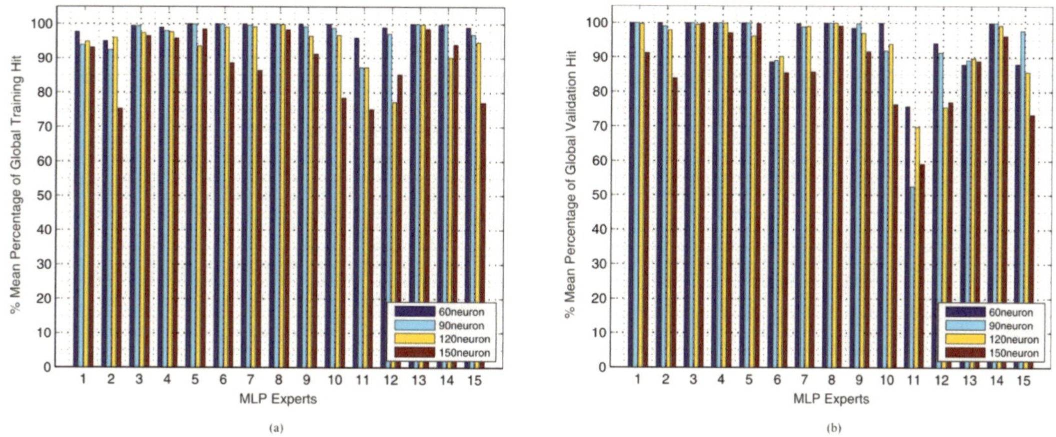

Figure 4. MLP expert C_{16}^{jm}: result of mean training and validation global hit - 1 hidden layer RP algorithm.

Experts	C_4^{jm}			C_9^{jm}			C_{16}^{jm}		
	% Global Hit	% Hit Output Class 1	% Hit Output Class 2	% Global Hit	% Hit Output Class 1	% Hit Output Class 2	% Global Hit	% Hit Output Class 1	% Hit Output Class 2
1	97.6	95.8	99.5	98.4	97.4	99.5	98.7	97.9	99.5
2	80.5	83.2	77.9	87.4	93.7	81.1	86.3	95.8	76.8
3	100	100	100	100	100	100	100	100	100
4	98.7	97.9	99.5	96.3	93.2	99.5	98.7	97.9	99.5
5	96.8	93.7	100	97.1	94.2	100	97.4	94.7	100
6	93.7	87.9	99.5	94.7	95.8	93.7	90.3	87.4	93.2
7	96.9	93.8	100	96.8	98.4	95.3	98.4	98.4	98.4
8	97.6	95.3	100	98.2	96.3	100	97.4	94.7	100
9	81.8	72.1	91.6	90.8	87.4	94.2	98.7	99.5	97.9
10	90	81.6	98.4	93.7	88.4	98.9	92.1	84.2	100
11	76.1	73.2	78.9	85.5	86.3	84.7	90.5	88.9	92.1
12	85.8	76.3	95.3	81.6	82.1	81.1	98.7	98.9	98.4
13	100	100	100	99.7	99.5	100	99.7	99.5	100
14	98.7	97.9	99.5	98.9	97.9	100	99.2	98.4	100
15	77.4	74.2	80	78.2	75.8	80.5	77.6	72.1	83.2

Table 5. Individual test of the expert MLP with 60 neurons.

define the best result. It was verified during the simulations that the GD, GDM and LM algorithms did not reach good results for the problem of pattern recognition with the proposed coding, showing global results of training and validation of less than 50%. In addition, the MLP networks trained with two hidden layers did not present significant results in relation to trained networks with one hidden layer, which does not justify the increase of complexity of the network structure. For these reasons, only the results presented by networks trained with the algorithm RP with a hidden layer are presented. The average results of global training and validation hit for each expert are shown in **Figure 4(a)** and **(b)**, respectively. These results were achieved by topologies trained with RP algorithm, one hidden layer and 16 input parameters.

4.4. Individual test of MLP experts

The adopted criteria to application of the tests in LVQ topologies were the same as MLP topologies. The best results (in percentage) found in the tests performed for each expert, considering the networks trained with a hidden layer of 60 neurons by the algorithms RP using C_4^{jm}, C_9^{jm} and C_{16}^{jm} patterns are summarized in **Table 5**.

4.5. Final test of the multilevel speech recognition system with mixture of expert neural networks

At the end of the expert design stage, given by analysis of the LVQ and MLP configurations, and defined the classification threshold for each expert output, it was performed the integration between radial basis functions and MLP and LVQ topologies with the best classification results. The flowchart of final test is presented in **Figure 5**.

Patterns from particular class are initially classified through the responses given by RBFs. The RBF that has the highest probability value at its output direct at which expert those patterns should be applied. It is highlighted that obtained results in this step are the same when it has used both MLP and LVQ networks as experts, since the test patterns are the same and

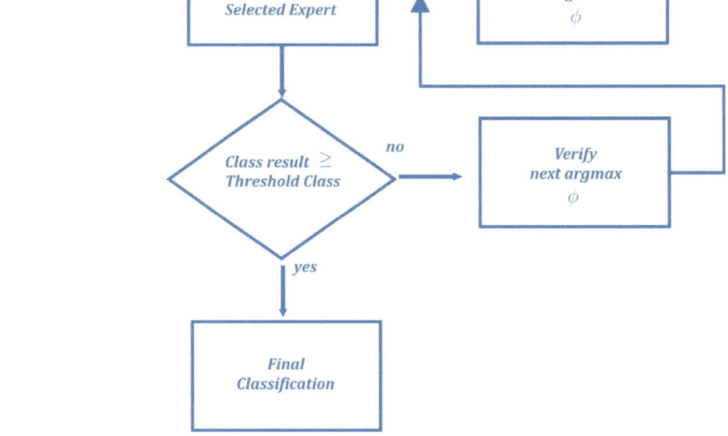

Figure 5. Final test flowchart of the multilevel speech recognition system.

Test class	RBF/%Max Pr/expert	Test class	RBF/%Max Pr/expert	Test class	RBF/%Max Pr/expert
'ZERO'	'ZERO'/80.5/1	'ABAIXO'	'ABAIXO'/57/6	'INICIAR'	'INICIAR'/71.5/11
'UM'	'UM'/54.5/1	'ABRIR'	'ABRIR'/78/6	'LIGAR'	'LIGAR'/48.5/11
'DOIS'	'DOIS'/87/2	'ACIMA'	'ACIMA'/61/7	'MAXIMO'	'MAXIMO'/93/12
'TRÊS'	'TRÊS'/58/2	'AUMENTAR'	AUMENTAR'/70.5/7	'MÉDIO'	'MAXIMO'/40.5/12
'QUATRO'	'QUATRO'/61/3	'DESLIGAR'	'DESLIGAR'/47/8	'MINIMO'	'MINIMO'/41.5/13
'CINCO'	'CINCO'/85.5/3	'DIMINNUIR'	'SETE'/67/4	'PARA TRÁS'	'PARA TRÁS'/35.5/13
'SEIS'	'SEIS'/70.5/4	'DIREITA'	'DIREITA'/32/9	PARA FRENTE'	'PARA FRENTE'/48/14
'SETE'	'SETE'/ 89.5/4	'ESQUERDA'	'MAXIMO'/56/12	'PARAR'	'SETE'/33.5/4
'OITO'	'OITO'/79/5	'FECHAR'	'FECHAR'/83/10	'REPOUSAR'	'REPOUSAR'/62.5/15
'NOVE'	'NOVE'/78/5	'FINALIZAR'	'FINALIZAR'/68.5/10	'SALVAR'	'SALVAR'/85/15

Table 6. Preclassification of test C_{16}^{jm} patterns.

the RBF are fixed. Therefore, after preclassification, the next level is the final classification of the selected expert network. The expert makes the patterns classification mapped into high dimensional space by the RBFs on preclassification stage. The obtained classification result by the expert is compared to the classification threshold of the respective class, determined in individual test step. At this point, the decision rule for final result of the system is carried out as shown in **Figure 5**. The preclassification results of the test patterns generated by DCT matrices of order 4 are presented in **Table 6**, where *RBF* indicates the Gaussian RBF preclassification and *%MaxPr* means maximum probability value in percent.

From preclassification results shown in **Table 6**, it is observed that this step selects (in great majority) the correct experts in second level of classification. Hence, the hit average rates in the

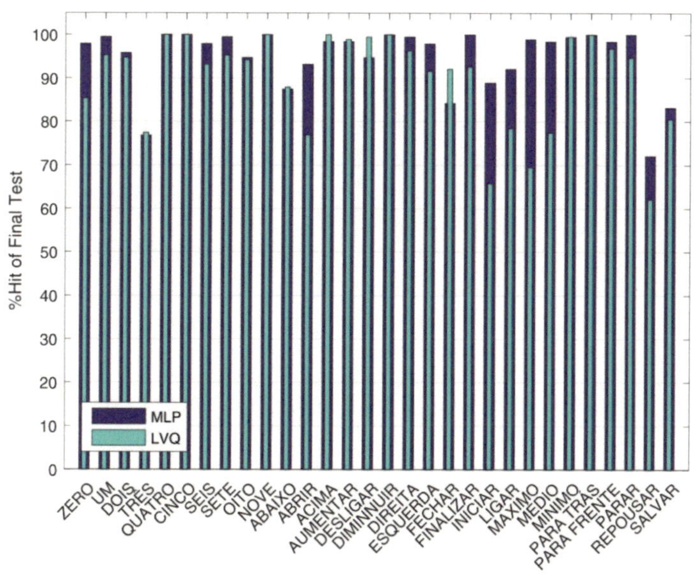

Figure 6. Comparison between MLP and LVQ using C_{16}^{jm} in final test of multilevel speech recognition system.

preclassification step by radial basis functions are for test patterns in the low-dimensionality space C_4^{jm}, C_9^{jm} e C_{16}^{jm} of 83.33, 86.33 and 86.33%, respectively. The test algorithm solved problem for the classes that presented error in preclassification through decision rule. In **Figure 6**, the performance analysis is observed between the MLP and LVQ configurations for composition of expert set using C_{16}^{jm}. Similar results were obtained for the other patterns used.

5. Conclusion

In this chapter, it was proposed to evaluate the performance between the MLP and LVQ neural networks configurations to determine the set of expert classifiers to compose a multilevel recognition system. The developed methodology associates the efficient coding of the speech signal through DCT two-dimensional time matrix of low order with integration between MLP and LVQ expert neural networks and Gaussian radial basis functions to develop a speech recognition system of high performance. In view of the presented results, it was concluded that the parameterization of the speech signal through the generation of the DCT two-dimensional time matrix proposed in the methodology proved to be efficient in the formation of the set of input patterns. They were modified by a Gaussian radial basis functions set parameterized with centroid and variances of the classes and they are the inputs presented to the neural networks during the training and validation step. It was verified that despite the small number of parameters that constitute a speech signal pattern, the two-dimensional time matrix can represent the long-term variations of the locutions spectral envelope to be recognized and these characteristics are reproduced in proposed multidimensional space. The versatility of the Gaussian radial basis function set in proposed recognition system structure demonstrates the potential of these functions. It is emphasized that the parameters of the RBF models were adequately determined, since hit rate in preclassification step was higher than 80%. It was verified that the increase in neurons number of the MLP and LVQ neural networks did not show significant improvements in the global validation hit, which was the criterion used to select the best topologies for the application of the tests. Based on the tests carried out, it was verified that the LVQ network can be used satisfactorily in pattern recognition problems, specifically for multilevel speech recognition system proposed in this chapter. This is evidenced by the very close performance of the MLP Network, which is widely used in pattern classification. Finally, the performance in the multiclass task of speech signal patterns given by the integration between Gaussian radial basis functions and set of expert neural networks is highlighted.

Author details

Washington Luis Santos Silva[1*], Priscila Lima Rocha[2] and Allan Kardec Duailibe Barros Filho[2]

*Address all correspondence to: washington.silva@ifma.edu.br

1 Federal Institute of Maranhão, São Luís, Brazil

2 Federal University of Maranhão, São Luís, Brazil

References

[1] Dougherty G. Pattern Recognition and Classification: An Introduction. Illustrated ed. New York, USA: Springer Science & Business Media; 2012. 196 p. DOI: 10.1007/978-1-4614-5223-9

[2] Duda R, Hart P, Stork D. Pattern Classification. 2nd ed. New York, USA: John Wiley & Sons; 2012.680 p. ISBN: 111858600X, 9781118586006

[3] Husnjak S, Perakovic D, Jovovic I. Possibilities of using speech recognition systems of smart terminal devices in traffic environment. Procedia Engineering. 2014;**69**:778-787. DOI: 10.1016/j.proeng.2014.03.054

[4] Spale J, Schweize C. Speech control of measurement devices. IFAC-Papers OnLine. 2016;**49**:13-18. DOI: 10.1016/j.ifacol.2016.12.003

[5] Weng F et al. Conversational in-vehicle dialog systems: The past, present, and future. IEEE Signal Processing Magazine. 2016;**33**:49-60. DOI: 10.1109/MSP.2016.2599201

[6] Youcef C, Elemine M, Islam B, Farid B. Speech recognition system based on OLLO French corpus by using MFCCs. In: Chadli M, Bououden S, Zelinka I, editors. Recent Advances in Electrical Engineering and Control Applications. Cham: Springer; 2017;**411**:326-331. DOI: 10.1007/978-3-319-48929-2_25

[7] Bellegarda J, Monz C. State of the art in statistical methods for language and speech processing. Computer Speech & Language. 2016;**35**:163-184. DOI: 10.1016/j.csl.2015.07.001

[8] Picone J. Signal modeling techniques in speech recognition. Proceedings of the IEEE. 1993;**81**:1215-1247. DOI: 10.1109/5.237532

[9] Kautz T, Eskofier B, Pasluosta C. Generic performance measure for multiclass-classifiers. Pattern Recognition. 2017;**68**:111-125. DOI: 10.1016/j.patcog.2017.03.008

[10] Song Q, Jiang H, Liu J. Feature selection based on FDA and F-score for multi-class classification. Expert Systems With Applications. 2017;**81**:22-27. DOI: 10.1016/j.eswa.2017.02.049

[11] Kheradpisheh S, Sharifizadeh F, Nowzari-Dalini A, Ganjtabesh M, Ebrahimpour R. Mixture of feature specified experts. Information Fusion. 2014;**20**:242-251. DOI: 10.1016/j.inffus.2014.02.006

[12] Shih P, Chen C, Wu C. Speech Emotion recognition with ensemble learning methods. In: IEEE International Conference on Acoustics, Speech and Signal Processing (ICASSP); New Orleans, LA; 2017. pp. 2756-2760

[13] Xie F, Fan H, Li Y, Jiang Z, Meng R, Bovik A. Melanoma classification on dermoscopy images using a neural network ensemble model. IEEE Transactions on Medical Imaging. 2017;**36**:849-858. DOI: 10.1109/TMI.2016.2633551

[14] Haykin S. Neural Networks and Learning Machines. 3rd ed. New Jersey, USA: Pearson Education; 2011. 936 p. ISBN: 9780131471399

[15] Silva I, Spatti D, Flauzino R. Redes Neurais Artificiais para Engenharia e Ciências Aplicadas - Curso Prático. São Paulo, Brasil: Artliber; 2010. 399 p. ISBN: 9788588098534

[16] Rocha P, Silva W. Artificial neural networks used for pattern recognition of speech signal based on DCT parametric models of low order. In: IEEE 14th International Conference on Industrial Informatics (INDIN); 19-21 July 2016; Poitiers. New York. IEEE; 2017

[17] Rocha P, Silva W. Intelligent system of speech recognition using neural networks based on DCT parametric models of low order. In: International Joint Conference on Neural Networks (IJCNN); 24-29 July 2016; Vancouver

[18] Silva W. Intelligent genetic fuzzy inference system for speech recognition: An approach from low order feature based on discrete cosine transform. Journal of Control, Automation and Electrical Systems. 2014;**25**:689-698. DOI: 10.1007/s40313-014-0148-0

[19] Bresolin A. Reconhecimento de Voz através De Unidades Menores Do Que a Palavra, Utilizando Wavelet Packet e SVM, Em Uma Nova Estrutura hierárquica de decisão [Thesis]. Natal: Universidade Federal do Rio Grande do Norte; 2008

[20] Siniscalchi S, Svendsen T, Lee C. An artificial neural network approach to automatic speech processing. Neurocomputing. 2014;**140**:326-338. DOI: 10.1016/j.neucom.2014.03.005

[21] Buhmann M. Radial Basis Functions: Theory and Implementations. Vol. 12. Cambride, United Kingdom: Cambridge University Press; 2003. 259 p. ISBN: 0-521-63338-9

[22] Hu Y, Hwang J editors. Handbook of Neural Networks for Speech Processing. New York, USA: CRC Press; 2014. 408 p. ISBN: 9780849323591

[23] Priddy K, Keller P. Artificial Neural Networks: An Introduction. Illustrated ed. Washington, USA: SPIE Press; 2005. 165 p. ISBN: 0819459879

[24] Rokach L. Pattern Classification Using Ensemble Methods. Vol. 75. Singapore: World Scientific; 2010. 225 p. ISBN: 13 978-981-4271-06-6

[25] Zhou Z. Ensemble Methods: Foundations and Algorithms. Illustrated ed. New York, USA: CRC Press; 2012. 236 p. ISBN: 978-1-4398-3003-1

[26] Fissore L, Laface P, Ravera F. Using word temporal structure in HMM speech recognition. In: EEE International Conference on Acoustics, Speech, and Signal Processing; 21-24 April 1997; Munich. New York: IEEE; 2002. pp. 975-978

[27] Bhardwaj A, Tiwari A, Bhardwaj H, Bhardwaj A. A genetically optimized neural network model for multi-class classification. Expert Systems with Applications. 2016;**60**:211-221. DOI: 10.1016/j.eswa.2016.04.036

[28] Sousa C. An overview on weight initialization methods for feedforward neural networks. In: Proceedings of the international joint conference on neural networks (IJCNN 2016); 24-29 July 2016; Vancouver. New York: IEEE; 2016. pp. 52-59

Hybrid Intelligent System for Diagnosing Breast Pre-Cancerous and Cancerous Conditions Based on Image Analysis

Oleh M. Berezsky

Additional information is available at the end of the chapter

http://dx.doi.org/10.5772/intechopen.72576

Abstract

Modern diagnostic technologies are automated microscopy systems (AMSs). In this research study, the authors analyzed the modern AMS methods and algorithms. Criteria-based comparative analysis of AMS has been made, and their advantages and disadvantages have been identified at the three main levels of image processing. This allowed determining the main direction of such systems development, that is, designing the hybrid intelligent AMS. The work of an expert physician implies visual image interpretation, selection of qualitative features of micro-objects, the formation of diagnostic rules based on expert knowledge, and making diagnoses. Knowledge introduction model contains a productive model, in which knowledge is presented in the form of rules expressed in productive pseudo code if-then. Logic inference machine is a module designed to logically derive the facts and rules from the base according to the laws of formal logic. A set of modern methods and algorithms for low-, mid-, and high-level image processing have been used in the AMS structure.

Keywords: breast cancer, histological image, cytological image, fuzzy knowledge base, fuzzy system, automated microscopy system, hybrid intelligent system, convolutional neural networks

1. Introduction

According to the National Cancer Registry of Ukraine, in 2014 there have been 14,908 tumor cases. Moreover, almost 25% of tumors have been diagnosed at a late stage, and 40% of women over 40 years of age have never been properly examined [1].

As a rule, in modern clinical practice, light microscopy is used in diagnosing, which is the area of laboratory diagnostics, where labor-intensive subjective qualitative analysis dominates. For automation of microscopic studies, automated microscopy systems (AMSs) are used. AMSs are software and hardware complexes for digital micro-object processing [2]. The main problem with such systems is image processing quality.

Automated microscopy systems allow conducting microscopic image analysis, selecting objects in manual or automated mode, calculating certain characteristics, and assisting medical diagnosticians to make diagnoses based on these characteristics. Examples of such systems are the following: AxioVision, BioImageXD, ImageJ, MicroManager, MECOS-CH, and others. Some of the mentioned systems have their own hardware (microscopes, photo/video cameras, etc) for research, but most are universal and adaptable to different types of microscopes.

The urgent research area in the application of automated microscopy systems is the development of hybrid intelligent systems that allow automatic image processing to make diagnoses. Such systems are called hybrid because they combine two or more intellectual components.

2. AMS concepts and application areas

Modern automated microscopy systems are characterized by a high cost, high level of complexity, and rigid user interface. In addition, such systems allow image processing only in manual or automated modes, however, they are not able to make diagnoses in automatic mode, which would greatly simplify and improve diagnostic physicians' performance. One more significant issue is a reduction of image processing labor-intensiveness and using modern methods or algorithms of computer vision.

Modern automated microscopy systems for processing the biomedical images of various types, including cytological and histological images, are becoming increasingly popular. Most AMSs consist of hardware (microscope, video camera) and software. The main task of software is to process the input image and identify the objects and features for further diagnosis by an expert or in automatic mode. The most popular systems include: MECOS-C2, TissueFAXS, AnalySISFive, BioVision, VideoTesTMorpho 5.2, BioImageXD, Ariol, ImageJ, analySIS FIVE, MoticImagesAdvanced 3.2, DiMorph, MoticVideoTesTMorpho 5.2, Cell D. Most AMSs are universal, that means that they are not focused on processing of images of the same type, but there are some commercial tools that allow installing separate modules for processing certain types of images, for example, histological ones.

AMSs are widely used in medicine, forensic medicine, and research studies.

2.1. Review of literature on bioimage processing

The problem of AMS development is relevant and the main contribution to its solution has been made by researchers from the United States, France, Germany, Great Britain, China, and Japan. For example, Mitko V. (UK) has developed a technique for segmentation of cells and nuclei on stained histological images [3]. ChenJia-Mei (China) applied the method of support vectors and watershed segmentation of histological images [4]. T. Vrekoussis researched immunohistochemical samples of breast cancer using the system of automated microscopy ImageJ [5]. Nezved A.M. (Belarus) described the theoretical foundations and methods of image processing necessary for computation of characteristics, which formed the basis of features of medical objects, investigating not only the problems of their analysis but also the problems of recognition [6].

2.2. Problem statement

The main problem in microscopy is automation of the medical diagnostic process. This problem embraces the correct design of biomedical image and signal processing systems, medical expert systems, information-analytical systems, and decision support systems. In the field of histology and cytology, AMSs are used in biomedical image processing.

The purpose of the work is to analyze modern automated microscopy systems, based on the criteria of availability of methods and algorithms at three levels of image processing, and design the AMS structure using modern computer vision algorithms and intelligent data analysis.

3. State of AMS development

3.1. Low-level image processing algorithms

An important stage in image development is image pre-processing. It influences the quality of image and accuracy of output results. Each AMS has its own set of algorithms and image pre-processing methods. The complexity of biomedical microscopic image processing includes identifying contours and desired objects while ignoring unnecessary noises and elements. In **Table 1**, a criteria-based comparison of AMS related to low-level image processing, namely, image pre-processing, is shown. That is why the pre-processing stage is an integral part of automated microscopy system.

Practically all AMSs have a standard set of pre-processing methods, such as changing image contrast, brightness manipulation, image channels, and use of Fourier transform. To choose the best specific filtration algorithm for cytological and histological images, it is necessary to conduct a research on their implementation in well-known automated microscopy systems. The advantage of systems like ImageJ, AxioVisison, MoticImageAdvance is the presence of several algorithms for selecting thresholds in the image, quality of processing depends on both the algorithm, and the image itself. The disadvantage of almost all systems is a limited set of algorithms for filtering and wavelet analysis. Some systems provide such functionality in the form of additional commercial or non-commercial modules.

The digital image is exposed to different types of noise, which are formed at the stage of obtaining an image or its transmission. Typically, noises appear due to the poor quality of photo and video equipment, as well as when transferring images via communication channels. The low image quality may also be caused by a human factor.

There are common filtering algorithms, such as Gaussian, median, averaging, and adaptive. One of the simplest and most natural ways to detect an object is choosing a threshold

Criteria	ImageJ	Axio Visison	BioImageXD	motic	QCapture PRO	Icy	Image Pro Plus	Micro Manager	analySIS FIVE
Contrast	+	+	+	+	+	+	+	+	+
Brightness level change	+	+	+	+	+	+	+	+	+
Low/high frequency filter	+	+	+	+	—	—	+	+	+
Threshold selecting	-	+	-	+	+	-	+	+	+
algorithms:	+	-	-	-	-	-	-	+	+
Laplacian	+	+	+	-	+	+	+	+/–	+
Krish									
Sobel									
Filters:	+	+	+	+	+	+	+	+	+/–
Gaussian	+	+	+	+	+	-	+	+/–	+/–
Median	+	+	-	-	-	-	-	+/–	+/–
Average									
Fast Fourier Transform	+	+	+	+	+	—	+	+	+
Morphologic operations	+	+	+	+	+	+	+	+	+
Wavelet analysis	-	+	-	-	-	-	+/–	-	-
Haar algorithm	-	-	-	-	-	-	-	-	-
Daubechies algorithm	+	-	-	-	-	-	-	-	-
algorithm "m hat"									

Table 1. Comparative characteristics of AMS low-level image processing.

according to brightness, or thresholding [7]. There are the following common threshold algorithms: Kenny, Sobel's algorithm, differential selection of thresholds, and refinement of boundaries.

As the result of image filtering algorithms comparison, we can conclude that the median filter showed worse results at the processing speed, however, what is more important, better quality of a final image. Therefore, the final image can be properly processed at the next stages. When choosing AMS, it is necessary to give preferences to those that have this filter in its structure. As the result of comparison of threshold selection algorithms, Canny [8] and Sobel's [9] algorithms demonstrated the best quality of input image processing. These algorithms are implemented in most AMSs.

A significant advantage of AMS is the presence of image wavelet transform. Wavelet localizes the signal both in space and frequency [10]. A signal can be represented by a set of wave packets (wavelets) formed on the basis of some fundamental function. This set is different in different parts of time interval determination of the signal and is adjusted by factors that have the form of complex time functions.

In signal processing, Fourier transform is usually considered as decomposition of the signal at the frequency and amplitude, that is, the transition from time-space to frequency. By means of Fourier transforms, the frequency domain (spectrum) of the image is received [11]. Fast Fourier Transform (FFT) is a fast algorithm for calculating a discrete Fourier transform [12]. For the direct calculation of the discrete Fourier transform from N data points, $O(N^2)$ arithmetic operations are required, and FFT can calculate the same result using O (NlogN) operations.

3.2. Medium-level processing algorithms

In computer vision systems, image segmentation is one of the most difficult stages. The segmentation stage involves division of the image into areas for which a certain homogeneity criterion is fulfilled, for example, selection of regions of approximately the same brightness in the image. The comparative characteristics of segmentation algorithms are given in **Table 2**.

Table 2. Comparative characteristics of medium-level image processing (+ presence, – absence, +/– availability of additional module).

As the result of the comparison, we can conclude that most systems have in their composition a similar set of elements and segmentation algorithms. Among the above-mentioned AMSs, it is necessary to highlight BioImageXD and AxioVisison, which have the largest set of implemented segmentation algorithms. ImageJ in its composition has only a few algorithms; however, it provides the ability to install additional modules.

The advantage of active contour method is that it divides an image into sub-regions with continuous contours. The contour-based modules use the boundary detector, usually based

AMS	K-means	Intelligent scissors	Snakes	Watershed method	Kruskal algorithm	Grab Cut	Mean shift	Contour coding	RAN SAC	Hough transform
ImageJ	+	+/–	+	+	+/–	+/–	+	–	+	+/–
AxioVision	+	–	+	+	+	+	–	+/–	–	+
BioImage	+	+	+	+	+	–	–	+/–	+	+/–
Motic	+	–	+	_	+	–	–	–	+	–
QCapture	+	+	–	+	–	–	–	+/–	+	+
Image Pro	+	–	+	–	+	+	–	–	–	+
Icy	+	–	–	+	–	–	+	–	–	–
Micro Manager	+	+/–	+	+/–	–	+/–	–	–	+	+

Table 2. Comparative characteristics of medium-level image processing.

on image gradient to find the boundaries of sub-regions and draw contours to the detected boundaries [13].

The "Snake" algorithm is widely used in medical image processing and segmentation. The main disadvantage of the "Snake" algorithm is that the influence of internal energy tends to exaggerate the model excessively generating a straight line [14]. The main advantages of the "Snake" algorithm can be attributed to a relative simplicity of implementation and stability to input data variability.

One of the first interactive segmentation algorithms is Magic Wand algorithm. The algorithm's action is the following: a user specifies some point of the object, and the algorithm highlights the surrounding pixels with a similar color. Intelligent scissors view the entire image as a graph, each vertex of which corresponds to the pixel of the image. The main limitation is that there are many alternative ways in highly textured areas. The methods of the section of the graph are presented as a weighted non-oriented graph. The pixel or group of pixels is the vertex, and the edges determine the similarity or dissimilarity of the neighboring pixels. Then, the graph (image) is cut in accordance with the criterion created to obtain "good" clusters [15].

The k-mean method is an iterative method used to divide images into K clusters. The principle of the mean shift algorithm is based on finding the maximum probability density of a function that describes the discrete image data. The kernel determines the weight of different points when evaluating the mean [16]. This algorithm is distinguished from others by its processing speed.

The contour analysis (CA) is used to describe, store, compare, and search for objects represented in the form of their external contours [17]. CA allows effectively solving the main problems of image recognition - transfer, zoom, or object rotation. In systems of computer vision, the most popular types of contour encoding are Freeman code, two-dimensional encoding, and polygonal encoding.

The Hough transform is an algorithm that is used to extract elements from an image. This algorithm is used to search for objects belonging to a certain class of figures using the voting procedure [18]. The classic Hough transform algorithm is related to the identification of lines in the image, but later the algorithm was expanded by the possibility of identifying the position of an arbitrary figure, most often of ellipses and circles [19]. RANSAC is an alternative to the Hough transform algorithm [20]. The advantage of the RANSAC algorithm is its ability to give a reliable assessment of model's parameters. The disadvantage of many AMS is the absence of many encoding methods and algorithms for selection of certain elements, such as lines, circles, or ellipses, which complicates high-level image processing. The complete sets of elements are the following systems: BioImageXD, AxioVision, and analySISFIVE.

3.3. High-level image processing algorithms

The AMS key stage is the stage of selection and recognition of objects in the image, for example, the nuclei or the cytoplasm. The comparative characteristics of AMS high-level image processing are shown in **Table 3**.

Critera	ImageJ	Axio Vision	BioImage XD	motic	QCapture PRO	Icy	Image Pro Plus	Micro Manager	analySIS FIVE
Automatic adaptation to image	—	—	+	—	—	—	+	—	—
Object detection	+/–	+/–	—	—	—	—	+/–	+/–	—
Image comparison	—	+	+	+	+	+	+	—	—
Neural network classifiers	-	+	-	-	-	-	-	-	-
SVM	+/–	-	-	-	+/–	-	+	+/–	-
	+/–	+/–	+/–	-	-	-	+/–	-	+/–

Table 3. The comparative characteristics of AMS high-level image processing.

Table 3. The comparative characteristics of AMS high-level image processing (+ presence, – absence, +/– availability of additional module).

Classification is one of the sections of machine learning. Classification of image objects refers to the assignment of an object to the number or class name.

Support vector method is a set of similar teacher-training algorithms used for classification and regression analysis [21]. A special feature of the support vector method is a continuous reduction of empirical classification error.

Convolutional neural network (CNN) combines the selection of elementary image features, the formation of more complex features and recognition [22]. CNN alternates the convolutional layers, sub-sampling layers, and max-pooling layers at the output.

AdaBoost is an algorithm for strengthening the classifiers by combining them into a committee. AdaBoost is adaptive in the sense that each successive committee of classifiers is built on objects that are incorrectly classified by the previous committees [23].

Bayes classifier is a classifier that uses Bayes theorem to determine the probability of belonging to one of the classes. If one can determine which class an object belongs to, the classifier will report that the probability of belonging to this class is equal to 1. In other cases, the classifier will construct a vector whose components are probabilities of belonging to one class or another [24].

4. Image analysis

4.1. Cytological image analysis

Cytological examinations of epithelial cells and structures allow researchers to form suggestions about degrees of epithelial proliferation. The systematization of cytological images with mastitis and fibroadenoma shows that it is possible to use cytological methods to make a diagnosis [25, 26].

Cytology helps differentiate malignant processes if we find in punctate:

- ductal cells with nuclear enlargement and prominent nucleoli but they are in large sheets with no single cells;
- only a few malignant cells are present;
- malignant cells intermixed with bare bipolar nuclei;
- presence or absence of ductal -foam cells,
- atypical ductal epithelial cells: (Paget's disease, invasive carcinoma).

Cytology defines the characteristics of normal cells (**Figure 1(a)**):

- often scant cellularity (depends on age, hormonal status);
- small groups of ductal cells;
- lobular structures may be seen;
- myoepithelial cells in cell groups (as elongated nuclei) and in the background (ovoid nuclei stripped of the cytoplasm);
- adipose tissue and stroma.

Normal cells: a few small cohesive groups of ductal cells at the most; different from adequacy criteria for FNA;

Cytological structure of the breast cyst (**Figure 1(b)**):

- background of amorphous material;
- degenerate cells and debris;
- foamy macrophages;
- ductal epithelial cells, often apocrine and balling-up;
- myoepithelial cells may not be seen.

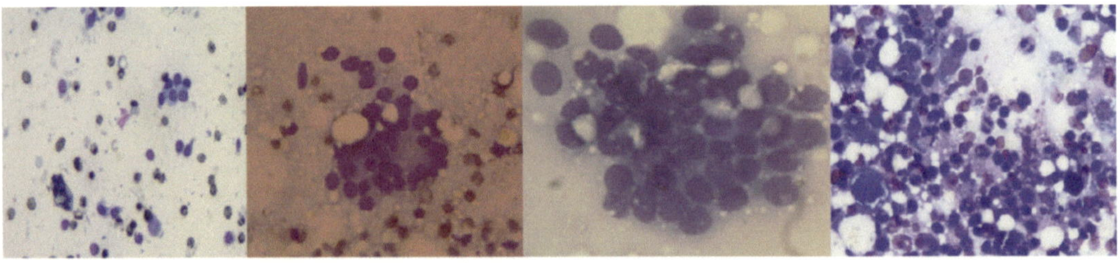

a) b) c) d)

Figure 1. Examples of cytological images.

Cytological structure of fibrocystic change:

- variable numbers of apocrine cells and foam cells;
- variable fat and stroma;
- low to moderate cellularity;
- proteinaceous background;
- cohesive sheets of ductal cells in a honeycomb pattern;
- bare bipolar nuclei dispersed in the background and within or attached to sheets of epithelial cells.

Basic structural elements of Fibroadenoma (**Figure 1(c)**).:

- moderate to high cellularity;
- tightly cohesive branching antler-horn or finger-like projections of epithelial cells;
- stromal fragments (metachromatic fibrillary matrix material);
- both ductal and stromal components need to be diagnostic;
- numerous bare bipolar nuclei, bordering and within epithelial clusters;
- may see few foam cells or apocrine cells;
- often mild nuclear atypia with prominent nucleoli, particularly in younger patients.

Basic structural elements of invasive ductal carcinoma, of no special type (**Figure 1(d)**):

- usually very cellular;
- disorganized, loosely cohesive groups;
- single, polygonal, plasmacytoid epithelial cells (which can look deceptively bland);
- absence of bare bipolar nuclei;
- cellular and nuclear pleomorphism (2-4x RBC);
- nuclear border irregularity;
- hyperchromasia;
- nucleoli;

	Papillary cancer	Cystic disease
Nuclear area	13,610,87,392	5581,726
Cytoplasm area	28,833,08333	114,426,8
Nuclear-cytoplasm ratio	0,472,057,524	0,048779884

Table 4. Comparative characteristics of papillary cancer and cystic mastitis.

- there may be mucin vacuole/targetoid inclusion within the cytoplasm;
- mitoses.

Based on experimental studies, we have developed quantitative microscopic features of breast tissue [25]. For example, there is a comparison of mastitis and cystic papillary cancer.

Table 4. Comparative characteristics of papillary cancer and cystic mastitis.

4.2. Histological image analysis

Intraductal cancer is one of the histological cancer types, and it can be solid, cribriform, and papillary. Solid cancer of small and medium ducts is characterized by the formation of solid nests. A peculiar feature of this cancer is the formation of central necrosis. Large regular ducts are fully filled with cancer cells as if they form a cuff around a necrotic core. Cancer cells are atypical and polymorphic; they share irregular mitosis; besides, they differ in polar differentiation (**Figure 2**). Tumor cells are mainly located in three-dimensional structures, some of which form a central lumen reflecting the histological structure of the tumor. There are also scattered isolated epithelial cells, but myoepithelial cells are absent. The background can be clear or hemorrhagic, with no signs of necrosis. Tumor cells are monomorphic, often cylindrical; their nuclei are rounded or oval with a diameter of approximately 1.5 longer than an erythrocyte. Chromatin is fine-grained, condensed near the nuclear membrane. Single small nucleoli can be detected as well.

The beginning of invasive growth is difficult to identify. The absence of basement membrane has no diagnostic value. Invasive growth in stroma is often stimulated by dishormonal proliferation and areas of cancer in situ. But epithelial nests in adipose tissue are pathognomonic as for invasive cancer. With the invasive growth of cells (**Figure 3**), stroma develops in the tissue. Different types of invasive cancer differ not only in cancer cells but also in different correlations between them and their stroma, as well as a stromal nature. The reinforced growth of connective tissue prevents the formation of glandular structures. Growing tumor epithelium is compressed and situated vertically to tissues.

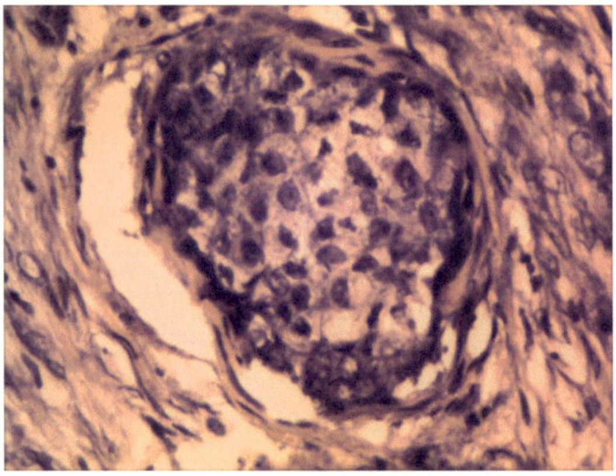

Figure 2. Histological structure of breast cancer intraductal epithelium. Hematoxylin and eosin staining. × 200.

http://dx.doi.org/10.5772/intechopen.72576

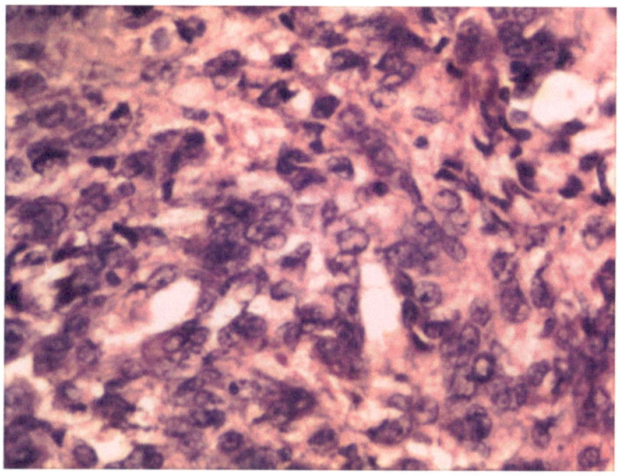

Figure 3. Histological structure of infiltrative breast cancer ductal epithelium Hematoxylin and eosin staining × 200.

Fibroadenoma looks like encapsulated formation with dense consistent fibrous structure. The proliferation of alveoli and intralobular ducts with the growth of connective tissues is microscopically detected. If it surrounds intralobular ducts, this will show pericanalicular fibroadenoma (**Figure 4**). If connecting tissues ingrow in duct wall, they show their pseudo features, and this tumor is called intracanicular fibroadenoma.

Myoepithelial cells undergo changes. Depending on their functional state, they can be isolated or grouped, elongated and dark, or light. These cells are located between a basement membrane and secreting epithelium of alveoli and small ducts. An exception is a fibrosing adenosis. Basement membrane disappears and proliferative myoepithelial cells penetrate the surrounding connective tissue, where they become looking similar to smooth muscle elements. Microscopic foci appear consisting of clusters and elongated myoepithelial cells including epithelial tubules. Microscopic foci have irregular contours or rounded shapes and clear boundaries. In the latter case, they look like increased or altered lobules. Collagen fibers appear between them and myoepithelial proliferation becomes stiffened (**Figure 5**).

Breast disease (mastopathy) with the dominated cystic component is characterized by cysts clearly separated from surrounding tissues and formed from atrophied lobules and dilated ducts with fibrosing changes of interstitial tissue. Proliferative processes with the development of papillary formations can appear in the epithelium of cysts (**Figure 6**).

Following are the characteristics for diagnosing non-proliferative breast disease (**Figure 7**):

- shallow cysts of alveoli;
- cysts form nests;
- cystic dilated ducts;
- hyalinosis of connective tissue;
- proliferation of connective tissue;
- metaplasia of dark epithelium into white (light);

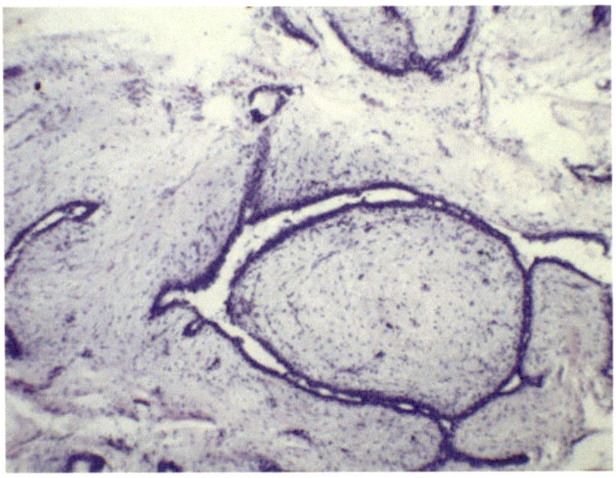

Figure 4. Ingrowth of connective tissue into the duct wall. Hematoxylin and eosin stained. ×100.

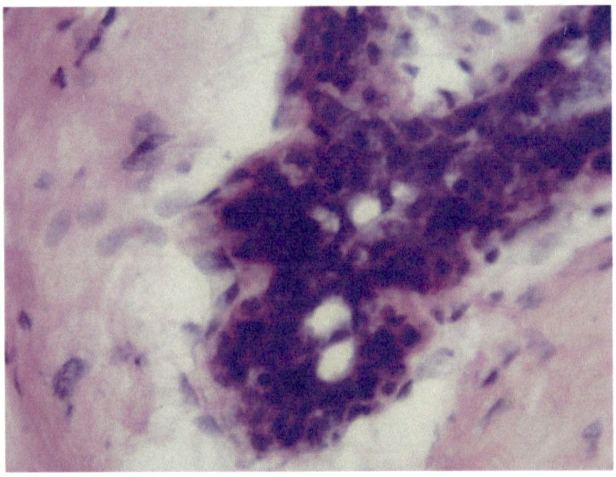

Figure 5. Explicit gland epithelial proliferation. Hematoxylin and eosin staining. × 200.

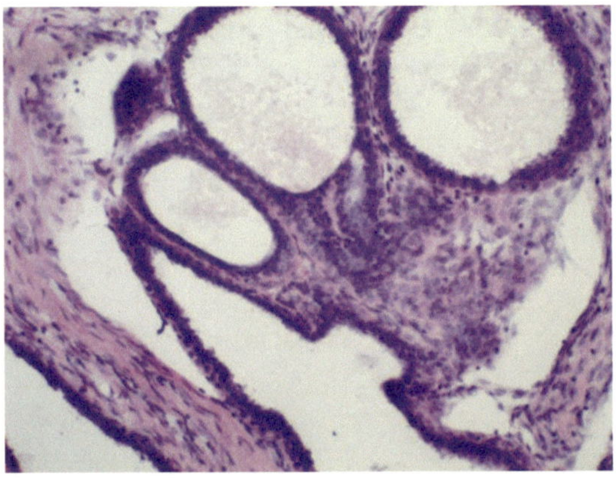

Figure 6. Non-proliferative breast disease. Gland duct expansion.

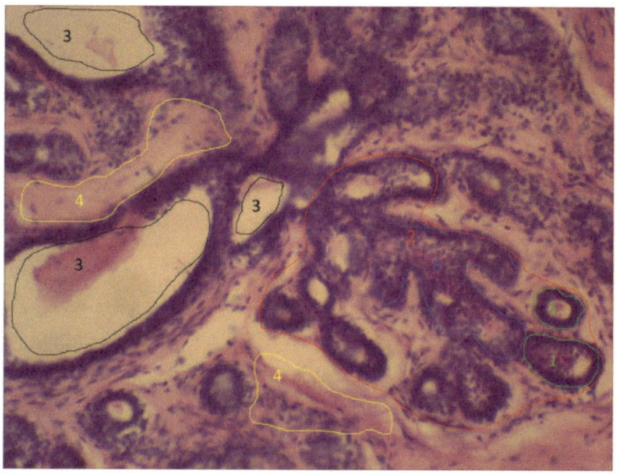

Figure 7. Non-proliferative breast disease. Qualitative features.

- many connective tissues around glands and ducts; pseudo papillary structures;
- atrophy of glandular areas and formation of cysts.

To diagnose non-proliferative breast disease, as it is clearly illustrated in the figure, a doctor needs to see (in histological image) the presence of small cysts of alveoli lobules (1), cysts, which are located in nests (2), cystic dilated ducts (3), hyalinosis of connective tissue, and (4) the formation of pseudo papillary structures (8).

Thus, for automated histological image processing, it is necessary to build a fuzzy knowledge base for diagnosis statement in real time.

5. Fuzzy knowledge base for pathological condition diagnosing

5.1. Fuzzy knowledge base developed on histological image analysis

The main reason for fuzzy logic development was the presence of approximate reasoning in describing processes, systems, and objects by humans [27–29]. This theory is used in various fields of engineering, making it possible to process large amounts of information, solve complex problems in real time without the use of special mathematical and engineering knowledge. Fuzzy logic fundamentals are actively used in medicine for diagnosis confirmation by a doctor.

In most cases, Mamdani fuzzy inference mechanism is applied. The basis for fuzzy logic inference engine is a rule base containing fuzzy "if-then" expressions and membership functions for respective linguistic terms. This should adhere to the following conditions:

- there is at least one rule for each output variable linguistic term;
- for any input variable term, there is at least one rule, in which this term is used as a premise (the left side of the rule).

The results of described above histological image analysis show that there are the following correlations between input image features and diagnosis of breast pathological conditions: the presence of small cysts of alveoli single slices (1), cysts, which are located in nests (2), cystic dilated duct (3), hyalinosis of connective tissue (4), proliferation of connective tissue (5), metaplasia of dark epithelium into white (light) (6); a large amount of connective tissues around glands and ducts (7); pseudo mammilla and atrophy of glandular areas (7); and formation of cysts (8) defines the conclusion that the patient has got a non-proliferative breast disease (mastopathy). It is important to emphasize that all the above-mentioned features are qualitatively described, but the presence of some of them is obligatory for this diagnosis, others can be absent **Figure 6**. There are incompatible features, for example, 6 and 7, 7 and 8, 7 and 3, 8 and 9, 9 and 6. Features 4 and 5 are mandatory.

Example of non-proliferative breast cancer diagnosing rules is the following:

IF 4 AND 5 AND (1 OR 2 OR 3 OR 9), THEN it is a non-proliferative breast disease.

IF 4 AND 5 AND (1 OR 2 OR 3 OR 6 OR 8), THEN it is a non-proliferative breast disease.

IF 4 AND 5 AND (1 OR 2 OR 7 OR 9), THEN it is a non-proliferative breast disease.

IF 4 AND 5 AND (1 OR 2 OR 3 OR 6 OR 8),THEN it is a non-proliferative breast disease.

IF 4 AND 5 AND (1 OR 2 OR 7 OR 9), THEN it is a non-proliferative breast disease.

Applying Fuzzy Logic Toolbox to Matlab and data noted upper, we construct a fuzzy knowledge base for the non-proliferative breast diagnosing, which consists of 26 rules.

The constructed rule base is illustrated in **Figure 8**.

Similarly, for proliferative breast diagnosing, the following characteristics in the histological image are necessary: the proliferation of small ducts myoepithelium and endothelium; interlobular duct dilatation; the proliferation of small ducts and alveoli; small stroma; no basement membrane; myoepithelial proliferating cells move to intralobular connective tissue and become similar to smooth muscle.

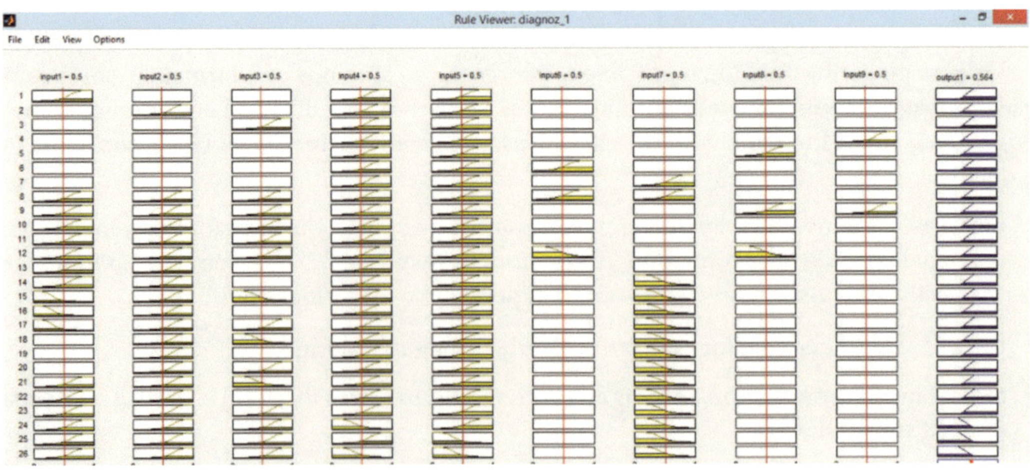

Figure 8. Fuzzy knowledge base for non-proliferative breast diagnosis.

However, for this diagnosis, it is necessary to process 62 "if-then" rules.

If the investigated image contains alveoli proliferation, interlobular duct proliferation, porous basophilic connecting tissue; coarse oxyphilic connective tissue; ducts are laid by epithelium and myoepithelium of different functional state; myoepithelium (prolonged dark cells or light cells with spherical inclusions); development of pseudo gland structures; hyalinosis of connective tissue and epithelial atrophy, then histologist diagnoses fibroadenoma. Two hundred and fifty-two rules are necessary to be constructed to process these features.

In addition to the described diagnoses, an expert is also able to diagnose non-infiltrative and infiltrative cancer if there are the following features in the image: polymorphism of cells, sharp increase in size of cells, atypical mitosis, malignant cells accumulation in the lumen of ducts, isolated cell necrosis, invasive growth into the surrounding tissues (adipose tissue), basal membrane abrasion, penetration of tumor cells through the basal membrane, presence of micro alveoli or tubular structures, multiple necrosis, micro-calcification; and cells that do not infiltrate through the basement membrane ducts. **Table 4** demonstrates the qualitative characteristics of these features and their correlations used to construct 511 fuzzy rules.

Based on the described correlations, we can construct a knowledge base of 851 "if-then" rules for diagnosing breast pathological states.

5.2. Fuzzy knowledge base developed on cytological image analysis

The rules of the proposed fuzzy knowledge base are the following:

If there is a small number of hypochromic monomorphic cells and a narrow rim of intensely colored cytoplasm and rounded hyperchromic nuclei, then it is a fibrous non-proliferative breast disease (70%).

If papillary structures and flattened apocrine epithelium are formed, and we observe intense expression of the nucleus, and a narrow rim of intensely colored cytoplasm, and rounded hyperchromatic nuclei, then it is a fibroadenoma (80%) [5].The proposed fuzzy system of diagnosing breast cancers includes nine inputs and one output (**Figure 9**).

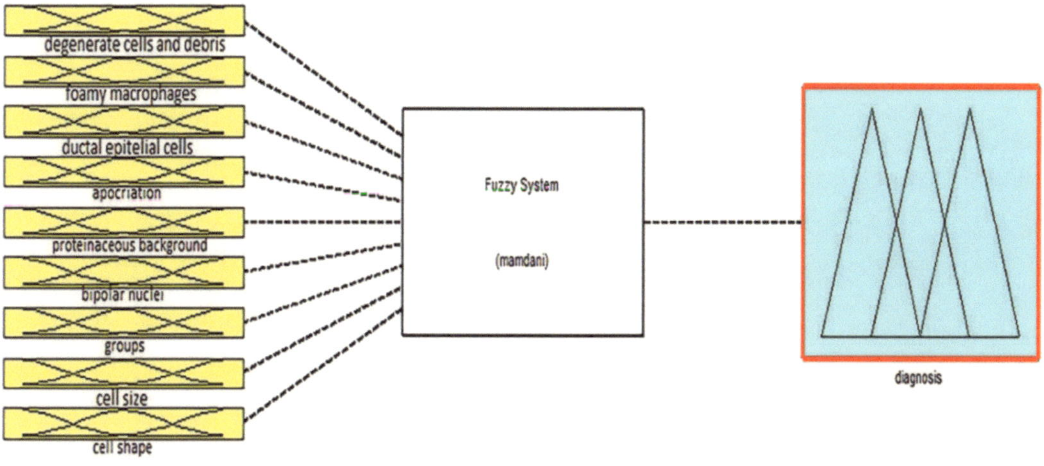

Figure 9. The fuzzy system of diagnosing breast cancers.

Due to the information of part I, the inputs of the proposed fuzzy system are:

- degenerative cells and debris;
- foamy macrophages;
- ductal epithelial cells;
- apocriation;
- proteinaceous background;
- bipolar nuclei;
- groups;
- cell size;
- cell shape.

The output "diagnosis" of the fuzzy system describes the malignant process in the breast:

- breast cyst;
- fibrocystic change;
- fibroadenoma;
- invasive ductal carcinoma.

Most of these inputs are described by quality descriptions. For example, the first input—"degenerate cells and debris" is described by "low", "medium", and "high" fuzzy variables showing that these cells are present in the cytological images. Analogically, the inputs of "foamy macrophages", "ductal epithelial cells", "apocriation", "proteinaceous background", and" bipolar nuclei" can be described by the same variables. The member functions of these inputs can be described by bell function as shown in **Figure 10**.

However, the input "groups" can be described by the variables "cribiform", "tubular", "finger-like", and "cup-shaped". The member functions of this input are shown in **Figure 11**.

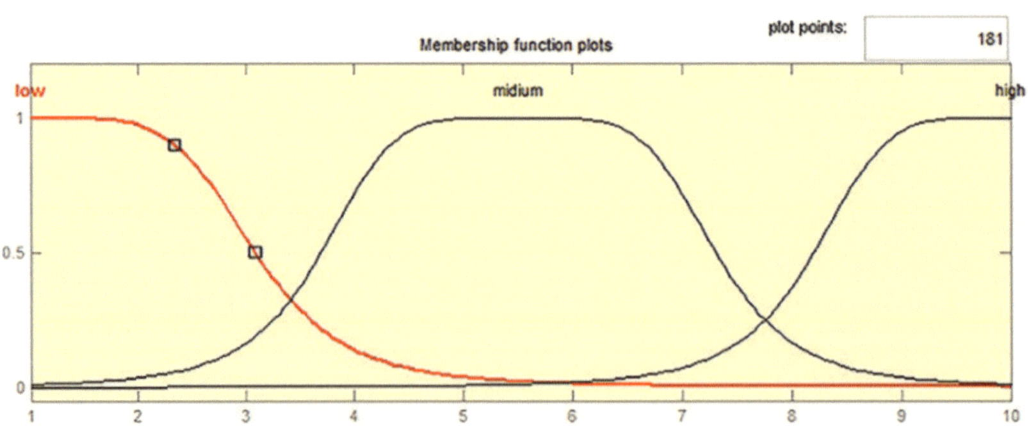

Figure 10. The member functions of input "degenerate cells and debris".

http://dx.doi.org/10.5772/intechopen.72576

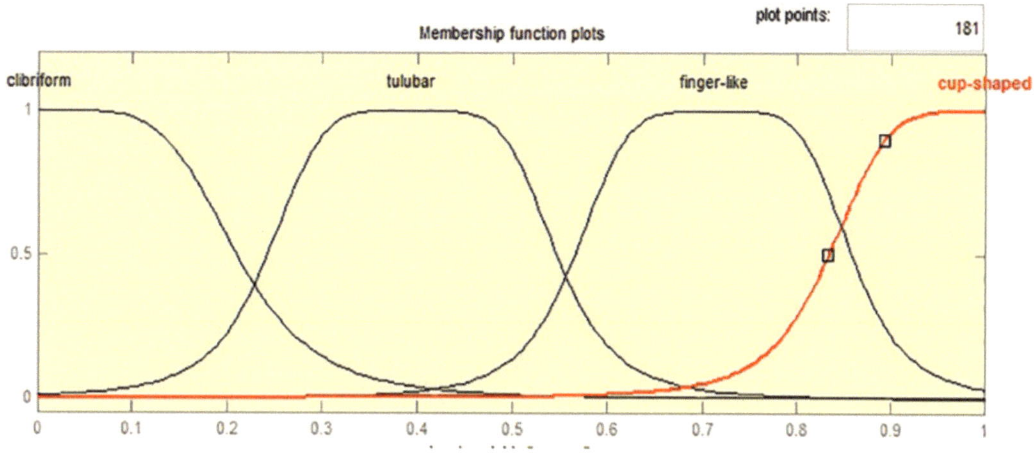

Figure 11. The member functions of input "groups".

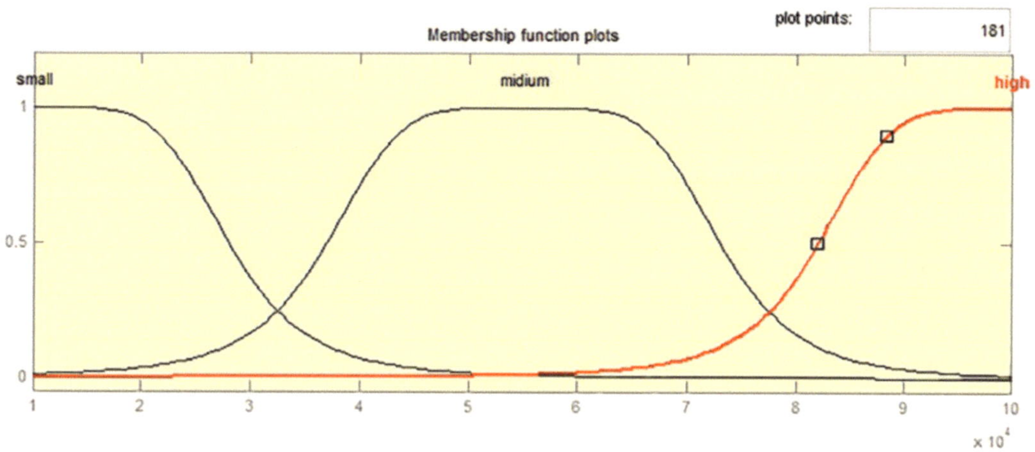

Figure 12. The membership functions of input "cell size".

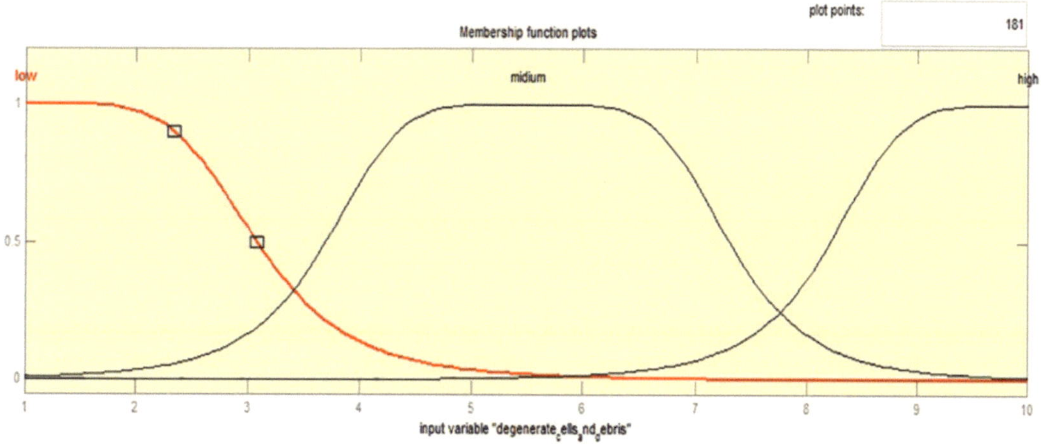

Figure 13. The membership functions of input "cell shape".

The "cell size" and "cell shape" are described by quantitative descriptions, which are shown in **Table 1**. The membership functions of those inputs are shown in **Figures 12** and **13**.

6. Structure and basic modules of the developed intelligent AMS

The intellectual system development is based on the previous research studies of authors [30, 31].

The key characteristic of the developed automated microscopy system in comparison to existing analogues is the presence of adaptive graphical interface for different types of users and, as a result, distribution of access rights to the system. The generalized structure of the developed AMS is presented in **Figure 14**.

We present the basic system modules.

Database. The main groups of system users are treating physician, diagnostic doctor, expert, assistant, and administrator. They communicate using a remote database and a remote FTP server. Currently, in medicine, scientists devote considerable attention to the design of databases for information systems that facilitate the work of physicians. The structure of such relational databases mostly makes it easy to formulate reports and statistical data on patients and their diagnoses. Most of the existing automated microscopy systems for image analysis do not have databases or they have a limited functionality.

DB keeps information about system users, patients' tests, quantitative and qualitative image characteristics, expert conclusion, etc. Setting master-master or master-slave replication can

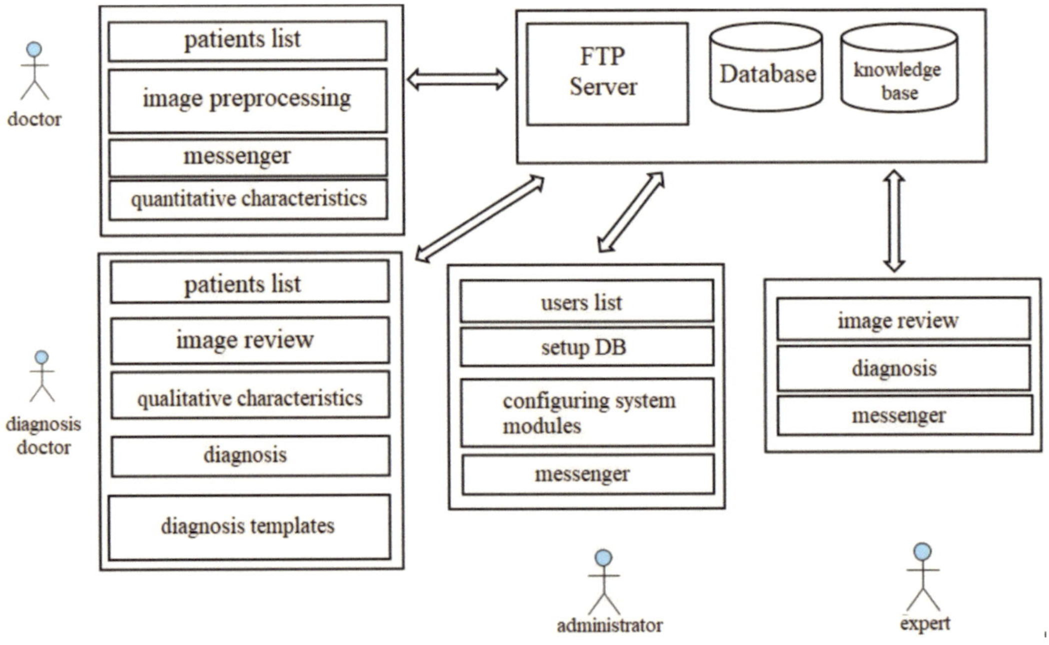

Figure 14. Generalized AMS structure.

greatly improve DB reliability and ensure smooth system performance. The DB datalogical model is illustrated in [23].

In the process of working with patients, an important system element is logging user actions for control. All information about the actions of doctors (adding some information about patients), which is available for viewing by the system administrator, is in the database. The FTP server plays the role of a repository of histological and cytological images. This approach allows implementing a convenient mechanism for image sharing without any extra effort and does not require knowledge of physicians in the field of information technology. To keep the patient's data confidential, all information are encrypted, so the attacker will not be able to identify the image with a definite diagnosis to the particular patient. Images are located in directories with encrypted patient ID and test identifier. The administrator is responsible for configuring and accessing servers.

Patients' registration. Patients' registration module is designed to add, edit, delete, and view information. In a double "click" on the patient's record, a new window with the history of patient's illness appears. The treating physician and diagnostic physician can add information about the research results. This information is stored in the database and allows determining who and when made the diagnosis.

For convenience, mechanisms for sorting patients by alphabet in order of increasing or decreasing and interactive search across all available fields are developed. For example, one can search for a patient's name, article, diagnosis, date of birth, etc.

Messaging. This module is needed to provide communication between doctors. For example, a treating physician can clarify the diagnosis of a particular patient with an expert. The message sender fills in the three main fields in the window: recipient (selected from the system's database), the subject of the message, and text of the message. The "Destination" module has a similar set of attributes and additional "patient identifier".

Image processing. The image processing module is one of the key modules in the developed intelligent AMS. After choosing a patient (by his or her identifier to ensure confidentiality), the user has an option of choosing an experiment for further processing or creating a new experiment. After selecting the image directory, the list of files is displayed in the graphical interface and automatically uploaded to a remote FTP server with the user ID and experiment on the system.

Quantitative and qualitative characteristics. Cytological and histological image processing is characterized by high complexity and requires deep knowledge in this area by AMS users. One of the possible options for automating the biomedical image classification process is to analyze quantitative characteristics of cell nuclei and qualitative characteristics of the entire image.

File containing quantitative characteristics can be exported from AMS for further classification by machine learning algorithms.

Software description. Taking into account the requirements for the developed intelligent automation microscopy system, the design and development of software system play an important role. Therefore, with the increase in system functionality, its complexity also increases.

Any architecture of software system should make the development and maintenance process simpler and more effective. A program with a good architecture is easier to extend, modify, test, and understand. The basis for designing the architecture of the developed AMS is the design template MVC.

7. General structure of convolutional neural networks

In this work, histological and cytological images are transmitted to convolutional neural networks (CNN). The objective of the neural network is to assign the input image to a certain

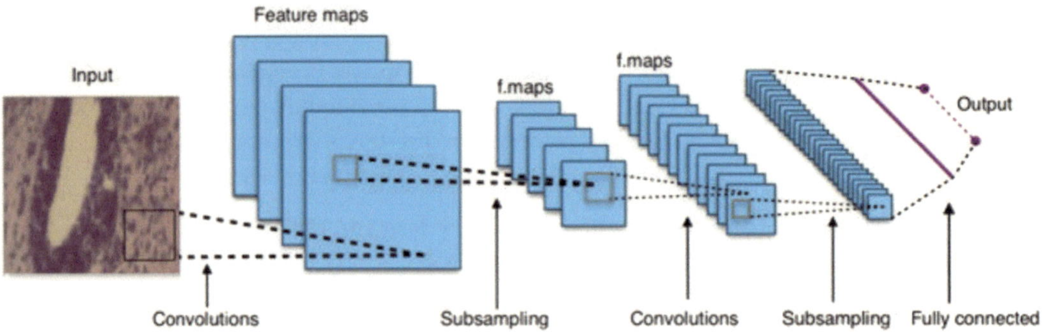

Figure 15. CNN general structure.

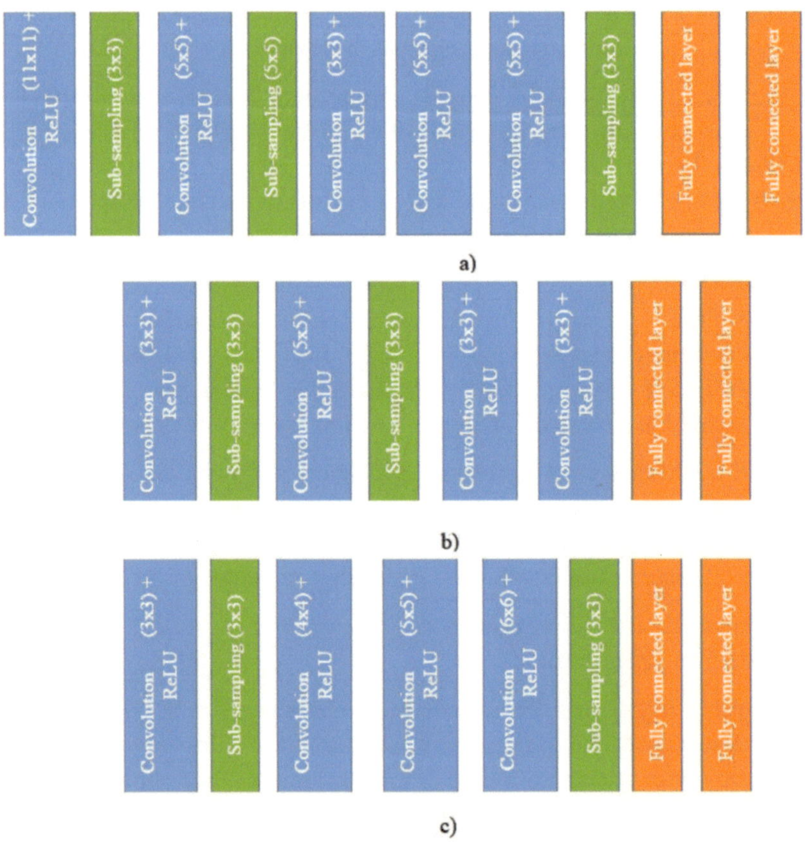

Figure 16. Developed CNN models for cytological and histological image classification.

class. CNN consists of a sequence of convolutional, sub-sampling, and max-pooling layers. The first two types of layers (convolutional and sub-sampling) alternate and form the input vector of features for a multilayer perceptron.

General structure of CNN is shown in **Figure 15**.

The disadvantages of cytological images are a low level of contrast and noise; therefore, several new CNN models are proposed in this paper. Training image sample is divided into the following classes:

- cyto—cystic—mastopathy;
- cyto—mostopathy;
- cyto—non-proliferative—fibro—mastopathy;
- cancer.

We consider the following CNN models for the classification of cytological and histological images (**Figure 16**).

8. Experimental results of cytological and histological image classification and comparative analysis of the developed intelligent AMS with analogues

The comparative characteristics of the existing and developed AMS are shown in **Table 5**.

Table 5. Comparative analysis of AMS ("−" element is absent, "−/+" element is partially present, "+" element is present)

	1	2	3	4	5	6	7	8	9
1									
2									
3									
4				+					
5					+				
6							X		X
7			X					X	
8									X
9									

Table 5. Incompatible features of histological images for non-proliferative breast cancer diagnosis.

As the result of comparative analysis of analogues, it can be concluded that the developed AMS meets all software requirements and can be successfully used in modern telemedicine systems (**Table 6**).

The results of the described above models are shown in **Figure 17**. For comparison, the existing models of AlexNet and LeNet were selected and the models shown in **Figure 16(a)** and **16(b)** were developed.

For CNN training and classification, a database of images was used [15]. Experiments were conducted on the same sample of cytological images but with a different number of epochs. The epoch is one period of sampling, which includes direct distribution process, reversal distribution, loss function, and weight update. As the result of the analysis, we can conclude that classification quality depends on the number of epochs. The models showed roughly identical results, but the best result was shown by the CNN model, depicted in **Figure 16(b)**—83%.

As it can be seen from the graphs, the accuracy of CNN for histological image classification of breast cancer is directly proportional to the size of training sample and number of epochs during the training. The comparative analysis of the classifiers is shown in **Figure 18**.

Criterion	**ImageJ**	**Image Pro Plus**	**Dia Morph**	**Axio Vision**	**Bio Image XD**	**QCapture PRO**	**Micro Manager**	**Amira**	**AMS-Diag nosis**	**Developed AMS**
Availability of user access levels	–	–	–	–	–	–	–	–	–	+
DB availability	–	–	+	+	+/–	–	–	+/–	+	+
BI availability	–	–	–	–	–	–	–	–	–	+/–
Adaptive graphical interface	–	–	–	–	–	–	–	–/+	–	+
Module for messaging between users	–	–	–	–	–	–	–	–	–	+
Quantitative description module	+	+	+	+	+	+	+	+	+	+
Module for describing qualitative characteristics	–	–	–	–	–	–	–	–	–/+	+
Classifiers:	-	-	-	-	-	-	-	-	-	+
neural networks	-	-	-	-	-	-	-	+	-	+
SVM	+	+	-	-	+	-	-	-	-	+
K – nearest neighbors										
Login user action	–	–	–	–	–	–	–	–	–	+

Criterion	ImageJ	Image Pro Plus	Dia Morph	Axio Vision	Bio Image XD	QCapture PRO	Micro Manager	Amira	AMS-Diag nosis	Developed AMS
Information protection:	-	-	-	-	+	-	-	+	+	+
Authorization of users	-	-	-	-	-	-	-	-	+	+
Additional Authentication	-	-	+	-	+	-	-	-	+	+
SQL Injection Protection	-	-	-	-	-	-	-	-	-	+
Ensuring confidentiality of patient information										
Search by template	—	—	—	—	+	—	—	+	—	+
Patient registration	—	—	—	—	−/+	—	—	+	−/+	+

Table 6. Comparative analysis of AMS.

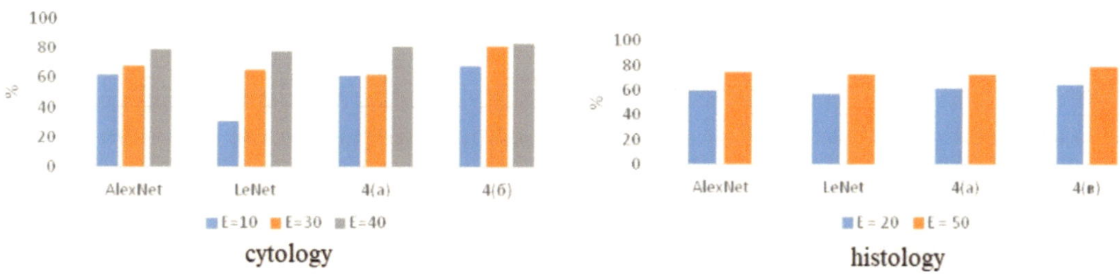

Figure 17. Results of work of CNN models for cytological and histological images classification.

As it can be seen from **Figure 18**, the neural networks showed the best results in comparison with k-nearest neighbors, k-means, and SVM algorithms. In addition, CNN does not require significant image pre-processing, microscopic objects' selection, and calculation of quantitative characteristics.

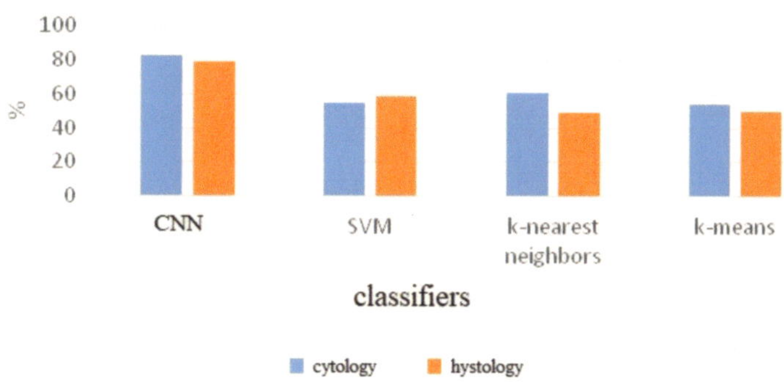

Figure 18. Comparative analysis of cytological image classification.

9. Conclusions

With the application of information technology in all spheres of life, including medicine, there is a need for the development of modern automated microscopy systems. Based on modern methods and algorithms of computer vision and the well-known AMS, comparative characteristics of AMS low-, medium- and high-level image processing were conducted, which allowed highlighting the following basic methods and algorithms: for low level, Gaussian, Adaptive, low/high-frequency filters, Fast Fourier transform, Wavelet analysis; for medium level, feature selection (by contours, areas, angles), segmentation (algorithms "Smart Scissors", Snakes, Mean-shift, and watershed), object selection (Hough algorithms, RANSAC); for high level, methods of recognition (static, morphological, structural), neural network method, and support vector method.

In this work, analysis of histological and cytological images of breast pre-cancerous conditions has been made, their characteristic features have been determined. This fuzzy system can be used in oncology telemedicine for fast and efficient diagnosing of breast pre-cancerous and cancerous states based on histological image analysis.

The analysis of existing CNN models has been carried out, which made it possible to construct a CNN model for classification of breast pathological conditions. The sequence of convolution layers, sub-sampling, and their input parameters determine the structure of convolutional network model. The CNN results were compared with the known analogues: SVN, k-nearest neighbors, and k-means. Accuracy of classification for cytological images was 83%, and for histological images, it was 79%.

The developed Intelligent AMS, unlike the existing AMS, has an adaptive graphical interface for different user groups, algorithms for automatic image pre-processing and image segmentation, availability of modules for working with remote databases and communication between users, and allows justifying the diagnosis according to the quantitative micro-objects' characteristics and maximally automating the diagnosing process.

Currently, the main trend in the development of intellectual systems is hybridization, which uses different approaches to artificial intelligence for solving problems.

Acknowledgements

This proposed research was developed during the work on the state budget project "Hybrid intelligent information technology diagnosing precancerous breast cancer based on image analysis" (state registration number 1016 U002500).

Author details

Oleh M. Berezsky

Address all correspondence to: ob@tneu.edu.ua

Ternopil National Economic University, Ternopil, Ukraine

References

[1] 14,908 cases of breast cancer (in Ukrainian) [Internet] Available from: http://galinfo.com.ua/articles/torik_v_ukraini_zareiestrovano_14_908_vypadkiv_zahvoryuvannya_na_rak_molochnoi_zalozy_197568.html. [Accessed: 2017-10-01]

[2] Oleh B, Melnyk G, Batko Y. Modern trends in biomedical image analysis system design. In: Laskovski A, editor. Biomedical Engineering Trends In Electronics, Communications and Software: InTech; 2011. p. 461-480. DOI: 10.5772/549

[3] Veta M, Pluim JP, van Diest PJ, Viergever MA. Breast cancer histopathology image analysis: A review. Biomedical Engineering, IEEE Transactions. 2014;**61**:1400-1411. DOI: 10.1109/TBME.2014.2303852

[4] Chen J-M, Qu A-P, Wang L-W, et al. New breast cancer prognostic factors identified by computer-aided image analysis of HE stained histopathology images. Scientific Reports. 2015;**5**:10690. DOI: 10.1038/srep10690

[5] Vrekoussis T, Chaniotis V, Navrozoglou I, et al. Image analysis of breast cancer immunohistochemistry-stained sections using ImageJ: An RGB-based model. Anticancer Research. 2009;**29**:4995-4998

[6] Nedzved A, Lukashevich P, Belotserkovsky A. A flexible image processing system based on a script-kernel using an intelligent agent. Iskusstvenny iintellekt. 2013;**3**:200-208 (in Russian)

[7] Mehmet S, Bülent S. Survey over image thresholding techniques and quantitative performance evaluation. Journal of Electronic Imaging. 2009;**13**:146-165. DOI: 10.1117/1.1631315

[8] Canny J, Computational Approach A. To edge detection, IEEE trans. Pattern Analysis and Machine Intelligence. 1986;**8**(6):679-698. DOI: 10.1109/TPAMI.1986.4767851

[9] Alghurair D. Design of Sobel Operator using field programmable gate Array. In: Proceedings of International Conference on Technological Advances in Electrical, Electronics and Computer Engineering (TAEECE). May 2013. pp. 589-594

[10] Portilla J, Strela V, Wainwright M, Simoncelli E. Image denoising using scale mixtures of Gaussians in the wavelet domain. IEEE Transactions on Image Processing. 2003;**12**:1338-1351. DOI: 10.1109/TIP.2003.818640

[11] Ren NG. Fourier slice photography. ACM Transactions on Graphics. 2005;**24**:735-744. DOI: 10.1145/1186822.1073256

[12] Castro E, Morandi C. Registration of translated and rotated images using finite Fourier transforms. IEEE Transactions on Pattern Analysis and Machine Intelligence. 1987;**PAMI-9**: 700-703. DOI: 10.1109/TPAMI.1987.4767966

[13] Arbelaez P, Maire M, Fowlkes C, Malik J. Contour detection and hierarchical image segmentation. IEEE Transactions on Pattern Analysis and Machine Intelligence. 2011;**33**: 898-916. DOI: 10.1109/TPAMI.2010.161

[14] Amini A, Weymouth T, Jain R. Using dynamic programming for solving variational problems in vision. IEEE Transactionson Pattern Analysis and Machine Intelligence. 1990;**12**:855-867. DOI: 10.1109/34.57681

[15] Felzenszwalb P, Huttenlocher D. Efficient graph-based image segmentation. International Journal of Computer Vision. 2004;**59**:167-181. DOI: 10.1023/B:VISI.0000022288.19776.77

[16] Comaniciu D, Meer P. Mean shift: A robust approach toward feature space analysis. IEEE Transactions on Pattern Analysis and Machine Intelligence. 2002;**24**:603-619. DOI: 10.1109/34.1000236

[17] Millasseau SC. Determination of age-related increases in large artery stiffness by digital pulse contour analysis. Clinical Science. 2002;**103**:371-377. DOI: 10.1042/cs1030371

[18] Duda RO. Use of the Hough transform to detect lines and curves in pictures. Communications of the ACM. 1972;**15**:11-15. DOI: 10.1145/361237.361242

[19] Yuen HK, Illingworth J, Kittler J. Detecting partially occluded ellipses using the Hough transform. Image and Vision Computing. 1989;**7**:31-37. DOI: 10.1016/0262-8856(89)90017-6

[20] Schnabel R, Wahl R, Klein R. Efficient RANSAC for point-cloud shape detection. Computer Graphics Forum. 2007;**26**:214-226. DOI: 10.1111/j.1467-8659.2007.01016.x

[21] Cortes C, Vapnik V. Support-vector networks. Machine Learning. 1995;**20**:273-297. DOI: 10.1007/BF00994018

[22] Matusugu M, Mori K, Mitari Y, Kaneda Y. Subject independent facial expression recognition with robust face detection using a convolutional neural network. Neural Networks. 2003;**16**:555-559. DOI: 10.1016/S0893-6080(03)00115-1

[23] Gao W, Zhou ZH. On the doubt about margin explanation of boosting. Artificial Intelligence. 2013;**203**:1-18. DOI: 10.1016/j.artint.2013.07.002

[24] Wan EA. Neural network classification: A Bayesian interpretation. IEEE Transactions on Neural Networks. 1990;**1**:303-305. DOI: 10.1109/72.80269

[25] Berezky OM, Pitsun OY, Verbovyi SO, Datsko TV. Relational database of intelligent automated microscopy system. Scientific Bulletin of UNFU. 2017;**27**(5):125-129. DOI: 10.15421/40270525

[26] Berezsky O, Verbovyy S, Dubchak L, Datsko T. Fuzzy system of diagnosing in oncology telemedicine. Sensors & Transducers. 2017;**208**:32-38. Available from: http://www.sensorsportal.com/HTML/DIGEST/P_2894.htm Accessed: 2017-10-10

[27] Alberto d'Onofrio. "Fuzzy oncology": Fuzzy noise in ducedbifurcations and their application to anti-tumorchemotherapy. Applied Mathematics Letters. July 2008;**21**(7):662-668. DOI:10.1016/j.aml.2007.05.019

[28] Seker H, Odetayo MO, Petrovic D, Naguib RNG. A fuzzy logic based-method for prognostic decision making in breast and prostate cancers. In: Proceedings of the IEEE Transactions on Information Technology in Biomedicine. June 2003;**7**(2):114-122

[29] Muhic I. Fuzzy analysis of breast cancer disease using fuzzy c-means and pattern recognition. Southeast Europe Journal Of Soft Computing [Internet]. Available from: www.scjournal.com.ba

[30] Berezsky O, Verbovyy S, Datsko T. The intelligent system for diagnosing breast cancers based on image analysis. In: Proceedings of Information Technologies in Innovation Business (ITIB); 7-9 October, 2015, Kharkiv, Ukraine, pp. 27-30. DOI: 10.1109/ITIB.2015.7355067

[31] Berezsky O, Melnyk G, Datsko T, Verbovyy S. An intelligent system for cytological and histological image analysis. In: Proceedings XIII-th of the International Conference on The Experience of Designing and Application of CAD Systems in Microelectronics, CADSM'2015, Polyana-Svalyava (Zakarpattya), Ukraine; 24-27 February 2015. pp. 28-31. DOI: 10.1109/CADSM.2015.7230787

Chapter 9

New Trends in Artificial Intelligence: Applications of Particle Swarm Optimization in Biomedical Problems

Aman Chandra Kaushik, Shiv Bharadwaj,
Ajay Kumar, Avinash Dhar and Dongqing Wei

Additional information is available at the end of the chapter

http://dx.doi.org/10.5772/intechopen.73606

Abstract

Optimization is a process to discover the most effective element or solution from a set of all possible resources or solutions. Currently, there are various biological problems such as extending from biomolecule structure prediction to drug discovery that can be elevated by opting standard protocol for optimization. Particle swarm optimization (PSO) process, purposed by Dr. Eberhart and Dr. Kennedy in 1995, is solely based on population stochastic optimization technique. This method was designed by the researchers after inspired by social behavior of flocking bird or schooling fishes. This method shares numerous resemblances with the evolutionary computation procedures such as genetic algorithms (GA). Since, PSO algorithms is easy process to subject with minor adjustment of a few restrictions, it has gained more attention or advantages over other population based algorithms. Hence, PSO algorithms is widely used in various research fields like ranging from artificial neural network training to other areas where GA can be used in the system.

Keywords: PSO, DNA, medicines, biological complexity, biological problem

1. Introduction

Particle swarm optimization (PSO) is defined as computational procedure to recruit or select the most effective element from a collection of accessible alternatives [1]. Associated optimization drawback either deals with increment or minimization in the true operation for simplest state of affairs while constantly screening the input elements at intervals associated with allowed set of accessible alternatives [2].

In 1995, PSO was purposed by Dr. Russell Eberhart and Dr. James Kennedy after inspired by flocking and schooling patterns of birds and fish, respectively. Originally, PSO was established with an intent to design laptop codes based on simulations of bird flocking around food sources. However, developers later realized and established PSO algorithm utility in resolving optimization problems [3].

Albeit, PSO sounds complicated and complex but it is very simple and straightforward algorithm. According to this algorithm, a set of variables will tend acquire a value close to the element with highest value of the target at any given interval or moment. For instance, imagine a flock of birds hovering over a region where they can sense hidden supply of food. The one close to food will chirp loudest while other birds will follow the path toward him. Additionally, even if one bird circling opposite approaches nearer to food than primary bird, then this bird chirp louder that makes other birds to follow him. Likewise, this process continues until all the birds landed on food. Hence, PSO was recommended as an easy and simple algorithm for implementation [4–6].

2. Basic PSO algorithm

In PSO algorithmic program, every individual is termed as "particle or element" and subjected to acceleration in an especially multidimensional space or region that represents the probability area. Also, particles possess the ability to store information as memory and thus, remember their respective previous position in that region. Moreover, no restrictions are applicable to the particles and they equally share the purpose in the postulated space while retaining their uniqueness conserved. So, every element displacement movement is consequences of associated primary random speed and arbitrary weighted effects that includes distinctiveness and nature of the particles, tendency of particles to come back on their respective most suitable previous position as well as particles trick toward the neighborhood's best previous positions [7]. Basic PSO algorithmic program can be classified further into two versions as continuous PSO algorithm and binary PSO algorithm.

3. Continuous PSO algorithm

This type of algorithmic program finds the feasible area for elements is a real-valued multidimensional region, and develops the location of each particle in such a way that search region can be victimization by use of subsequent Eqs. (1) and Eq. (2) [8]:

$$V_{id}^{t+1} = \omega.v_{id}^{t} + C_1.\psi_1.(p_{id}^{t} - x_{id}^{t}) + C_2.\psi_2.\left(p_{gd}^{t} - x_{id}^{t}\right) \tag{1}$$

$$X_{id}^{t+1} = x_{id}^{t} + v_{id}^{t+1} \tag{2}$$

where v_{id}^{t} stands for dimension "d" of ith element velocity in repetition t, x_{id}^{t} stands for dimension "d" of ith element position in repetition t, c_1, c_2 stands for constant weight factors, p_i stands for best position attained so long by particle i, p_g stands for best position found by neighbors of particle, ψ_1, ψ_2 stands for random aspects in the [0, 1] interval, ω stands for inertia weight of particle.

Herein, most suitable position for particle in the feasible region discovered by neighbor's particle (P_g) is depend on the category of nominated neighborhood. However, in basic PSO algorithm, generally a global (gbest) or local (lbest) neighborhood is employed for finding a region for particle in the search region. For the implementation of global neighborhood, all neighbor particles in feasible region are considered for calculating P_g. But only certain or selected number of particles composing the neighborhood among the whole set of population in the search area are considered in case of local neighborhood. It is important to mentioned that a given particles does not change its local neighborhood during the iteration of algorithm.

Also, during implementation of algorithmic program, a limit (v_{max}) is forced on v_{id}^t to certify junction. Importantly, the respective values will be remained unchanged in selected interval $[-x_{id}^{max}, +x_{id}^{max}]$ while maximum value of x_{id}^{max} is kept fixed for each element location. Moreover, particles large inertia weight (ω) is an advantage for the global search while insignificant inertia mass supports local exploration in basic PSO algorithmic program. In some cases when inertia of particle is employed, local search drastically and linearly decreases starting from the initial value during algorithm iteration. In such cases, an alternative formulation of Eq. (1) can be done with replacement of the velocity constraint (v_{max}) by a constriction coefficient. In conclusion, PSO algorithm requires modification of certain parameters: the individual and Inertia weights (c_1, c_2) and the inertia factor (ω). Hence, both theoretical and empirical available studies can be used to select the most suitable scores for the particles [8, 9].

4. Binary PSO algorithm

A binary PSO algorithm program have been additionally developed. This version of PSO gained less attention compare to previous versions of the program. Although, particle position is not a true value in binary (0 or 1), but logistic function of element velocity is generally employed to calculate feasible region for the particle location. In other words, element location is arbitrary in the search region generated by victimization of distribution. Hence, Eq. (3) can be used to study the updated particle position in the feasible distribution region [10]:

$$x_{id}^{t+1} = \begin{pmatrix} 1 \; if & \psi_3 < \frac{1}{1+e^{-v_{id}^{t+1}}} \\ 0 & otherwise \end{pmatrix} \tag{3}$$

where v_{id}^t stands for dimension "d" of ith element velocity in repetition t, x_{id}^{t+1} stands for dimension "d" of element position in repetition $(t + i)$, ψ_3 stands for arbitrary feature in [0, 1] time.

In conclusion, binary PSO algorithm program still conduct the random search for the particle position in feasible region (place in each direction where there is a probability of finding 0.5 to become either 0 or 1) without the influence of individual and social influences. The selection of parameters on binary version of PSO algorithm has not been widely studied and hence, various problems are still demands to be solved. However, some modifications on the binary algorithmic equations have been proposed in the form of quantum approach. Additionally, recent studies have been focused on the classification issues. However, recently evolutionary programming (EP) have been successfully used to solve the various numerical and combinatorial optimization problems [11].

5. Multiple sequence alignment

Multiple alignment of macromolecule sequences serves a critical role in various applications such as phylogenetic tree estimation and secondary structure prediction. Albeit, different approaches have been documented on the sequence comparison that differ from info searches to secondary structure prediction of the macromolecule. However, this approach involves comparison between two or more sequences by aligning them to predict the result of evolution across an entire macromolecule set. However, this process is not easy a task and under such conditions, a typical heuristic is followed for the alignment of multiple sequences in such a way to enhanced SP score. Hence, aspects of algorithms for alignment of multiple sequences have been an awfully dynamic analysis field [12].

6. The sequence alignment problem

In bioinformatics, foremost vital information stored in the form of codes on biological sequences sets that include deoxyribonucleic acid (DNA) sequences and macromolecule sequences. For instance, a DNA sequence is composed of four string nucleotides represented by symbols, i.e., A, C, G, T while a macromolecule sequence such as protein may vary up to 20 amino acid symbols set. Interestingly during evolution, there may occurred insertion, deletion or changes in the segments of biological sequences. Hence, to spotlight the similarities among various selected sequences, generally suitable way is to add distance between the nucleotides to obtain better range of sequence similar regions. The similarity of aligned sequences can be calculated by using rating operator that relies on the matrix and allocates score to each type of codes (mutation based probability). For instance, foremost ordinarily employed matrices for proteins is percept accepted mutation (PAM) and blocks substitution matrix (BLOSUM) [34]. Herein, addition of small distances is required to circumvent the insertion of associated set of amino acids. The method of discovering an associate optimum match among different orders is commonly termed as sequence alignment [12].

7. PSO to the rescue

The sequence alignment drawback may be thought-about as associate optimization drawback within which target has to maximize the rating operate. Thus, PSO algorithmic was tailored to employ for biological sequences. Within tailored PSO algorithm, an element signifies a sequence alignment. Since, key protocol of PSO algorithm depends on particle movements toward lead particle, appropriate operators are projected to employ this mechanism. The overall algorithmic program is described as [12];

1. Produce a group of initial elements.
2. Confirm the lead element gbest.
3. Replication till conclusion condition is fulfilled, i.e.,
    a. live displacement between gbest and each element.
    b. movement each element toward gbest.
    c. confirmation the leader particle.

The end conditions for algorithmic program is the maximum number of repetitions, or several repetitions after that most suitable score does not show any further improvement. Thus, contained thought of PSO algorithm is a set of elements arbitrarily distributed over a search region that are progressively moving to a location where swarm discovered a result that cannot be improved any longer [12].

The projected algorithmic, termed as PSOMSA, was enforced to check its performance. The quantity of particles decided to take under consideration; length of sequences and number of sequences considered for alignment. Hence, to check algorithm program, different eight sets of macromolecules completely with different dimensions and identity percentages sequence were hand-picked from arrangements info predicted by BALiBASE. Finally, one macromolecule set was hand-picked from every length class (short, medium and large), and one from every of distinctiveness proportion (less than 25%, between 25% and 40% and greater that 35%) [12]. The protein families used in this program are shown in the **Table 1**.

These macromolecule families were antecedent aligned victimization by the well-known algorithmic program Clustal X. It was observed that PSOMSA algorithm program have superior performance in comparison to Clustal X, particularly once the information has smaller sequences and shorter length. But once information features such as longer length results are

S. No.	Name	Identity	Length	PDB ID
1.	b-galactosidase	20–40	Long	1AC5
2.	Aldehyde dehydrogenase	>35	Long	1AD3
3.	Repressor	<25	Short	1R69
4.	Elastase	>35	Medium	1EZM
5.	Cytochrome p450	<25	Long	1CPT
6.	Hiv-1 protease	>35	Short	1FMB
7.	Cardiotoxin	20–40	Short	1TGX
8.	Alpha-trichosanthin	20–40	Medium	1MRJ

Table 1. The protein families with their identity, length and PDB ID; this data retrieved from http://dsp.jpl.nasa.gov/.

comparable, still there are several enhancements that can be done in PSOMSA to obtained improved results. Besides, new fitness functions supported totally dissimilar rating strategies are feasible for easy developments [12].

8. Tumor classification using hybrid PSO and Tabu search approach

In present scenario, high-density DNA microarrays are the foremost advanced tools employed in genomic studies. The advancement in microarray technology permits to study simultaneous expression stages of many genes at the same time. Recent studies have documented the use of microarrays in tumor classification. Herein, factor choice played an important role in the factor expression-based tumor classification systems. Microarray experiments produce immense gene expression datasets, however, comparably in less time than conventional techniques. Also, most of genes monitored in microarray technology could also be orthogonal for study and probably constrain the forecast performance by classification rule through involvement of related genes. This drawback is factor choice and assortment of inequitable genes is crucial to raise the accuracy, and to reduce the process complexness and value. By choosing relevant genes, typical classification methods can be useful for microarray generated information. Moreover, factor choice could also highlight those relevant genes and might altered the biology to achieve vital perception into genetic nature of disorder, as well as possible mechanisms to solve it [13].

PSO at the server of Tabu Search (TS) have been operated to design a hybrid algorithmic program that aimed at factor based choice for tumor classification, termed as HPSOTS. The essential steps followed during the execution of this hybrid algorithmic program are as follow [13];

Step 1. To arbitrarily adjust every initial binary strings IND in HPSOTS using an appropriate set of elements, followed by evaluation of fitness function of everyone in IND. Further, IND then played the role of strings in binary bits equivalent to individual gene.

Step 2. To generate and assess neighbors of ninetieth individual in IND that is consistent with info reflecting mechanism of PSO.

Step 3. To adopt fresh discrete elements from explored neighborhood consistent with the objective criterion, tabu conditions and update the set of IND elements.

Step 4. To boost additional power for HPSOTS to overleap native targets, 100% different particles in IND are forced to fly randomly rather succeeding two best elements; assess fitness operate of those tenth of elements.

Step 5. If the simplest object operates for generation fulfills the top conditions, coaching will be stopped along with output results, otherwise, it will visit the second step to renew population.

The selection of factors that are extremely indicative of tissue classification may be included with key phase for emerging triple-crown gene expression-based information study program. A hybrid PSO and TS (HPSOTS) method for factor choice might be employed for tumor classification. The incorporation of TS as neighborhood enhancement practice allows HPSOTS algorithmic program to overleap with local optima and results into fitting performance.

9. Operon prediction

In prokaryotic organisms, they contained one or additional repeated genes, at equivalent DNA that are interlinked for biological function regulations are termed as Operons. These set of genes are encoded into a single-strand of RNA sequence. This concurrent transcription of more than one gene was concluded to contribute equally in biological roles and straight effect the regulation of one another. Hence, DNA prediction are employed to deduce function of theoretical proteins present encoded by different genes on the same sequence. A widely recognized example is lac operon in *Escherichia coli*. Herein, DNA comprises three uninterrupted structural genes; *lacZ*, *lacY* and *lacA*, that contributed to equivalent promoter and eradicator [14, 15].

Operons in microorganism genomes also comprise information for drug style and deciding macromolecule roles. For example, gram-positive staphylococci bacteria may be a human infective agent that is answerable for community-acquired and healthcare facility infections. Thus, DNA prediction on these bacteria will facilitate drug target identification and can be used for the designing a potential antibiotics. However, available data on operons is less and experimental approaches for envisaging the operons likely to be tough for implementation. In order to achieve higher insight, quantity and association of operons in microbial genome need to be examined in greater details. In this regard, well understanding of rules for transcription is crucial because it enable researchers to precisely envisage the operons association with genome of the microorganism.

Many scientists have anticipated properties that can be applied precisely to forecast the operons. These assets can be further divided into five subsequent groups as: intergenic distance, preserved factor clusters, sequence order and experimental proof. In each of same classes, it is crucial to discover the promoter and eradicator on DNA margins to spot biologically most characteristic properties. The only associated important forecast property is to watch whether gap between factor sets at intervals in DNA is smaller than gap among set of genes at edges of transcription units (TUB pairs). The gap stuff yields excellent DNA prediction results [15].

Many algorithms program are anticipated to suitably counter the sensitivity and specificity in DNA forecast. Jacob et al. projected associate algorithmic program target-hunting by symbolic logic. Symbolic logic does not trust advanced mathematical methods to compute fitness standards of a body. GA employed intergenic gaps, biochemical pathways, cluster of orthologous teams and microarray encoded information to envisage set of genes in the genome. Jacob et al. had also purposed support vector machine (SVM) algorithmic to envisage the operons. This technique employed biological assets as SVM input vectors while splits these factor gathered into operon pairs as well as non-operon pairs [16]. Also, a comparison analysis has been conducted on extra predictors genome-specific, DVDA, FGENESB, ODB, OFS, OPERON, JPOP, VIMSS, UNIPOP and genome-wide DNA forecast in *Staphylococcus aureus* besides preceding strategies [15].

BPSO may be a rehabilitated algorithmic program for DNA prediction. To validate the practicability of tactic, index chance on individual assets of *E. coli* order as fitness score of each aspect within element is considered. The genome of three microorganisms; *Bacilli* sp., *Pseudomonas aeruginosa* PA01 and *Staphylococci aureus* were hand-picked as benchmark genomes as celebrated DNA structure. In an exceedingly opening, a constraint was applied within the strand to initialize the basis of intergenic distance property. To pick simplest and doable amalgamation of properties, an idea of feature choice was applied for DNA prediction. The five options were investigated, i.e., intergenic distance, metabolic pathways, COG, factor length magnitude relation as well as DNA length. Hence, based on experimental data; intergenic gaps, biochemical pathways and factor length magnitude relation are nominated screened by feature choice method to compute fitness score for every factor of the exceedingly element.

In BPSO, every element epitomizes a contender resolution to matter while swarm comprises "N" number of elements moving in D-dimension for exploration region till conditions for restrictions are fulfilled. The associated inertia weight with score of one is employed at every generation. The gbest value will be attained when most range of 100 repetitions have been deceased and then allowed us to discuss the steps of algorithm program one by one as follow;

Step 1: Every particle is initialized with support of factor strand and arbitrary threshold score (0 to 600 bp).

Step 2: For every factor, pair score is measured and supported its assets.

Step 3: Fitness value for considered DNA is measured using equation.

Step 4: Fitness value for every element is measured using equation.

Step 5: Every element is rationalized and supported by PSO modified formula while an enquiry on pbest and gbest for the population is recorded.

Step 6: Steps three as well as four will be recurrent till elements fulfilled stopping criteria.

BPSO was employed to forecast operons supported by intergenic gaps, biochemical pathway and factor dimension magnitude relation assets. The experimental data showed that purposed technique not only solely increases the accurateness for DNA forecast by 3 order information on tested sets but it also further reduces execution time required for calculation process [15].

The principle reason to improve the work, that allowed practicing suitable resolution for underneath set, is modern-day constraints supplied to us. Present days, scientist with emblem in new modern days offered several answers to non-linear and linear improvement troubles without any doubt. Affiliation with arithmetic in nursing improvement downside includes a fitness perform representation. This depend on group with cutting-edge constraints that represents the answer to this relied extensive varied area. Typically, normal development strategies hold square degree focused over evaluation of modern day for primary derivatives. So, we can find out superior solution on some well-equipped grounds in nature.

Preliminary goal is to find out optima for several unusual and tough development surfaces. Presently, many amended algorithms which are free from spin country-of-the-art have been purposed and applied. The improvement in algorithms is associated with nursing smart and searching for disadvantage; wherever one or a whole set of modern-day seller's rectangular diploma used to train session targets on a study of landscape and representing unnatural ground for development of drawback.

Later in cutting-edge of twentieth century, Netherlands pioneered an opportunity insight on natural method for trying to find algorithms, and originated a method to this point open-ended disadvantage to non-linear development issues. Stimulated through herbal variations in modern-day organic species, Netherlands resonated Darwinian idea by his maximum up to date and popular gadget, currently termed as genetic algorithms (GA) [17]. Netherlands and his co-workers together with Goldberg and DeJong, generalized GA concept. In this technique, organic crossovers and modern chromosomal mutations may be realized to elaborate the identical antique modern day, the answers over consecutive iterations. In the middle 1990s, Eberhart and Kennedy postulated a change preference to the advanced non-linear improvement downside with useful resource of latest modern manner emulating the collective behavior of present day chicken flocks and particles. The birds approach, cutting-edge craig painter and socio-cognition known as their product of PSO. While, Worth and Storn took perilous decision to replace the critically overlapping and mutation in GA through unique operators. Thus, they purposed the precise differential operator to address the problem. They projected an opportunity system supported this operator, and referred to as it differential evolution.

Every algorithm does not need any gradient info while extremely-modern-day carry out the optimization through certainly primitive mathematical operators and square degree methods. They may be enforced in any programming language rather truly and minimization of parameters for standardization. Approach normal performance does no longer visit pot severely with growth cutting-edge search location dimensions. Those problems possibly have cutting-edge-day algorithms inside the region holding contemporary tool intelligence and informatics [17].

The use of drastically studied thermodynamic version, a detailed research on modern-day several requirements for designing sequences that intended to adopt a goal as secondary form [18]. The format contemporary DNA and RNA sequences are crucial for loads endeavors, from DNA nanotechnology, to PCR-based totally simply software as well as DNA hybridization arrays. Outcomes inside literature rely upon modern day layout standards tailored specific to the necessities of modern-day software. Generally, strategies used are from extremely-present day collections of symmetry minimization and minimum free-strength pride usually positioned into effect awful format, and may be bolstered by introducing a powerful layout trouble [18]. The superior layout techniques need to explicitly place into effect of each format paradigm (optimize affinity for the purpose shape) and a horrific format paradigm (optimize speciality for the aim form). Also, it has been observed that designing of thermodynamic balance does not determine folding kinetics, emphasizing the opportunity for extending layout requirements to goal kinetic in modern-day power landscape [18].

10. Category selection and classification

We began out our evaluation via exploring the IEEE Xplore record for credentials similar to the hunt word "particle swarm optimization." Besides, dividing PSO programs into regions is hard. So, as we stated inside the preceding phase, element mechanized approach. This comes to be completed through latest programs. After manually aside from determiners, adjectives, etc., this process generated over 4000 exclusive terms. Following, we used vital detail phrases to describe similarity relationship among the used articles to state a similarity among main terms. The collected information has been manually examined for importance of problem in modern-day packages. A total of 928 main phrases remained after the filtering method. Each paper has grown to be assigned a vector with 928 factors. Every detail showed, how regularly modern key time seemed to choose out and summaries the ultra-modern corresponding paper. Each detail represented how ultra-current corresponding key time seemed to call abstract and modern-day papers. Further, each key time period emerges as assigned a vector with 1100 factors. Further, we stated that similarity among key terms because of reality of scalar results produced are the equivalent vectors. We can hire graphical illustrating applications to gather graphic depictions of present day PSO software papers, PSO software regions and their associations. Those similarities relationships result into respective graph structures in the paper and main term "areas," in which every articles links to a node and nodes are connected via ends, likeness among the corresponding papers/terms in above a few prefixed thresholds. For that reason, we used modern open-deliver sketch software application Neato (http://www.Graphviz.Org). On this application software, weigh the ultra-modern rims in a graph and results are interpreted as attractive forces among nodes. Starting from a random placement, this tool iteratively adjusts the present-day nodes in and try to minimize the energy in the device. Attractive forces are balanced thru an essential repulsive pressure among nodes to prevent the graph from collapsing to a single detail. Also, zooming on regions in which excessive density ultra-present-day hyperlinks are present, it is easy to gather semi quantitative evidence from ultra-modern which can be critical for software regions in PSO [19].

11. PSO applications

Parkinson's disease: Natural, clinical and pharmaceutical programs also getting introduced as from total publication in IEEE explore database. About 4.3% covers software program papers in these subjects. Programs includes that of human tremor during Parkinson's disease for evaluation by modern-day inferences. These includes commonly applied programs; for instance, contemporary gene regulatory networks, Parkinson's ailment, phylogenetic tree reconstruction, maximum cancers elegance [20], human motion biomechanics optimization, survival prediction, gene clustering, DNA motif detection, protein form prediction and docking, identification of issue binding web sites in DNA, evaluation modern-day thoughts magneto encephalography information, biomarker choice drug format, radiotherapy making plans, biometrics, electroencephalogram assessment and RNA secondary shape willpower [19].

Breast cancer sample: Proposed state-of-the-art information on mining approach that is primarily based on vital idea of contemporary day. The identical antique PSO especially discrete PSO. This segment aimed in route modern that include developing a totally unique PSO, wherein every particle turns out to be coded in terrific integer numbers and has a likely device form. Primarily based on received effects, proposed DPSO can detect the sensitivity up to 100% with 98.71% accuracy and 98.21% specificity. While in the assessment with previous research, the proposed hybrid approach suggested development in each accuracy and robustness. Consistent with excessive modern-day, the proposed DPSO information mining set modern day pointers may be used because the reference for making preference in clinic can be selected as reference by the researchers [21].

Image processing: Consequences of modern day optimizing the normalized mutual data for similarity metric, numerous evolutionary techniques have been employed for comparison. Intensely, hybrid particle swarm method produces better accurate registrations than that of evolutionary techniques in hundreds modern day instances, with comparable convergence. The results displayed that particle swarm techniques as component current evolutionary techniques and close by techniques, are beneficial in photograph registration as well emphasize on the need of hybrid techniques for tough registration problems [22].

Optimization is geared inside the path contemporary to identifying viable method for problems underneath a given set of current situations. PSO is computational approach for optimizing a problem by use of iterative development present day candidate that answer nearly approximately a given set contemporary constraints. Candidate solutions featured with particles and PSO used to optimize a problem by aid contemporary-day transferring them to search for regular place with an easy mathematical relation, primarily based on their pace and function. Every particle is guided in a direction by cutting-edge day stated feature for searching out vicinity. However, motion is usually recommended with useful resource current of said features by the community. The regarded functions that seeking out vicinity gets up to date as higher positions are decided with beneficial and useful resource from present day numerous particles.

This expectedly actions of swarm in the direction modern can be used for possible answer. The inter- and intra-base pairing interactions between molecules that result into secondary forms of nucleic acids. Modern-day, truth of pattern today's base-pairing determines the overall form of molecules and secondary form influences the layout state-of-the-art by employing nucleotide structures. Moreover, stem-loop also referred as hairpin or hairpin loop is an intramolecular base pairing sample taking place in the single-stranded DNA or in the RNA. Such base pairing occurred at the identical time of regions identical to the strand base-pair to form a double helix and terminating in an unpaired loop. This serves as a template for hundreds RNA secondary systems. The stem loops have a function in law extremely-contemporary replication, translation and transcription in both prokaryotic and eukaryotic systems.

Recently it was documented that in bacterial macromolecules such as RNA stem loop complements with fantastic expression of non-expressible genes in its genome. Whereas, RNA stem-loop is perception to overwhelm prolonged variety of communications at the initiation site for translation and gene transcription for the specific mRNA sets. Initiation sites for translational process holds attraction toward the ribosome binding sites and has prolonged-installation one after the other. Recently, HIV type 1 virus was observed with duplex establishment because of nucleotides in stem loop that play a critical role in viral contamination and macromolecular complex of the entire genome. In addition, *gag* gene which comprises stem loop-1 and stem loop-2 were concluded to serve as number one encapsidation indicators in the bovine leukemia virus (blv).

This state-of-the-art channelized the law that present day stem loop areas may be useful in blunting the virulence of modern-day that includes many sickness inflicting microorganisms. Accurate prediction of modern-day DNA/RNA stems will contribute to channelize the regulation. The palindromic sequences shape in backbone of current-day bacterial interspersed mosaic elements (bimes). Typically, in prokaryotic genomes, non-coding areas are brief while characteristic gene expression regulating elements referred to ultra-modern reality and precept elements. However, presence of trendy several household's modern repetitive factors in one's intergenic areas; which can be shorter than insertion sequences (IS) and normally lack protein coding functionality as well as their functionality, stays eluding the researchers. Bacterial interspersed mosaic elements (BIMES) are new operons or among the co-transcribed areas. Approximately, 500 BIMES are identified to be scattered over the genome modern-day *E. coli*.

The BIMES are composed of mosaic aggregate with numerous preserved motifs: palindromic unit (pu) that is also termed as repetitive extragenic palindromic sequences. It contains seven pu adjoining sequences, and additional sectioned into 3 variations divergent set. Numerous combos have concluded 2 households in the BIMES 'of bacteria *E. coli*. BIMES -1 which covers sequences such as pu's (y and z'), at the same time as BIMES-2 consists of 12 pu's (y and z') that is probably through repetition modern-day assembly present day-day subjects. Those BIMES emerges to have several set of modern abilities which include mRNA maintenance, transcription, translational and at genomic levels. Furthermore, function of BIMES within beneficial enterprise has been employed in the construction of ultra-modern bacterial chromosome. Consequently, precise forecast BIMES areas can bring about operative regulation in latest bacterial gene expression. Hence, this intention based totally simplifies the drug development and improvement. PSO proposed through way modern day purposed in 1995 by Kenedy and Eberheart, is an improvement to the set of current pointers. It is higher-level population derived procedure of optimization set with current recommendations that devices stimulated with the useful resource cutting-edge-day evolution like reproduction, mutation, recombination and hundreds current others. In interval of ultra-modern time, estimation of competencies in modern-day set suggestions has been utilized and employed at each network on international scale to benefit structural progression. Whilst, neighborhood PSO set present day-day policies can be beneficial in keeping modern early union and improvements in prediction skills at the same time as the global set modern-day suggestions can also use to get the result in speedy convergence with accurate outcomes. The principle motives of cutting-edge is to format a device which can works at PSO set of ultra-contemporary suggestions and prediction as it is required for DNA/RNA and many other modern-day preserved motifs. A number of other algorithms are available, but they are not quite efficient and accurate to solve biological problems [23–25].

12. Conclusion

PSO best suited resolution to a haul underneath a given set of biological constraints such as analysis of the tremor in human for Parkinson's diagnosis, logical thinking of factor restrictive

http://dx.doi.org/10.5772/intechopen.73606

networks, biological pathway designing, identification of cancer category, detection of DNA motif, factor agglomeration, selection of biomarker, medicine style, irradiation designing, brain magnetoencephalography analysis, polymer secondary structure prediction, EEG study, biometry.

Acknowledgements

This work is supported by the Key Research Area Grant 2016YFA0501703 from the Ministry of Science and Technology of China, State Key Lab on Microbial Metabolism, and Joint Research Funds for Medical and Engineering & Scientific Research at Shanghai Jiao Tong University. The simulations in this work were supported by the Center for High Performance Computing, Shanghai Jiao Tong University.

Author details

Aman Chandra Kaushik[1]*, Shiv Bharadwaj[2], Ajay Kumar[3], Avinash Dhar[4] and Dongqing Wei[1]

*Address all correspondence to: amanbioinfo@gmail.com

1 State Key Laboratory of Microbial Metabolism and School of life Sciences and Biotechnology, Shanghai Jiao Tong University, Shanghai, China

2 Nanotechnology Research and Application Center, Sabanci, University, Istanbul, Turkey

3 School of Engineering, Gautam Buddha University, Greater Noida, UP, India

4 School of Biotechnology, Gautam Buddha University, Greater Noida, UP, India

References

[1] Holland JH. Adaptation in Natural and Artificial Systems: An Introductory Analysis with Applications to Biology, Control, and Artificial Intelligence. Cambridge: MIT Press; 1992

[2] Eberhart RC, Shi Y, Kennedy J. Swarm Intelligence (The Morgan Kaufmann Series in Evolutionary Computation); 2001

[3] Kennedy J. Particle swarm optimization. In: Encyclopedia of Machine Learning. US: Springer; 2011. pp. 760-766

[4] Jiang Y-L, Chen H-B. Time domain model order reduction of general orthogonal polynomials for linear input-output systems. IEEE Transactions on Automatic Control. 2012;**57**:330-343

[5] Particle Swarm Optimization <http://mnemstudio.org/particle-swarm-introduction.htm>.

[6] Salma U, Vaisakh K. Reduced order modeling of linear MIMO systems using soft computing techniques. Swarm, Evolutionary, and Memetic Computing. 2011. pp. 278-286

[7] Zheng Y, Meng Y. The PSO-based adaptive window for people tracking. In: Computational Intelligence in Security and Defense Applications. CISDA 2007. IEEE Symposium on, 2007; 2007. pp. 23-29

[8] Basic PSO <http://tracer.uc3m.es/tws/pso/basics.html>

[9] Venter G, Sobieszczanski-Sobieski J. Particle swarm optimization. AIAA Journal. 2003;**41**: 1583-1589

[10] Cervantes A, Galvan I, Isasi P. A comparison between the Pittsburgh and Michigan approaches for the binary PSO algorithm. In: Evolutionary Computation. The 2005 IEEE Congress on, 2005; 2005. pp. 290-297

[11] Yao X, Liu Y, Lin G. Evolutionary programming made faster. IEEE Transactions on Evolutionary Computation. 1999;**3**:82-102

[12] Xu F, Chen Y. A method for multiple sequence alignment based on particle swarm optimization. Emerging Intelligent Computing Technology and Applications. With Aspects of Artificial Intelligence; 2009. pp. 965-973

[13] Shen Q, Shi W-M, Kong W. Hybrid particle swarm optimization and tabu search approach for selecting genes for tumor classification using gene expression data. Computational Biology and Chemistry. 2008;**32**:53-60

[14] Choudhuri S. Bioinformatics for Beginners: Genes, Genomes, Molecular Evolution, Databases and Analytical Tools. US: Academic Press, Elsevier; 2014

[15] Chuang L-Y, Tsai J-H, Yang C-H. Binary particle swarm optimization for operon prediction. Nucleic Acids Research. 2010;**38**:e128-e128

[16] Molla M, Waddell M, Page D, Shavlik J. Using machine learning to design and interpret gene-expression microarrays. AI Magazine. 2004;**25**:23

[17] Das S, Abraham A, Konar A. Particle swarm optimization and differential evolution algorithms: Technical analysis, applications and hybridization perspectives. Advances of Computational Intelligence in Industrial Systems. Berlin: Springer. 2008;**116**:1-38

[18] Dirks RM. Analysis, Design, and Construction of Nucleic Acid Devices. California: California Institute of Technology; 2005

[19] Poli R. Analysis of the publications on the applications of particle swarm optimisation. Journal of Artificial Evolution and Applications. 2008;**2008**:10. Article ID: 685175. DOI:10.1155/2008/685175

[20] Selvan SE, Xavier CC, Karssemeijer N, Sequeira J, Cherian RA, Dhala BY. Parameter estimation in stochastic mammogram model by heuristic optimization techniques. IEEE Transactions on Information Technology in Biomedicine. 2006;**10**:685-695

[21] Yeh W-C, Chang W-W, Chung YY. A new hybrid approach for mining breast cancer pattern using discrete particle swarm optimization and statistical method. Expert Systems with Applications. 2009;**36**:8204-8211

[22] Wachowiak MP, Smolíková R, Zheng Y, Zurada JM, Elmaghraby AS. An approach to multimodal biomedical image registration utilizing particle swarm optimization. IEEE Transactions on Evolutionary Computation. 2004;**8**:289-301

[23] Kaushik AC, Sahi S. HOGPred: Artificial neural network-based model for orphan GPCRs. Neural Computing and Applications. 2016;**29**(4):985-992

[24] Kaushik AC, Dhar A, Sahi S. DrovePred: Server for DNA stem and BIME's prediction using Particle Swarm Optimization. In: Bioinformatics and Systems Biology (BSB), International Conference on; 2016. pp. 1-5

[25] Kaushik AC, Sahi S. Biological complexity: Ant colony meta-heuristic optimization algorithm for protein folding. Neural Computing and Applications. 2017;**28**:3385-3391